THE MONEY MASTERS

The Money Masters

BY

JOHN TRAIN

HarperBusiness
A Division of HarperCollins*Publishers*

Designed by Sidney Feinberg

Library of Congress Cataloging-in-Publication Data

Train, John.
    The money masters.
    "Perennial Library."
    Includes index.
     1. Capitalists and financiers—United States—Biography. 2. Investments—
United States. I. Title.
HG172.A2T7   1987
332.6′092′2
[B]   78-20192

ISBN 0-88730-638-1(pbk)
94 95 96 97 98 CW 10 9 8 7 6 5 4 3 2 1

To Virginia Hilu

Contents

Foreword

I should reveal at the outset that in addition to being a client of John Train's firm I am his cousin, and so perhaps not a completely disinterested commentator.

Still, I can attest that he picks winners. The investment pool which his firm maintains and of which I am a part has risen more than seven times since the beginning of 1975, compared to two and a half times for the Dow Jones Industrial Average.

Further, *The Money Masters* is the most illuminating book I have ever read on how money is really made (and lost) in the stock market. It is also fun to read as well as profitable.

CLAIBORNE PELL

Preface

This is a new presentation of a book first published in 1980. I have brought the text up to date in places, but not throughout; continuous updating would be impractical. Fortunately, the lessons seem to apply as well today as they did then.

So let me instead take this opportunity to sum up a few later developments. Warren Buffett, to start with, has continued to enrich his Berkshire Hathaway shareholders, notably himself. If you had bought his stock when this book first came out, you would have made about fifty times on your money; his own net worth has grown from about $100 million to some $8 billion. He lives the same way as ever, has no great philanthropic activities, and continues making money for its own sake. I have written a study on Buffett called *The Midas Touch* (Harper & Row, 1987).

His transactions since this book first appeared illustrate several of his techniques. A central one is his belief in buying cash-generating companies (page 19, point 3; likewise Larry Tisch, page 179) that have cash hoards themselves. This enables you to deploy that excess cash either to buy other cash-rich companies or to shrink the company's capitalization. That idea, retiring stock, has caught on in the corporate world and, indeed, become almost excessively popular in recent years.

One should note that Berkshire's performance is not quite comparable to that of any other investor in this book, except to some extent

Larry Tisch, because of the leverage inherent in insurance companies, which can turn their portfolios essentially into margin accounts. Insurance companies, like banks, hold large amounts of cash corresponding to their obligations to others. If this cash is successfully invested, they can keep the profit beyond what goes back to their policyholders or depositors.

In 1987 Buffett bought a 13 to 14 percent stake in Salomon Brothers. Minorco, Inc., wanted to sell a large stock position. Fearing that an unfriendly buyer might be a threat to management, Salomon bought the bloc at the then market value of $38 a share, and created a like amount of 9 percent preferred stock, convertible at $38, which it sold to Berkshire, which thus got a higher yield and higher security than Minorco—or other shareholders—had enjoyed, together with a tax advantage. This triple enhancement was worth hundreds of millions of dollars to Berkshire and provoked many lawsuits. Joining Salomon's board, Buffett voiced ringing support for Chairman John Gutfreund. However, Salomon was a rough, tough outfit, as readers of *Liar's Poker*—and, one would have thought, the directors—were aware. The Treasury bill bid-rigging scandal in due course blew the roof off the firm. Buffett had to come east, remove Gutfreund *et al.*, and pitch in himself to save the situation. He then returned to Omaha, his "aw, shucks" image tarnished.

In the Introduction I describe "the freakish operator, whose method is so personal that it's virtually inimitable, and who is indeed a dangerous model to follow. Stanley Kroll is such a figure but has been included in this book to help the reader understand what an impossible casino commodities are." That was true even for Kroll. He got bored with life on the Lake of Geneva and returned to the hurly-burly of commodities. Unfortunately, he was no longer in tune with the market, and his performance was poor. In this he was not alone. He had told me of a commodities broker who was supposed to be outstanding—perhaps the most highly regarded in New York. As mentioned in the footnote on page 130, this broker's performance turned out disastrously, and has been worse since.

What seems to have happened to Kroll specifically, and to other commodity speculators who followed similar methods, is that too many brokers were attracted to the huge commissions that this business generates. Most of them followed rules similar to Kroll's: identifying a major trend, putting on the position during secondary reactions within that trend, and so on. With so many competitors—so many billions of dollars—trying to do the same thing, you had to act faster than you wanted to. Finally, the profitable tactic became almost the opposite of what Kroll liked: you didn't wait for the reaction but instead bet on the trend instantly and liquidated on the first sign of a reaction. Then nothing really worked. This is now such a closely followed area that I doubt if any "system" can survive for long without being swamped by imitators.

John Templeton's career since this book appeared has been remarkable. As mentioned on page 177, when I first visited him his fund had *grown* to only $20 million after many years of being among the top performers of all funds. In other words, during its best-performing period it was much smaller than even that. By the time the book came out the fund had reached $200 million and he had started another. Since then, those two funds have grown hugely, his firm has started several more, has gone into pension fund management in a big way, and is running tens of billions in all. Its very success made it inevitable that the performance should become mediocre. Finally Templeton sold the whole kit and retired.

Larry Tisch, who thought the market was high in 1980, was wrong: It almost quadrupled. Indeed, he has usually been too cautious on the market. It's in his specific choices that he has done well. Just as Buffett became the largest stockholder of Capital Cities/ABC, Tisch, in the course of saving CBS from a takeover, obligingly took it over himself.

Robert Wilson recovered from his catastrophic short sale in Resorts International and fought his way back into the financial big league. Then, however, he found that he couldn't seem to make real progress. His performance became about the same as the market's. So he turned his fortune over to others to manage and is enjoying life. In 1980 Wilson thought (page 206) "that the bankruptcy of New York City means the discrediting of big government, that as a result there will be less government, and that things in general will go much better. From today's depressed levels the market could rise to twenty times doubled earnings, or almost fivefold in five to seven years." Well, he caught the new temper of the times, and he wasn't too far off on the market.

However, Wilson is no longer as optimistic as he once was. He finds some deterioration in the moral and intellectual qualities of what shoud be the leadership class in America, and he is discouraged by American education.

As to the book's "Conclusions," they pretty well stand. I see no reason to soften my strictures against "technical analysis"—page 219 *et seq*. I still haven't been able to find a practitioner who is consistently successful for long periods. After James Dines, cited in the book, came Howard Ruff, who was swept out to sea on a river of blunders. Joe Granville was the next universal prophet. He announced that he had finally gotten everything absolutely straight and never expected to make a wrong prediction. Alas, in the trough of the great bottom in 1982, on the verge of one of the most powerful rises in market history, Granville took his disciples not only right out of stocks but *short*. He has had a disastrous record since.

The overcongestion of the Grahamite "value" school as compared to the "growth" school (discussed on pages 107–8 and elsewhere) has indeed gone very far. Not tens of millions but hundreds of billions are poised to snap up any opportunity that appears.

My suggestion that investors would look abroad was borne out to an astonishing extent. The emerging markets have been the most exciting area of recent years. A fund of which I am a director, Genesis Emerging Markets Fund (London), advanced 86 percent in 1993. Indeed, this sector, while full of promise for the very long term, seems to be boiling over.

In looking over the careers of the great investors described in this book, one is struck by how many of them discovered a whole approach to investing that had been overlooked until then. They became masters of this particular technique, and on the basis of that advantage were able to record outstanding performances for many years. Graham, for instance, codified methods of discerning neglected values in humdrum companies; Buffett studied the strengths of business franchises; Price focused on the persistency of growth; Templeton unearthed values in countries where his peers dared not to venture; Wilson sought the "new wave," the dream that will transform its industry and that investors don't yet understand (or in reverse, as a short sale candidate, the false dream that investors are paying too much for).

There is, in other words, a philosophical thread in most of these careers, a main idea. When the main idea matures, then comes the great test of the investor: to lay aside his overexploited discovery and find a new one. this need to adapt is implied in the epigraph of the book: "Times change, and we change in them." Change is indeed the investor's only constant.

I suspect this to be the cardinal secret of master-play in this business after one reaches a certain level of competence. Thus Templeton on page 176 and Wilson on page 198. Graham and Price *did*, of course, change their methods.

A difference between a master and a journeyman is that the journeyman has learned the rules but the master knows the truths *behind* the formulations needed to explain the craft to an apprentice. And it's the same in much of human thought. A great thinker or artist often rises above earlier principles. Then second-rate critics codify his discoveries, and a new constricting orthodoxy arises. So we have a paradox: to do well, you have to know the rules, but a master will know when the situation has changed enough so that they no longer apply. My hope in this book is that by studying the masters side by side the reader can get a feeling for what worked for them, and why, as well as for the underlying reality. He may then develop an approach that will work for him while the world and the investment markets change around him, as they will.

1994

Introduction

I have always liked to develop relationships with great investment managers. In the 1950s I went to work for and indeed became a client of Imrie de Vegh, whose fund had the best of all performance records in that decade. Some time later, when his company was about one-twentieth as large as it later became, I got to know T. Rowe Price and put money under his management, as I did with A. W. Jones and other highly successful investors. I also sought out some Europeans whose names would be less familiar to American readers.

I intended this book to be a voyage of exploration through the ideas and practices of some of the most notable portfolio investors of our time—not famous administrators of large amounts of capital, who are primarily executives and only rarely great individual investors, but men whose own decisions to buy and sell have actually made money grow. How do they think? What sources of information do they use? How much do they depend on fact and how much on psychology? What criteria do they apply in picking investments? And of course, why do they like the stocks they're buying now?

My subjects were chosen to represent the principal schools of investing, among them "growth," "value," "technology," "specialties," and the "gut operator."

A clear common thread emerged from my analysis of these great investors' techniques: in very different idioms they all say much the same thing. There are basically two ways of looking at a job: either as an exercise in futurology—peering into the fog a little farther than the crowd—or as laboratory analysis—studying with a little more care and imagination what's under the microscope right now. The reader is invited to join me in my voyage of exploration, and then at the end, in "Conclusions," we can examine what we have found out.

I might say that there's no luck to professional portfolio investing. It is a craft, involving thousands of decisions a year. You can no more pile up a superlative record by luck or accident than you can win a chess tournament by luck or accident. A single individual may well have a lucky strike, but to the year-in, year-out manager of a diversified portfolio, no one event is likely to make an overwhelming difference. He will have his share of the breaks, but that's to be expected; and, equally to be expected, his share of bad luck.

The reader will observe that most of my subjects are older men. I have also stuck with investors who have followed a definable technique over most of their careers, so that a reader can contemplate their ideas in action: the longer the record of a particular approach, the more convincing.

Youth is bliss, but not the so-called "New Breed" of investors—the gunslingers and hedge fund operators, described so amusingly (and alarmingly) in "Adam Smith's" *The Money Game.* In the blowoff phase of a bull market some of these men record marvelous performances for a while, but in the downdraft that follows, many of their favorite holdings go bankrupt, and virtually all plunge into the drink like Icarus. Quite a number of these wizards get washed out of the business altogether. Go-go "performance" investors skate around like daddy longlegs on a pond; pile too much weight on, and they sink. These managers lost much more money than they made for their customers; traveling light going up, they carried huge followings down with them when they collapsed.

A category of investor I've generally avoided is what might be called the freakish operator, whose method is so personal that it's virtually inimitable, and who is indeed a dangerous model to follow. Stanley Kroll is such a figure but has been included in this book to help the reader understand what an impossible casino commodities are. (Commodity speculation is not investing, cannot be carried out with consistent success by the retail investor, and should not be offered to retail investors by reputable securities firms. I cannot see why it should be illegal to take bets on the horses and legal to solicit them from ignorant speculators on sowbellies.)

So in general I've tried to choose masters who illustrate useful methods, and are thus more instructive to study. Bismarck said that even fools profit from their own experiences; let us instead try to profit from the experience of others.

Tempora mutantur nos et mutamur in illis

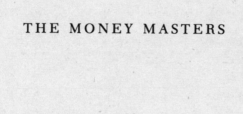

THE MONEY MASTERS

1

Warren Buffett

A Share in a Business

With the death of Benjamin Graham, the Maimonides of portfolio management, his disciple Warren Buffett of Omaha, Nebraska, may have succeeded to the title of the investor's investor. He disbanded his troupe of less than a hundred clients, collected in a single pool called Buffett Partnership, before his fortieth birthday, to become a solo operator. He has written no textbooks. Yet among investment professionals there is no more respected voice.

If you had put $10,000 in Buffett's original investing partnership at inception in 1956, you would have collected about $300,000 by the time he dissolved it at the end of 1969. He had never had a down year, even in the severe bear markets of 1957, 1962, 1966, and 1969. That achievement stands alone in modern portfolio management.

The portfolio of Buffett's partnership was often too concentrated in a few issues—some not readily marketable—for an investment counselor or fund manager, but not out of line with what might be done by a conservative professional with his own money. A masterfully competent investor (like an art collector) *should* buy what is out of fashion and thus hard to resell quickly, and indeed he should buy a lot of it, prepared to be patient with any particular holding. If he's right, the values will be recognized and his purchase gain liquidity in due course. Buffett now likes to own a dozen or so securities and characterizes traditional diversification as the "Noah's Ark approach." You buy two of everything in sight and end up with a zoo instead of a portfolio.

The essence of Warren Buffett's thinking is that the business world is divided into a tiny number of wonderful businesses— well worth investing in at a price—and a huge number of bad or mediocre businesses that are not attractive as long-term investments. Most of the time most businesses are not worth what they are selling for, but on rare occasions the wonderful businesses are almost given away. When that happens, buy boldly, paying no attention to current gloomy economic and stock market forecasts. Bonds are often better investment than stocks of bad or mediocre businesses—which include most of the stocks in the Dow Jones Industrial, Transportation, and Composite averages.

For Buffett, the key to a good business is what I call its "business franchise"—the extent to which it has attained a privileged position of some sort, so that another company can't muscle in to squeeze its prices and profits. However, as a general rule, the competitiveness built into the American economic system effectively prevents the creation of good franchises. Many steel companies actually earn only about 4 percent on equity, after allowing for inflation—much less than their own bonds yield. U.S. industry makes so little money, in fact, that it is increasingly unable to attract the investment capital needed to produce goods and services required by society. When it can't, the government does the job . . . badly. Witness the New York subway system, taken over by the city to protect the five-cent fare, which has increased to a dollar, or the fantastic wastefulness of the public housing the government puts up after rent control wipes out the small, efficient landlord.

One of the most unappetizing characteristics of many industries today is that the owners receive taxable "dividends" based on illusory taxable "profits" that do not take into account the real cost of replacing plant for much more money, thanks to inflation, than it cost originally. The owners, to stay in business, must keep putting in huge amounts of equity and debt capital—often more, after tax, than their dividends. (See page 38, "The Great American Jam Tomorrow Ponzi Scheme.")

The few businesses that Buffett thinks *are* worth owning—those with valid franchises—often fall into the category he calls "gross profits royalty" companies, perhaps better called "gross revenues royalty" companies: TV stations, international advertising agencies, iron-ore landholding companies, newspapers. Benefiting directly from the large capital investments of the companies they serve, they require little working capital to operate and, in fact, pour off cash to their owners. The unfortunate capital-intensive producer—Chrysler, Monsanto, or International Harvester—can't bring its wares to its customers' notice without paying tribute to the "royalty" holder: the *Wall Street Journal*, J. Walter Thompson, the local TV station, or all three.

Other valid franchises Buffett likes include the large insurance brokerage agencies and some specialized ad hoc situations such as Sperry and Hutchinson Green Stamps, but there aren't many that have both a substantial and well-secured niche.

I had a first-hand demonstration of a good franchise, that of *The New York Times*, when I went to visit Buffett for a few days in Omaha. I arrived at night at the Hilton, a mechanical and charmless establishment. Coming down for breakfast the next morning, I looked around for a newspaper. In place of the familiar *Times* or *Wall Street Journal*, I found the local Omaha offering, the *World-Herald*. It had an unreliable, tacky look. Instead of featuring national or world affairs and matters of cultural or philosophic moment, the front page was dedicated to local concerns of marginal significance, ephemera. I didn't buy a copy, but went straight in to breakfast.

Afterward I drove out to Buffett's office, on the top floor of a modern building about fifteen minutes from the center of town. The office is clean and anonymous, with framed documents on the walls and a box of fudge on a table, to which Buffett helps himself from time to time. It's delicious—made by a company he owns. A bookshelf on the wall holds, with other financial volumes, several editions of Graham and Dodd's *Security Analysis.*

Buffett, a genial, ruddy, muscular man with a wide, humorous mouth and an inquisitive expression behind his oversized horn-rimmed spectacles, put his feet on the desk, poured himself a Pepsi-Cola, and, in the somewhat toneless manner characteristic of midwesterners, cheerfully began to babble about what was on his mind. He speaks with a wry earnestness, and gives an impression of complete intellectual honesty. His delivery is so casual, rapid, allusive, and clever that unless you pay attention a lot could slip by. Much of what he says could be slowed down, delivered with gestures by a stand-up comic, and keep a Chamber of Commerce audience fascinated.

BUFFETT: When I was a kid at Woodrow Wilson High School in Washington [*business of refilling glass of Pepsi; pours cherry syrup into Pepsi, then pours more*] another kid and I started the Wilson Coin-Operated Machine Company. I was fifteen years old. We put reconditioned pinball machines in barbershops. In Washington you were supposed to buy a tax stamp to be in the pinball machine business. I got the impression we were the only people who ever bought one. The first day we bought an old machine for $25 and put it out in a shop. When we came back that night it had $4 in it! I figured I had discovered the wheel. [*Finishes glass of Pepsi, pours another, adds cherry syrup.*] Eventually we were making $50 a week. I hadn't dreamed life could be so good. Before I got out of high school I bought myself an unimproved forty-acre farm in northeast Nebraska for $1,200.

Buffett's father, a hyperconservative of messianic zeal who was revered by his children, served four terms as a Republican congressman and then became a stockbroker. A man of great personal integrity, he had little interest in money: when congressmen's salaries were increased from $10,000 to $12,500, he returned his raise to the Treasury. He was merely amused by Warren's moneymaking activities, and hoped his son would become a clergyman.

Buffett was well along in his career as a tycoon by the age of eleven, the period of his five-dollar "coup" in Cities Service Preferred (of which we'll hear more later) and his debut as a market technician. Soon after, we find him in the business of retrieving and reselling golf balls, and running several paper routes for the *Washington Post.** Delivery of papers accounted for most of his original stake of $9,000, with which he finished college.

At twelve, Warren became fond of handicapping horse races and compiled and sold a tip sheet called *Stable Boy Selections.* He persuaded his father to ask the Library of Congress for all the books they had on horse-race handicapping and betting, and today sometimes wonders what the Library made of Congressman Buffett's request.

He found few aspects of commercial life beyond his grasp, even at that age. "I always knew I was going to be rich," he has said.

The Graham Influence

As a boy, Buffett was fascinated by stock market technical analysis. He developed his own market indices and the like but it all made no real sense to him, and he discarded this approach in 1949, after reading *The Intelligent Investor* by Benjamin Graham while attending the University of Nebraska. The following year he went to Columbia University because both Graham and Dodd (of *Security Analysis*) were teaching there.

Buffett noticed in *Who's Who* that Ben Graham was a director of Government Employees Insurance Company (GEICO), which sold automobile insurance directly by mail, bypassing the brokers. He went down to the company's office on a Saturday and pounded on the door. Eventually a janitor opened up, and Buffett asked if there was anybody around he could talk to about the company. The janitor took him upstairs, where one man was in his office,

*Newsboy Makes Good. A substantial component of his wealth today is his holdings in newspapers and newspaper chains. He is the largest outside shareholder of the *Washington Post*—which he used to deliver—the *Boston Globe*, and the *Buffalo Evening News.* One of his newspaper investments, the *Omaha Sun*, didn't pay off financially, though the *Sun* won a Pulitzer Prize for exposing how Boys Town had become a fund-raising machine.

L. A. Davidson, later chief executive officer. Buffett questioned him for five hours, then went away very excited about the company and its stock.

After skimping to buy some shares, he discussed GEICO with two brokers who specialized in insurance issues; both pooh-poohed it, since the company didn't look cheap in their tables of insurance stock values. What the tables didn't show was that the company was making 20 percent on its underwriting activities as against a normal margin of 5 percent. At that time the entire company was selling for less than $7 million in the market; later it went to a billion and became a Wall Street favorite. Then mismanagement brought GEICO to the edge of bankruptcy. During that crisis, twenty-five years after his initial contact, Buffett bought 15 percent of the company and today thinks that it once again has a bright future.

Since Buffett believed in going to work for the smartest person available, on graduating he offered his services to Graham for nothing. When Graham declined, Buffett went back to Omaha and entered his father's stockbroking firm, pushing GEICO energetically but finding it extremely hard to place. Some insurance agents put pressure on Buffett's father to stop Warren from promoting an agentless underwriter.

After a while Warren had another idea, that one ought to be able to get the people who understand a company to buy stock in it. Kansas City Life, for instance, was trading for three times its statutory earnings, or a 33 percent "earning yield," while selling insurance whose policyholders' benefits were calculated on the assumption that the invested capital was only growing at 2.5 percent per annum compounded. Buffett thought that the general agent, who sold policies daily and mailed the checks to Kansas City, would have to know that Kansas City Life really did exist—people never were quite sure about GEICO—and would be a natural candidate to buy the stock. Quite the contrary. The agent was buying life insurance for himself and his family, content with the 2.5 percent compounding going on in the insurance, while rejecting the 33 percent compounding going on in the stock!

Buffett never could interest him in buying shares in his own company.

After leaving Columbia Buffett kept in touch with Graham, sending him ideas in the hope of receiving stock exchange business. Graham, in turn, was generous with his time and thoughts, and in 1954 he suggested that Buffett come to see him. Buffett went to New York and was hired to work for Graham-Newman Corporation, where he spent two instructive years. Today he finds it hard to describe what he did there, but it must have included analyzing hundreds of companies to see if they met Graham's investment criteria.

Ben Graham didn't distinguish between franchises. He never would have been able to buy American Express during the salad oil scandal, or Disney, two of Buffett's great coups. He did not believe in "qualitative" analysis—studying a company's products, how it operates, and its apparent future outlook. He never talked to managements. He believed in doing all his work by exhaustively studying the figures generally available: "quantitative" analysis. He didn't want to make use of any information that would not be available to his readers.

Comparing the qualitative approach with Graham's emphasis on numbers, I mentioned to Buffett the persistence of brand loyalty among smokers of cigarettes—which really are not very different—and the loyalty of newspaper readers. That very morning I had skipped the paper because the local product wasn't what I was used to. I wanted the book review in a certain place, and the company earnings reports in a certain size of type. And when I visit Paris, where I lived for some years, I go back to reading the comics in the *International Herald Tribune*, which I never do in a domestic paper. One grows accustomed to a paper's face, as to the furniture in one's room. As a result there's little happiness in trying to break into the territory of a well-entrenched newspaper.

Graham distrusted such ideas because they were subjective. Instead, he followed a series of mathematical criteria for analyzing stocks; for example, one should buy a sound company selling in the market for two-thirds of its own working capital and then sell it again when the market values it at 100 percent of its working capital. This technique was immensely profitable for Graham and his investors, but does not really satisfy Buffett, who finds such mechanical investing all too similar to filling out an application for group life insurance.

I asked Buffett how he thought one might do by purchasing the "Loaded Laggards" computed by *Forbes* magazine from time to time. Not too brilliantly, he felt. If you buy and hold on, you will do only about as well as the companies themselves do and, since they have a low return on capital, that means not outstandingly. To grow fast you need a high return on capital.

You must be sure to sell a "Graham" investment at the right time, whereas you can hold on to a higher-growth company for as long as it goes on developing rapidly.

After his two years of apprenticeship in the workshop of the master, Buffett was glad to set forth into the great world as a master himself. For the second time he returned to Omaha, where he bought a roomy house—to which he has been adding sporadically ever since—on a wooded corner, and started on his own. In retrospect, one is not too surprised that, given such mental equipment, such fascination for the subject, and such a thorough academic and practical preparation, Buffett should have done exceedingly well. Nobody, however, could have foreseen his record.

When it comes to money, Buffett enjoys the immense advantage of coming from Omaha rather than Boston, say, or Florence. I say advantage because everything in Omaha (as in many other American towns) seems dedicated to economic activity. No nonsense about solemn temples or gorgeous palaces; no quaint bookstores, no loggias or inviting arcades; no riverside benches for lovers, no museums or great collections. Instead, office buildings, the terminus of the Union Pacific, car rental agencies, farm equipment wholesalers, machine tool companies.

I doubt if there exists in Omaha an important building or business with whose economic history Warren Buffett is not familiar.

It is curious to walk around the downtown area with him and hear him rattle off the financial characteristics of every building and business he passes.

"I've been offered this one," he'll say, glancing up at a company sign overhead. "When I looked at the balance sheet it turned out they were only making 5 percent on sales. They turn over their inventory once every six months.

"That building was bought by a syndicate set up by Wertheim & Co. in 1946. They paid $1.6 million with a first of $800,000 and a second of $400,000. When they bought it, it was fully rented, but the major tenants didn't renew and after a while they couldn't cover charges. A group from Chicago took it over on an interest-only deal with a balloon. Even they can't make it, so I guess they'll take it down."

Some of these buildings are brick, others stone; some are turn-of-the-century Main Street, and others neo-Corbusier. I'm not sure, though, that Buffett actually sees their designs or remembers the colors. He seems to look through the walls into the financial dynamics: the ground lease foundation, the equity pillars, the mortgage roof, and the preferred stock buttresses supporting not a dome but a subordinated convertible debenture. Where the passerby contemplates a mural in the entrance of an office building, Buffett's inner eye, one feels, sees projected onto the wall the highlights of the original prospectus.

Just as a wise old family doctor often can recognize anemia before a new patient has taken a seat in his office, Buffett, glancing at an annual report, will start pointing eagerly here and there at the text, showing why there's too much inventory or not enough return on plant.

In short, of all the investors in this book, Buffett is the one who most perfectly understands the companies he owns stock in as businesses: living organisms, with hearts, lungs, bones, muscles, arteries, and nervous systems. It is madness, he would say, for an investor buying a stock to have anything else in mind than the operating realities of the underlying business: the condition of its plant, its customer and labor relations, its cash position, the amount of capital it has tied up—the animal reality of the enterprise. Buffett believes that those on Wall Street who talk of the stock trend or institutional sponsorship are ridiculous, combining laziness with ignorance, and compares them with astronomers setting aside their telescopes to consult the astrology page.

He thinks of a stock only as a fractional interest in a business and always begins by asking himself, "How much would I pay for all of this company? And on that basis, what will I pay for 1 percent of it?" There are very few companies he considers interesting enough to buy at all, and even those he will look at only when they are very unpopular. Of course, one must know for certain what the values really are if one is to have the confidence to buy in the teeth of a panic, but Buffett has succeeded often enough to make his fortune.

Buffett Partnership

In 1956, at the age of twenty-five, Buffett started a family partnership with $100,000 in it, after a while adding all his own capital. As manager he received 25 percent of the profits above a 6 percent annual return on capital.

As the partnership increased in value and his reputation spread, more money poured in. Homer Dodge, a physicist and former college president who excels at picking stock-pickers, came to see Buffett, then twenty-six, while on a canoe trip, with the canoe itself perched on top of the car. Long a friend and partner of Ben Graham, who had just retired, Dodge became Buffett's first partner outside the family, simply writing out a check to join the partnership after a brief talk. Normally he is extraordinarily careful and frugal. Even now, at ninety-one, though investing still commands his attention, spending holds no interest for him; but like all outstanding investors, he can make the bold decision when necessary.*

---

* I made the opposite decision when, looking for a good place to park some capital, I first met Buffett. At that very early stage he had no office at all, and ran things from a tiny sitting-room off his bedroom—no secretary, no calculator. When I found that the holdings could not be revealed, I decided not to sign up.

Every year Buffett wrote his co-investors:

"I cannot promise results to partners, but I can and do promise this:

a. Our investments will be chosen on the basis of value, not popularity.
b. Our patterns of operations will attempt to reduce permanent capital loss (not short-term quotational loss) to a minimum."

His stated goal was not absolute, but relative: to beat the Dow Jones by an average of ten percentage points per year.

In general, he bought undervalued listed stocks, but also was usually involved in merger arbitrage situations. Occasionally he bought a controlling interest in a public company or an entire private business on a negotiated basis.

Thus, in 1961 he became chairman of Dempster Mill Manufacturing Company of Beatrice, Nebraska, which made farm implements and was the biggest employer in town. In 1963 he decided to sell the business and the town raised money to help a new group buy it. Dempster continues to operate, but never has been particularly profitable.

In 1965 he took over Berkshire Hathaway in New Bedford, Massachusetts, a textile manufacturer with a long record of unprofitable operations, and installed new management. He now owns 47 percent of the company (former partners own another 35 percent or so) and it, in turn, holds many of his other interests. Experience with Dempster and the textile business contributed to his present firm conviction never to buy another "turnaround."

Through Berkshire he bought a number of entire companies: a candymaker (See's), a trading stamp company (Blue Chip Stamps), several insurance companies, banks, another textile company, a savings and loan association, one daily and one weekly newspaper, and, most recently, a steel service center. Negotiated purchases, he notes, simply can't be made on the bargain basis sometimes possible in common stock investment. A sole owner never becomes as crazy as the market sometimes does. The most he hopes for in a private purchase is a reasonable deal, not a great one.

He brought off perhaps his most spectacular transaction in 1964 when American Express collapsed in the market during the Tino de Angelis salad oil scandal. Studying the company carefully, he determined that the danger from those losses would be limited, while its basic strengths, the credit card operation and the travelers' checks, would be unaffected. He bought heavily, and saw the stock quintuple in the next five years.

In 1969, the stock market was booming, even junk stocks were selling at premium prices, and Buffett couldn't find bargains anymore.

He sent another letter to his partners:

I am out of step with present conditions. When the game is no longer played your way, it is only human to say the new approach is all wrong, bound to lead to trouble, and so on. . . . On one point, however, I am clear. I will not abandon a previous approach whose logic I understand (although I find it difficult to apply) even though it may mean foregoing large, and apparently easy, profits to embrace an approach which I don't fully understand, have not practiced successfully, and which possibly could lead to substantial permanent loss of capital.

Buffett had an additional problem: he had become fond of some of his principal holdings, such as Berkshire Hathaway, and no longer wanted to sell them at all. That, obviously, put him in potential conflict with his investors, in whose interest it might have been to sell. Buffett tries to avoid purchasing mediocre businesses but finds it hard to sell one, if he discovers that's what he has, once he becomes fond of the managers.

So after thirteen years, he decided to fold up the partnership. It had gained thirtyfold in its value per share, and through the addition of more than ninety new members and the success of its investments had grown to over $100 million. Buffett's profit participation as investor-manager, plus the compounding of his own capital, had made him worth some $25 million. Investors were given back their money and their proportional interest in Berkshire Hathaway (of which he became chairman). Some were guided to other advisors, some into municipal bonds. Buffett sent his partners a remarkable discussion of municipals, which appears as Appendix I on page 235.

When Buffett terminated Buffett Partnership, a few of the investors—in all cases divorced women—experienced acute anxiety about the required adjustment. An investment counselor to whom Buffett recommended some of his clients at the time told him that his experience had been similar; the investors who on occasion lose their balance most completely are those who spend considerably more than they earn from their own work and are thus very dependent on investment income, particularly divorced women.

Three years after the partnership was liquidated the market went into the 1973–74 collapse. Buffett (directly or indirectly through Berkshire Hathaway) was able to buy big pieces of some of his favorite "gross profits royalty" companies at giveaway prices: 8 percent of Ogilvy & Mather at 8, 16 percent of Interpublic, 11 percent of the *Washington Post* at 3, the *Boston Globe*, Capital Cities (an independent chain of television stations which also owns newspapers), Knight-Ridder Newspapers, Lee Enterprises, Media General, Pinkerton's. Several have tripled or quadrupled since. He also bought into a number of banks and other companies that have so far been uninteresting in the market. Even when markets disagree with him, however, he is happy with his stocks as long as the underlying businesses continue to do well. At this juncture he is no longer trying to maximize his investment profits, but rather to indulge his collecting instinct and to enjoy himself "playing several different games," in newspapers, insurance, and other areas.

He points out that Berkshire has a much easier time investing than do major corporate buyers of other corporations, since, as essentially an investment company, and quite small, it can buy in small quantities and not for control; the control sellout commands a much higher price than the market will sometimes attribute to shares of the same company.

"If one is ever going to buy common stocks, the time to buy them is now," said Buffet in mid-1979. "It screams at you." If the companies that are now purchasing other companies are acting rationally, then Berkshire will be enormously successful. If they are being merely stupid, Berkshire will still be successful, he adds.

Readers who want to follow Warren Buffett's fortunes—or buy an interest in his future—can do so directly by becoming shareholders of Berkshire Hathaway. An extract from the annual report is given as Appendix II on page 246. In the past you could buy a collection of Buffett's favorite holdings at a discount from their market value—getting the rest of the company free—through Berkshire. (In the future I'd think this discount would disappear.) The company's stock portfolio—in some instances held through subsidiaries—is listed in its annual report, and it's easy enough to add up the value per Berkshire share. A less satisfactory way to buy a piece of Buffett's action is through Blue Chip Stamps, which he also controls. Its portfolio appeals to me less than Berkshire Hathaway's, though. Still another way (although indirect) is to buy shares in Sequoia Fund, run in New York by Buffett's friend Bill Ruane, who took Benjamin Graham's class at Columbia when Buffett did. Sequoia's portfolio (see Appendix III on page 254) often parallels Buffett's thinking, as one can see by comparing it with Berkshire Hathaway's: the same big positions in Capital Cities, Ogilvy & Mather, the *Washington Post,* and banking; the same fondness for media companies in general; and an avoidance of high-technology and glamorous consumer stocks.

The rest of this chapter will describe the principles that Buffett follows. Though they are influenced by Benjamin Graham's, they have been modified to reflect the weakened position of capital in our society over the last fifty years, as compared with the increased strength of labor and government as well as the persistence of rapid inflation; there is also more emphasis on the unique-

ness of any situation and the strength of the business franchise.

Two Inches Above the Navel

The enormous advantage the independent investor has, Buffett
says, is that he can stand at the plate and wait forever for the
perfect pitch. If he wants it to come in exactly two inches above
his navel and nowhere else, he can stand there indefinitely until
an easy one is served up. Stock market investment is the only
business of which that is true. You can not only wait for the bargain, but for the particular one that you understand and *know*
to be a bargain.

I have a little paradox I offer to clients when I'm trying to
explain this point, and tried it on Buffett:

"How can you beat Bobby Fischer?"

Buffett finally gave up.

"Get him to play you any game except chess."

For best results, the competitive player should never depart
from his area of superiority.

Buffett observes that you might improve your investment performance by having a quota, a limit to the number of investment
ideas you could try out in your life: one a year, for instance . . .
or even fewer. You only have to do a very few things right in
your life, he says, so long as you don't do too many things wrong.
You should therefore resolve ahead of time to make only a few
big investment moves. Samuel Newhouse had one good idea, at
which he pounded away for the rest of his career: buying and
owning important newspaper franchises. He began penniless, and
now has assets worth about a billion dollars.*

This is sometimes called the strategy of the hedgehog, as distin-

---

* At thirteen, Newhouse went to work for two dollars a week as an office boy
for a magistrate who took over a Staten Island newspaper in satisfaction of an
unpaid debt and put him to work chasing up advertising. In due course he was
put in charge of the magistrate's interest in the paper. The magistrate died,
Newhouse acquired his interest from the estate, and went on from there.

guished from the strategy of the fox. The fox, so goes the saying, knows many little things, but the hedgehog knows one big thing.

"Swing, You Bum!"

Many times, though, the investment manager lets this advantage be turned into a disadvantage. Feeling obliged to remain active, he swings at far too many pitches, instead of holding off until he has an absolute conviction. He seems to hear the clients howling, "Swing, you bum!"

When he was eleven, for example, Buffett bought three shares of Cities Service Preferred at 38. His sister, who was fourteen, thought that she had better follow suit and bought three shares too. The stock declined to 27. She asked him about it every day. Finally it recovered to 40. To be rid of the headache and the questions, Buffett sold his stock and hers, making a total profit of five dollars, after commissions. The stock then went right on to 200! He never forgot the lesson.

He points out that if, for instance, he had reported to his partners that 40 percent of their money was in American Express, or that he was heavily long silver futures, his partners would have been concerned, asked questions, mailed him things to read. At best, he would have wasted a lot of time; at worst, he would have been influenced by their reactions. He says it would have been like a surgeon carrying on a running conversation with the patient during a major operation.

Nor does he like swapping stories with other investors, since he usually wants to buy more of any stock he owns, should the price come down. A golfer, Buffett says he doesn't want to putt for other golfers or have them putt for him. And if someone to whom he mentions an idea thereafter buys the stock, Buffett feels responsible for him.

The relationship between a truly effective advisor and his clients is no simple matter. Aside from anything else, if he's really successful the time comes when he doesn't need clients anymore, or finds that they cramp his style—witness Buffett himself.

The Investor

Buffett thinks that to succeed as an investor you must have six qualities:

1. *You must be animated by controlled greed, and fascinated by the investment process.* You must not, however, let greed take possession of you; you must not be in a hurry. If you are too interested in money, you will kill yourself; if not interested enough, you won't go to the office. And you must enjoy the game. The investment process always has fascinated Buffett more than the dollars themselves; he had just as much fun working with small sums as he now has with large sums.

2. *You must have patience.* He often repeats that you should never buy a stock unless you would be happy with it if the stock exchange closed down for the next ten years. Buy into a company because you want to own it permanently, not because you think the stock will go up. You can't determine the correct value for a stock in all cases, or even in most, but you can in a few cases, and they are all you need. Guessing stock movements, on the other hand, is just that: guessing. He says that if you are right about the company and buy it at a reasonable price, you will eventually be right about the stock.

3. *You must think independently.* Jot down your reasons for buying: "Harte-Hanks is undervalued by the market at $50 million because . . ."* When you have them all down, make your decision and leave it at that, without feeling the need to consult other people: no committees. Buffett reasons that if you don't know enough to make your own decisions, you should get out of decision-making. He likes to quote Ben Graham's dictum "The fact that other people agree or disagree with you makes you neither right nor wrong. You will be right if your facts and reasoning are correct."

4. *You must have the security and self-confidence that comes*

---

* But *cf.* footnote, page 37.

from knowledge, without being rash or headstrong. If you lack confidence, fear will drive you out at the bottom.

Buffett knew a man who in 1941 was "hard put to pay for a Good Humor bar." Then the man became an expert in a particular industry, water companies, and eventually knew how much of an impact somebody taking a bath had on the earnings of American Water Works. He became very rich indeed.

As an example of the folly of being too market-conscious, Buffett cites nervous investors who don't know the facts and are thus fond of selling stocks when they go down. Crazy, he says. It's as though you bought a house for $100,000 and immediately told the broker that you would sell it again if you got a bid of $80,000.

5. *Accept it when you don't know something.* In the days of his investing partnership, people often asked Buffett to look over lists of securities that they wanted to contribute to the partnership. He'd say, "I don't know this one, I don't know that one, I don't know that one. I don't want securities I don't know. Just give me a check."

6. *Be flexible as to the types of businesses you buy, but never pay more than the business is worth.* Calculate what the business is worth now, and what it will be worth in due course. Then ask yourself, "How sure am I?" Nine times out of ten you can't be. Sometimes, though, the bell rings and you can almost hear the cash register.

Nobody is clever enough to buy stocks he doesn't really want and resell them to someone else at a profit. The bigger fool in the "bigger fool theory"—that you can sell a bad buy to someone dumber than you are—is usually the buyer, not his intended victim.

As we talked out this list, I added four requirements that Buffett, but not necessarily someone else, can fulfill:

7. Have ten or fifteen years of intensive theoretical and practical training—including a number of years under the greatest investors—before you start in yourself.

8. Be a genius of sorts.
9. Possess perfect intellectual honesty.
10. Avoid any significant distractions.

Wonderful Businesses

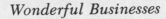

There are few wonderful businesses—only a handful in the entire country. What are the characteristics?

1. *They have a good return on capital* without accounting gimmicks or lots of leverage.

2. *They are understandable.* One should be able to grasp what motivates the people working in them, and why they appeal to their customers. Even IBM, which looks straightforward, has changed character several times, such as when it went from punch cards to magnetic tape, and again when it introduced the 360, betting the future of the whole company on the success of one system.

3. *They see their profits in cash.*

4. *They have strong franchises and thus freedom to price.* The number of truly protected areas in our economy is minute. Their very rarity is the greatness of capitalism. Start a Japanese restaurant and, if it works, the neighborhood soon has two, four, eight, then sixteen Japanese restaurants. Their profitability declines until the owners just have a job, not an exploitation.

American Express, for instance, has had two perfect natural business franchises: the first is its billions of dollars of cash "float" from the traveler's check business. Essentially the company is always borrowing without interest from the purchasers of these checks and relending the money at high interest. The second is the American Express credit card. It is clearly number one, and isn't price-sensitive. When Buffett saw the cost of the cards gradually increase from three dollars a year to twenty dollars, with no loss of acceptance even during the salad oil scandal, he knew that here was something unique.

5. *They don't take a genius to run.* While Tom Murphy of Capi-

tal Cities is the most able manager in the communications industry, even his ordinary counterparts do extremely well because
they are swimming with the tide.

6. *Their earnings are predictable.*

7. *They are not natural targets of regulation.*

8. *They have low inventories and high turnover of assets.* In
other words, they require little compulsory capital investment.
There are many high-growth businesses that require large infusions of capital as they grow and have done nothing for their
owners—a lesson investors periodically relearn.

9. *The management is owner-oriented.* Buffett observes that
one can sense quickly when management is not owner-oriented,
and when it isn't the investor had better stay away. He thinks
it an atrocity when controlling shareholders go public at high
prices in a bubbling market, then fail to perform, and eventually
force the public investors out at fifty cents on the dollar.* He
likes managements who regard stockholders as partners, not ad-
versaries.

One horror story Buffett cites specifically is Kennecott's message to its shareholders on the sale of its subsidiary, Peabody
Coal, at the government's insistence. Management could have
distributed the stock of Peabody or the proceeds of its sale to
the Kennecott shareholders in one way or another. That, however,
would have given management 1 billion fewer dollars in assets
to play with. So they told the shareholders that the whole thing
was too complicated for laymen to understand, and management
would decide for them—which management never would have
been allowed to do if Kennecott had been owned by U.S. Steel
or by a single family. Peabody, in turn, had an Australian subsidiary. Would Kennecott, the shareholder owner of Peabody, have

---

* Benjamin Graham deals harshly with this maneuver in Chapter 15 of *The
Intelligent Investor*, (4th rev. ed., New York: Harper & Row, 1973): "Financial
authorities have given little attention to the questions about fair treatment that
arise in such repurchases; the stockholders themselves have not thought about
it at all. It is time that a basic principle was adopted here—the principle that a
corporation should deal fairly with *all* its owners, and that it should pay a fair
price to those who are selling their interest back to it."

allowed the Peabody management to sell *its* subsidiary and redeploy the assets without the approval of its Kennecott parent owner? Buffett doubts it.

He points out that the disposition of a company's most important asset may be the chief issue the shareholders ever have to confront, and to say they can't be trusted to deal with it or that they shouldn't have a say in the utilization of proceeds is absurd. At least they should have the opportunity to express a preference. Certainly management can be trusted less to decide that question than the owners themselves.

10. *There is a high rate of return on the total of inventories plus plant.* (Receivables usually offset payables.) This test, only applicable in certain industries, exposes many bad businesses that seem to have high earnings but in fact are wormy—some of the conglomerates, for example. Stock promoters during frothy markets crudely but successfully dress up ordinary companies to fit the current fashion of the investment world, but this test is hard to fake.

Petrie Stores is one of the world's most wonderful businesses. Buffett doesn't know how Petrie does it, but it needs virtually no capital to operate.

11. *The best business is a royalty on the growth of others, requiring little capital itself,* such as Marsh & McLennan among the great insurance-broking firms, or the top international ad agencies.

The Wall Street Transcript *Indicator and Other Investment Techniques*

Buffett recommends looking less at earnings per share than at return on capital, which is what produces the earnings. There are ways of manipulating earnings per share and earnings growth; return on total capital is harder to play with.

I asked him about buying companies that were showing increasing profit margins and rising earnings, or were gaining institutional acceptance, or had just skipped dividends, or whatever.

Buffett replied that Benjamin Graham had examined any number of such techniques and found that nothing bettered the formula of buying a company at a substantial discount from its working capital and selling it when it was valued in the market at close to 100 percent of its working capital. One must, of course, have enough financial background to be able to understand the company's annual report.

I pointed out that while lack of marketability is unimportant to a true investor, the ordinary man can't know enough about a company to accept illiquidity. "In that case," Buffett replied, "I can't help him." We agreed that the correct solution in such an instance was a good mutual fund.

Buffett has a theory that the Dow Jones is worth one times book value if you expect Treasury Bills to yield an average of 11 percent in the future, 1.3 times book if your expectation is that they will yield an average of 8.5 percent, and close to twice book if you expect 5 percent. The trick, of course, is to make a reasonably good estimate of future average interest rates.

Buffet believes almost no one should ever go short, but if one does, it is best to go short the entire market—a representative list—rather than stocks one considers overpriced. Ben Graham tried going short overpriced stocks. Three out of four times it worked, but the fourth time he would get murdered as an already overpriced stock was run up to the skies by public enthusiasm. He himself has no interest in shorting.

Buffett says that he has never seen a major discrepancy between market value and intrinsic value maintained over an extended number of years. He tends to buy on weakness. If a stock he has bought advances an eighth, he stops and reconsiders. He says that for him to buy a stock on an uptick is about the equivalent of the Second Coming. It has to be the world's greatest idea. (He regards this as a quirk of personality, rather than a desirable technique, and adds that his best buys have been on a scale up when his conviction overcame his hesitations.)

I described visiting Tampax when the stock was in the dumps, and being told by the financial vice-president that a couple of years before, with the stock selling four times higher on lower earnings, he had been inundated by analysts, whereas I was the only one he'd seen in weeks. Buffett replied that it's always like that: one of the surest indices that you are on safe ground in buying a stock is that there is no mention of it in any recent index of the *Wall Street Transcript,* which reprints a great many brokerage house writeups.

Discussing the trading approach to the stock market, I mentioned having talked to Martin Sosnoff, whose *Humble on Wall Street* and guest columns in *Forbes* I had enjoyed. Buffett says that Sosnoff's method of hyperintensive investing, though most impressive, is excessively difficult, like a tournament of bridge experts in which each player can see the others' cards.* The stocks that Sosnoff describes dealing in are being followed by some of the best brains in the world. For example, he writes about buying and selling Hughes Tool at the time of the original public issue. At that moment it was perhaps the most discussed stock on Wall Street. When Buffett was buying Disney or American Express, there was virtually no competition. Buffett says he knows no one who has made and kept a significant amount of money by the method Sosnoff describes.

The One-Line Employment Form

In discussing qualifications for business managers, Buffett grinned and recommended a one-line employment form: "Are you a fanatic?" A manager must care intensely about running a first-class operation; if his golf game is what he thinks about while shaving, the business will show it. A good manager should be a demon on costs. He need not have fancy data processing equipment,

---

* This comparison also occurs in Chapter 13 of *The Intelligent Investor.* "Everyone is very brilliant indeed, but scarcely anyone is so superior to the rest as to be certain of winning a prize. An added quirk in Wall Street is that the prominent market analysts freely communicate and exchange their views almost from day to day. The result is almost as if all the participants in a bridge tournament, while each hand was being played out, gathered round and argued about the proper strategy."

or even a budget: he should *know* his costs, down to how many stamps he uses. Buffett mentioned Peter Kiewit, regarded as the leading businessman in Omaha, whose company may be the most successful construction firm in the world. There are no carpets in the executive offices, no consultants, and the bosses are there on Saturday.

Buffett doesn't mind having managers who are over seventy years old. Gene Abegg, for example, from whom he bought Illinois National Bank, ran it until he died in 1980 at eighty-one. Two other companies he controls are run by men in their mid-seventies.

The manager should feel and act as though he were the owner of the business. Buffett hates managers who exploit their position to the disadvantage of the owners—for instance, those who tell stockholders a tender offer at 40 is grossly inadequate shortly before or after selling part of the company to themselves (through liberal stock options) at 25; or who sell stock at less than intrinsic value to finance an acquisition at more than intrinsic value; or who fail to buy in their own stock in the market when it is far underpriced because they want to expand, not contract, their own domain, even though the shareholders' interests would be served by a repurchase program.*

Buffett considers that Henry Singleton of Teledyne has the best operating and capital deployment record in American business. When I asked if he did not consider Tom Murphy of Capital Cities to be equally outstanding, Buffett smiled and said, "Well, Murph plays a simpler game," but added that part of great business ability is to get into simple games. Singleton's return on assets, calculated in the way that Buffett likes to do it (inventory *plus* fixed assets), is unique. All four major industry groups in Teledyne are in fully competitive areas; none has a special pro-

---

* As Benjamin Graham says, management "almost always wants as much capital from the owners as it possibly can get, in order to minimize its own financial problems. Thus the typical management will operate with more capital than is necessary if the stockholders permit it—which they often do." (*The Intelligent Investor*, Chapter 4.)

tected niche; and yet all four earn 50 percent on assets. The company earns $250 million after tax, with very conservative accounting.

Singleton bought 130 businesses for "Chinese paper," as it used to be called, when his stock was riding high. Then when the market, and his stock, fell he reversed field and in the last eight years hasn't acquired a single company; on the contrary, by buying his stock back he has shrunk his capital from 40 million shares to 12 million.

According to Buffett, if one took the top 100 business school graduates and made a composite of their triumphs, their record would not be as good as that of Singleton, who incidentally was trained as a scientist, not an MBA. The failure of business schools to study men like Singleton is a crime, he says. Instead, they insist on holding up as models executives cut from a McKinsey & Company cookie cutter.

"There Ain't No 'Across the Street' from the Wall Street Journal."

Buffet considers the *Wall Street Journal* one of the most perfect business franchises, one you probably could not duplicate for a billion dollars. (Two others are *TV Guide* and the *Racing Form*, both apparently price-insensitive and both owned by Walter Annenberg.) The most profitable publication in the country, the *Journal* offers a product for which many users would gladly pay double the price. Both advertisers and readers get a bargain, while required capital investment to support growth is minimal.

Bernard Kilgore made the discovery that a newspaper is as good as its own city. The only problem was that all the cities were taken. So he created his own, the community of business readers, block by block. His city is a demographic dream, with no slums, and its readers have a vast buying capability. Columns one, four, and six on the front page now are the most read daily texts in America.

When a media executive asked a friend on the *Journal* why

it did not tie its ad salesmen's compensation more closely to their productivity, the friend replied, "Why, the salesmen would just go across the street."

The executive answered, "There ain't no 'across the street' from the *Wall Street Journal.*"

Advertising Agencies: A Royalty on Sales

The perfect business is a royalty on the sales of a major company, as distinct from its net profits. One example is the big international advertising agencies, which net 1 percent or so after tax on their clients' advertising expenditures, and often 5 percent or so on their own revenues. The clients, not the agencies, invest the capital to build those sales.

There are few big international agencies, and there will be fewer new ones, since it's getting harder and harder to break into the club. At this point a J. Walter Thompson controls so much business that it can just buy an agency in a new territory that becomes interesting, such as Brazil or the Middle East. A smaller agency would have trouble making a competitive offer.*

A local advertising agency is quite another matter. Buffett would not buy a share in a brain surgeon, but in the Mayo Clinic, yes: it's become institutionalized.

Interpublic and Ogilvy & Mather, two of the top five or six agencies worldwide, are to him the most interesting of them as investments. In 1974 Interpublic sold at less than two times pre-tax earnings per share, and half of the market price of its tangible assets, although this unique enterprise represents a well-earned royalty on the gross income of Exxon, Carnation, Buick, and Chevrolet. Small agencies at that time were being bought out at perhaps three times that price. In a way, the situation was actually better than in 1932, since by 1974 it was quite clear that the companies themselves would not fall apart.

---

* Further, since GM, Ford, Chrysler, American Motors, and VW each must use different agencies, as do the soap companies, big banks, cigarette companies, and the rest, there always must be business for each big international agency.

Television

Broadcasting companies enjoy superb growth and provide cascades of cash. As a result they have maintained strong values in purchases by private buyers. (Buffett thinks it might be an interesting idea to buy a TV station in partnership form, so that one could duck the corporate tax.)

Their stock market values are another story. In 1974 Capital Cities was appraised by the stock market for $125 million but was worth at least three times that. Capital Cities' only problem is the pleasant one of what to do with all its excess cash. Buffett felt it should buy its own stock; I mentioned that my firm, as shareholders, had urged Murphy to do just that.*

Television stations are not entirely without risk as investments. In theory, the government can fail to renew a license, although in practice that almost never happens. Regulation and new technology could change the economics of broadcasting. But at present the arithmetic of television stations is astonishing: they often net 50 percent on sales, have no need for working capital, have only minor fixed assets, and no inventories except for a supply of movies, which can be bought on credit. Buffett bought a major television station in Dayton, Ohio, for Grinnell College, of which he is a trustee. The purchase price in 1976 was $12.9 million; it was sold for four times that amount a few years later.†

Bad Investments

1. Buffett's worst investments have been in *retailing* (including trading stamps), a field he says he never has really understood. In addition to investment losses on several retailing securities, his negotiated purchase of Hochschild Kohn, a Baltimore department store, also proved a dud. Figures and close observation are

---

* After we talked, the company did decide to do so.
† In 1986 Berkshire made its largest investment ever, in Capital Cities/ABC.

not enough: you need a special flair to understand what's going on in that field. A store can report good figures year after year and then, as Buffett learned the hard way, suddenly go bankrupt. (In checking back with him before publication I found him buying another retailer: the moth returning to the flame.)

2. *"You bet your company"* situations, such as Lockheed. Periodically, they have to put the whole company on the line just to stay in business.

Other businesses to avoid include:

3. *Farm-related enterprises.* They have a very long inventory cycle (a whole crop year) and you have to finance the farmer, who never has any cash.* You may show a bookkeeping profit, pay taxes on it, and still end up with receivables that you have trouble collecting.

4. *Businesses heavily dependent on research.* Ben Graham always disagreed with the Wall Street belief that a company with an overwhelming advantage in research and development tends to maintain its lead over its competitors—a Merck, say, or an IBM (which spends over $1 billion a year on R&D). Graham felt that if the company had to spend so much to stay ahead it was a sign of weakness, not strength.

Buffett replies that in Graham's day there were lots of businesses with intrinsically privileged positions, which didn't need to spend massively on R&D to hold their lead; today there are very few, so Graham's antipathy to R&D companies is no longer applicable. Buffett nevertheless can't understand the high technology companies, and doesn't like them for that reason.

To that I in turn would reply that the ordinary investor isn't going to understand a large and complex business anyway, so

---

* I told Buffett the story of the two farmers in Georgia who were guests on a radio talk show. "What would you do, Jim," the MC asked the first farmer, "if a rich uncle left you a million dollars?"

Jim was thrilled. "Why, ah'd pay off the mortgage, get mahself a new tractor, send the kids to college, and put in a new kitchen. Then ah'd take Minnie 'round the world like we've always wanted to do."

"And what'd you do with your million, Josh?" the MC asked the other farmer.

Josh wasn't so sure. He rubbed his chin and thought. Finally he said, "Well, ah guess ah'd jest go on farming 'til it was all gone."

the historical excellence in research of Texas Instruments probably should give him a better indication of its future prospects than could be gained from an attempt to really understand a General Electric. Philip Fisher, as we will see, also disagrees with Buffett, believing that a successful commitment to innovation is an essential quality in a company that will build value for its owners, and outstanding research can keep you ahead.

4. *Debt-burdened companies*. A house with no mortgage obviously is worth more than one that is burdened with one.

5. *Chain-letter businesses*—those with geometric growth requiring more and more cash.

6. *Managements that don't tell the truth*. If they don't, then Buffett doesn't want to be in business with them. Many annual reports are a disgrace. If major mistakes are made or adversity threatens, the annual report should say so frankly, as one partner would talk to another. Instead, these reports are all too often exercises in optimism and flackery—sales pitches rather than honest expositions.

7. *Long-term service contracts*. Discussing casualty insurance, Buffett observed that it can be fatal to be short services and long dollars—obliged to provide something in the distant future with no idea what it will cost. If you write workmen's compensation and a policyholder is disabled, you are short doctors' fees and hospital costs for twenty years against dollars received today. . . . Disastrous. (Property and casualty insurance is Buffett's largest direct business interest, and the business of two of his largest passive investments, GEICO and SAFECO. Assuming top management, other characteristics of the insurance business enable it to cope with inflation.)

Insurance

Buffett doesn't believe in businesses that generate profits that you can't get your hands on, and where you must maintain a high net worth—that is, tie up capital.

An easy way to evaluate a life insurance company is to look at its intrinsic worth ten years ago, for instance, and then today: in almost all cases the rate of compounding is unexciting.

I commented on the life insurance companies' advantage in being able to use depreciated dollars to pay off their policies, and to use unrealistically low actuarial assumptions. Even so, says Buffett, life insurance is not a particularly good business. The present value of the future income, less future costs, is not enough to justify the cost of putting the business on the books today. It's only a good business if you sell gimmicky "Mickey Mouse" policies—and he doesn't want to own such a company. Travelers, Connecticut General, and the like are not attractive. When they make money, part goes into the policyholder's surplus account, which means another tax when it comes out again.

" 'Long tail' reinsurance is a terrifying business," Buffett says. "You can have an obligation pop up at you twenty years later with a huge price tag that you never anticipated. Reinsurance rarely turns out to be what it's sold as. Some of the slick fellows who sell it look as conservative and modest as you could possibly want—straight from Central Casting. But they'll stick you all the same."

Venture Capital

Venture capital propositions interest Buffett scarcely at all. Typically, the promoter invites you to put up all the money for a speculative undertaking in exchange for half to three-quarters of the company. Most new ventures soon fail, however.

In a market washout, on the other hand, you can buy a flawless company for one-quarter of what it's worth right then and there, without having to pay off the promoter or take the risk that his dream will never be realized.

Disney, for example, when Buffett bought into the company, in early 1966, at its low was selling for one-quarter of what it was worth to a private buyer, with the greatest creative management in the world already in place. The market was placing no value on its huge inventory of former hits, which can be reissued every few years forever, it seems.

The Fortune *500 Syndrome*

All too often, Buffett says, if you could put a chief executive under sodium pentothal and dig into the rationale behind his acquisitions, you'd find he was inspired by his yearning to move up a few places in the *Fortune* list of the 500 largest companies, not by concern for the value per share of his company. Many companies, including banks, are run into the ground because the president is concerned with size rather than quality: he becomes hypnotized by his company's rank in terms of gross size.

The Crocker Bank in San Francisco paid a premium of approximately $90 million over book value (about twice book, in fact) to buy a troubled bank one-sixth its size, U.S. National of San Diego. Crocker then sold its own stock well below book to pay a large part of the cost of this purchase. The CEO (now retired) did not take the attitude of an owner but of an empire-builder. The bank sold a portion of its stock at a discount in order to buy the inferior bank at a gigantic premium. The banker became more important, and the stockholders became poorer. Buffett quotes Morris Shapiro: "There are more banks than bankers."

Buffett says that for a cash-rich company to buy into a business that requires enormous amounts of cash is like going to a beautiful princess and announcing, "I have a poor sex-starved wretch here who desperately wants to meet you." A cash-rich company should buy other cash-rich companies.

It's usually better for a company not to have a formal acquisition department: he thinks it results in a pressure, usually misguided, to buy for the sake of buying. Too often the members of the department merely regurgitate what they know to be the inner desires of management.

Banking

Buffett points out that banking is one of the few industries in which there is no advantage to being number one. What counts is how you manage your assets, liabilities, and costs. And in those respects, size means practically nothing.

He considers banking a splendid business if you don't go crazy. Unfortunately, there is a real risk of precisely that. How do you control lots of eager young men, each with a pen, who can manufacture immediate earnings by incurring risks that are not apparent until much later?

Buffett is highly skeptical of the epidemic of loans to wobbly foreign credits that have been responsible for much of the earnings growth of the money-center banks in recent years. Very few Third World countries have repaid as much as they have borrowed. Anyone's credit looks good while he's borrowing more than he's repaying, but how will the countries react when they are asked to cut back services and consumption in order to repay the loans?

In discussing the contrast between a good, tough, businesslike bank manager and a romantic and unbusinesslike one, Buffett commented with amusement that David Rockefeller periodically announces that the only thing wrong with Chase is a few of his top subordinates.

Bufffett noted that the Freedom National Bank in New York, advised by several large banks, including Chase, lost money in 1975 *before* loan losses, and that it bought more New York municipal paper than its own net worth, even though it had a huge tax loss, so that buying tax-exempts was irrational. Buffett said that socially-oriented business activities still have to make sense; doing business in a half-assed way is no favor to anybody.

A minority-owned bank was started in Omaha and came to Buffett for support. He told them that if they raised a quarter of a million dollars in cash, he'd then raise another quarter-million. He refused to raise his part first or to accept IOUs for theirs;

only cash. They finally got the money and Buffett did his part. He is now on the bank's advisory board, and it is operated soundly and profitably by an able black manager.

Commodity Speculation

Buffett agrees with me that it's scandalous for Wall Street houses to encourage small investors to dabble in commodities. He says that one sometimes can analyze the long-term price outlook for a nonagricultural commodity, notably a metal. If the price gets way below production cost for an indispensable metal, it must eventually recover. But the prices of agricultural commodities are subject to weather and other vagaries of nature; investing in them becomes a matter of flair. Since he depends on analysis for success, Buffett never will invest in an agricultural commodity.

In twenty years he engaged in only two commodities transactions, recently in copper and, some years ago, before the price was freed by the government, in silver futures. Every time President Johnson announced that the price of silver would never rise, Buffett went out and bought more. In his copper speculation he bought a large position at 56 cents per pound, since, though the above-ground stock of the metal was enormous, many mines were closing down and eventually the price would have to go up. He would never buy more than he could afford to take delivery of in cash: if one buys a metal on margin, even though it reaches one's target eventually, it may first go down, wiping you out en route.

He finds ownership of actual metal far safer than ownership of a mining company. A Kennecott, for example, spends hundreds of millions of dollars to dig a hole and sell copper. Then it reinvests much of its profits in more and more development and facilities. Eventually the consumers have gotten all the copper and Kennecott is left with the hole. In theory this can be profitable; in practice, lots goes wrong.

The only thing worse is mining in South America. You spend

your money to sink the shaft and install the mill, and presently
a chap appears with a couple of MPs and tells you to get out.

How Buffett Buys a Whole Company

He bought Berkshire Hathaway, a bad business, at a good price.
It is largely owned by Buffett and his former partners. Because of
its acquisitions, it has had an outstanding growth in earnings per
share and in asset value for twenty-five years.

Since for Buffett a stock is a business, which he first analyzes
as a business, it follows that he can also buy a business itself with
little more time and effort. Although the approach is the same,
he cautions that you don't get bargains in businesses as you do
in stocks. He made Mr. See an offer for his candy company about
three hours after meeting him. To buy the Illinois National Bank,
he went on a Friday and spent two hours there. He said to Gene
Abegg, the seventy-one-year-old owner, whom he immediately
liked, "If we make a deal, I'm going to make four changes that
you won't like. I'll drop four shoes, but there are no more shoes
after that. If you accept them, I'll tell you my price on Monday
and, if you like my offer, I'll meet you at the Harris Trust on
Thursday with a check and a contract that you won't have to
change a word of." Mr. Abegg accepted the changes, and that
was that. When he bought National Indemnity Company, Jack
Ringwalt came to see him at 11:30 and everything was completed
so rapidly they couldn't even stretch the meeting out for lunch;
and he bought the *Buffalo Evening News* without interviewing
anyone on the staff.

When Bonds Are Better Than Stocks

For high-bracket individuals, tax-exempt bond income is often
more attractive than the expectable after-tax return from stocks.
A generous target for total return on a stock portfolio would

be 3 percent a year from the dividends, plus a 9 percent capital gain, or 12 percent in all. After a 50 percent income tax and a 30 percent capital gains tax, however, 1.5 percent is left from dividends and 6.3 percent from capital gain, a total return of 7.8 percent after tax. And when the general market is selling for, say, 1.5 times its own book value, the expectable return falls considerably from this level.

From time to time you can get a similar return from good quality municipals, such as industrial revenue bonds, without the risks of stock ownership. At such a time, municipals are preferable to stocks. Buffett mentioned that he had negotiated a direct purchase from K mart of an industrial revenue bond earning 7.5 percent, which should do better than many stocks, after taxes.

What did he think of the strategy of buying a very steady growth stock, such as Schlumberger, and then from time to time borrowing on the portfolio to cover spending needs? This means that one pays no taxes, since the bank recovers its loan from one's estate, and the taxable dividends from the stock usually are less than the interest going to the bank.

Buffett said that he had learned from his father and from Ben Graham never to borrow. For instance, there is the sad case of Jimmy Goodwin, son of Leo Goodwin, founder of GEICO. He had $100 million of GEICO stock and he borrowed on it for living expenses and miscellaneous ventures so as not to have to pay capital gains taxes on his holdings. When GEICO's stock collapsed, he not only lost his portfolio assets but had his house sold at a sheriff's sale. People usually borrow because they want to get rich soon; Buffett feels that the journey should be as much fun as the destination, so why take chances?

Liquidity in bonds is not very important, any more than it is in stocks. If one can sell in a week, or even a month, that's good enough—and far better than one expects in real estate. How long does it take to sell a farm?

The more one is a true investor, the less one need be concerned about liquidity.

Wall Street: I Don't Sell to Fish

Buffett observes that few Wall Street reports on stocks discuss a business as though one owned it privately: why would I want to put more money in this business and, above all, how can I get it out again? Buffett never has seen a stockbroker's report on a company that discussed a business the way its manager would discuss it with an individual owner he was reporting to, and in general does not find it worth reading them.

Buffett tells the story, which he said reminds him of Wall Street, of a fisherman who goes into a sporting supply store. The salesman offers him a fantastic lure for bass; painted eyes, half a dozen hooks, imitation bugs: a whole junk shop. The fisherman asks the salesman incredulously, "Do fish really like this thing?"

The salesman replies coldly, "I don't sell to fish."*

Buffett hates to go to Wall Street. A hotshot conglomerate president passes the word that he's going to give his earnings a jab. The professionals load up. Then a respected institutional brokerage house solemnly intones the tale, hoping that it will be picked up and relayed, chain-letter style.

In the hedge fund days of the 1960s the market was a series of concentric circles, he says. The go-go managers wanted to be in the exact center of the inner circle, to be sure that whatever they bought could be fobbed off on the outer circles. They really didn't care what the values were or even if the "story" was true; only if it would sell.

---

* This reminded me of the yachtsman down east who got tired of his own cooking. Next time he put into a cove he went to the little general store to ask for Angostura bitters. The proprietor seemed to remember that he had some of that stuff down in the cellar. They descended with a lantern, and indeed discovered a bottle on an upper shelf. The yachtsman noticed that the walls of the cellar were lined with bags of salt. As the storekeeper was making change the yachtsman asked him, "Is there a cannery in town? You seem to have an awful lot of salt down there." The storekeeper paused and looked at the yachtsman intently over the register. "Mistah," he said, "me, I can't hahdly sell a pinch of salt. But the man who sells *me* salt, can he sell salt!"

"Look at this!" cried Buffett, producing an old *Moody's* showing the holdings of the Manhattan Fund, Gerry Tsai's lamentable assemblage. "Four Seasons Nursing Homes, National Student Marketing, U.S. Financial, King Resources, Teleprompter, Career Academy, Deltona . . . they're *all* here!"

We went over the portfolio, and found that more than half of the holdings had, within a year or so, either lost 90 percent of their value or gone bankrupt! (For the list, see Appendix IV on pages 256–257.)

"These were people's savings!" said Buffett. "This guy was supposed to be an *analyst!*"*

Wall Street, he says, probably deserved the retribution it got.

The Future

Buffett doubts that the world can save itself from an exchange of atomic blows. He contributes to the Pugwash Movement, which hopes to improve U.S.-Russian understanding, but thinks that it's probably hopeless. He bases this opinion on his knowledge of how people act in a crisis rather than on any technical analysis of the problems, although he has read the usual studies. If a large number of proud men, any one of whom could set things off, time and again get on a collision course, at some point things are likely to spin out of control. We'll squeak by 999 times and then miss once; a 99.9 percent success ratio guarantees disaster.

I asked him once what he contemplated doing with the rest of his life. He doesn't want to manage outside money anymore. In fact it's bad tactics to sit at a desk all day long, fiddling with a portfolio. Doing very little is more profitable. He does enjoy working with people he likes in a number of businesses. He liked becoming a director of the *Washington Post,* and has the greatest admiration for its chairman, Kay Graham, and the publisher, Don

---

* Buffett later suggested that for Gerry Tsai specifically the catalogue of "reasons to invest" described on page 17 should be modified to read, "I believe King Resources will not go bankrupt for thirty-six months because . . ."

Graham. He has no feeling that he has solutions to the problems of the world, but believes he understands reasonably well what motivates people and organizations.

I asked him if he would enjoy working on a regulatory commission and he replied that it would depend on "how many tickets" he had. He enjoys transforming ideas into action, but if forestalled from doing so, would become impatient.

He finds that happiness comes from small improvements, not by getting somewhere once and for all. Being able to add on one room to your house is what makes you happy, not living in a palace. He believes in "a meritocracy based on equality of opportunity." Inherited wealth, with a life supply of "food stamps" presented upon birth based only on proper selection of parents, is "socially unjust."* Consistent with that philosophy, he is putting his money in a foundation rather than leaving it to his children.

The Great American Jam Tomorrow Ponzi Scheme

For me, Buffett's most important single message is his cry of alarm and recurring admonition to steer clear of the standard big American heavy industries requiring continuous massive investment. Most of them are in trouble.

The cause is competition, overregulation,† rising labor costs, and the like. The symptom is that just to stay in business many of these big industries need more money than they can retain out of reported earnings after paying reasonable dividends. To stay in the same place they require endless infusions of net new cash, like India or Egypt. To be sure, there are dividends on the new stock and interest on the new bonds that they constantly issue, but basically these dividends and interest payments are

---

* Obviously, those born with exceptional abilities favor *la carrière ouverte aux talents;* those born with money, the duty to husband one's patrimony; those with high social positions, the doctrine of *noblesse oblige.*

†Congress' General Accounting Office estimated that the yearly direct and indirect cost of *all* government regulation of business was $180 billion *(sic)* in 1980. The Executive branch's Office of Management and Budget puts it at $130 billion. Either is wildly higher than the imaginable benefits.

only a loss leader to induce the investor to buy the new securities being issued. He has only an outside chance of ever seeing his principal again in real terms. "Jam yesterday and jam tomorrow, but never jam today."

I call all this a Ponzi scheme because basically the *capital* raised by the endless new stock and bond issues pays the dividends and interest. The dividends, at least after honest depreciation, are often not being earned.

Buffett points out that after seventy years in the business, the Ford Motor Company doesn't ordinarily pay enough dividends to give its own shareholders after taxes the equivalent of 100,000 cars a year out of the 6-odd million that it makes. All that money, that huge plant, those many generations, and still the impact of higher costs, taxes, and foreign competition mean that the owners can't even claim 2 percent of the output.

I observed that this was in a way the subtlety of American capitalism. The owners are coaxed along into putting more and more money (or reinvesting more and more profits) into plant, but are not able to take out net cash that they can go home to spend. It's like fishing with cormorants: they have bands around their necks so they can have the satisfaction of diving for the fish and filling their gullets, but not of actually swallowing the fish, which are taken away by the boss—in the case of American corporations, by the government and everyone else except the shareholders.

Buffett regards investing in the "smokestack" companies, the heavy industries whose obsolescence is often more rapid than their allowable depreciation, as, in essence, participating in a series of constant mandatory rights offerings, where you have to put up more money to maintain your percentage interest. Instead of distributing their earnings to the shareholders in dividends, these companies need to retain them to build more capacity, either to replace rapidly aging facilities or to meet competition. This increases output, which further lowers profit margins, so that the companies are even less able to make real money in their basic businesses.

My conclusion is that, as a result, the investor in a "heavy" company that cannot pay an adequate dividend is really acting as its curator in its intermediate stage between private and public ownership. That holds for almost all railroads and many utility, chemical, and domestic oil companies here, for example, and a great many companies abroad.

Buffett goes so far as to maintain that it may hold for almost all capital-intensive industries: unexciting businesses, often run at profitability levels which do not allow their owners to maintain purchasing power, let alone obtain a real return on their investment.

For this reason, he feels a newspaper should not develop its own sources of newsprint except as a defensive measure; it's cheaper to buy the newsprint in the market.

Discussing American Airlines, Buffett mentioned that it turns over its capital (including leased equipment and facilities) only once a year. On that basis it would have to realize close to a 20 percent pre-tax profit margin on sales in order to net 10 percent if financed by equity capital. In fact, the company makes nothing like a 20 percent profit margin on its sales, which would, indeed, be one of the highest margins in all industry.

I noted that to stay in business through the 1980s General Motors will have to raise some $15 billion of new money; more than the whole company was selling for, and more than it will pay in dividends between now and then. Can it really be said to be making money at all? And ATT by its own account has to keep raising its dividends in order to raise immense amounts of stock in the market through repeated rights offerings and, of course, even larger bond offerings. If ATT extracts more money from the market than the shareholders are receiving from it net in dividends, after paying their own taxes, are they really making money?

Buffett once met a leading executive of a capital-intensive business giant at a time when the company was selling in the market for one-quarter of its replacement value.

Buffett asked the executive, "Why don't you buy back your

own stock? If you like to buy new facilities at one hundred cents on the dollar, why not buy the ones you know best and were responsible for creating at twenty-five cents on the dollar?"

Executive: "We should."

Buffett: "Well?"

Executive: "That's not what we're here to do."

2

Paul Cabot

The Realist

By general consent, the dean of institutional investors in Boston is Paul Cabot. (And although perhaps not everyone in Wall Street would agree, Boston is still the Vatican of trust investment.)

Paul Cabot ran Harvard's endowment for seventeen years, during which time the money grew 500 percent, from $200 million to $1 billion, not including capital additions. He also founded and has for more than fifty years been a partner of State Street Management and Research, which runs a stable of mutual funds, endowments, and private portfolios. The most important is State Street Investment Company, one of the first American mutual funds, which has been in business over half a century—since 1924. If you had bought $1,000 worth of stock at its inception, the 1980 value came to about $100,000, including dividends and reinvested capital gains distributions. Very few money managers indeed have a comparable record.

Even without that distinction, Paul Cabot would certainly still rank as one of the great characters of the Boston business scene. While still a young man, Cabot was elected to the board of J. P. Morgan & Company, at once the most powerful and the stuffiest of American banking firms. (Mr. Morgan's desk stood in the middle of the street floor at 23 Wall Street, but he did not require a receptionist or secretary to keep people from approaching him. Nobody dared.) At one directors' meeting Cabot appeared sporting a big purple shiner and a cut on his forehead. A fellow director commiserated respectfully on his wound—a fall while fox hunting, presumably?

"Christ, no!" bellowed Cabot across the boardroom. "Haven't any of you bastards ever been drunk?" At another Morgan board of directors meeting, Cabot was sitting next to Alfred P. Sloan, creator of the modern General Motors. Many of the concepts of today's largest enterprises were worked out under Sloan's management, among them decentralized operating management within centralized financial control, return on capital as a cardinal responsibility and test of managers, and the systematic positioning of different makes of GM cars at key points in the market's price spectrum.

To this sage, with his tall, stiff collar, grave manner, and incalculable responsibilities, the young Cabot addressed the cheerful question, "How's it going?"

Sloan courteously started to describe the point that he and his finance committee had reached in developing corporate policy on the relationship between the wholly-owned suppliers, such as Fisher, and the different divisions, such as Buick and Chevrolet.

"No, no!" Cabot interrupted after a while. "The hell with that! What I want to know is, when is it going to make some real *dough?*"

If you ask them in Boston how Paul Cabot got this way, if he's showing off or trying to sound like a sailor or had troubles with his mother, they all say the same thing: "It's not that. I don't know. He's just *always* been that way."

One of Cabot's finest hours came in 1972. For several years McGeorge Bundy of the Ford Foundation had been broadcasting his call to American colleges to invest their endowments aggressively so they would "go up" faster, and then to live dangerously on the "total return" from their portfolios: not just on the income but also on the market appreciation—and even what the market appreciation ought to be. Heady times!

The Foundation is the chief private source of largesse for American universities, and sounds awfully money-wise to a board of trustees in Savannah, Georgia. When its call came for this Children's Crusade there were many who felt they better string along. The Ford Foundation's pronunciamento came right at the top of the bull market—the only time people will believe in a repeal of common sense—and lured a significant number of American institutions of learning onto the rocks—and the foundation itself, which later had to jettison one-third of its activities.* Yale succumbed; Harvard, yea even Harvard, was tempted. The president and fellows started wondering if there might not be something to it.

Across the Charles River, over in Boston, Paul Cabot blew his stack. No longer Harvard's treasurer, he fulminated an open letter to the president of the university which promptly attained circulation among the governing bodies, faculty, and alumni. It is still vividly remembered both in educational and in investment circles.

Here is the text (I've left out some statistics and examples):

Dear President Bok:

I have heard that you and other members of the Harvard Corporation are considering the use of capital for current expenses (specifically part of capital gains) in addition to your present policy of using *all* of income on the endowment funds of the University.

The purpose of this letter is to dissuade you from adopting this dangerous, unfair, unwise, and possibly disastrous policy.

Ever since Harvard was founded in 1636, we have had (other than for short periods) higher prices and a declin-

---

* It would be interesting to try to calculate whether the foundation's championing of the "total return" heresy cost the universities more than the foundation had previously given them. Very possibly, after the arguments over Vietnam have subsided and Henry Ford's noisy resignation from the Ford Foundation board has been forgotten, the Bundy campaign for "total return" investing will survive in Wall Street lore. It sums up the unrealism of its era much as did Professor Irving Fisher's famous opinion that stocks had reached a "permanently high plateau" just before the Great Crash.

ing value for the dollar, i.e., inflation. I guess that you and the other members of the Corporation would agree with me that this will continue in the future, regardless of rather futile attempts which, at best, may only slightly slow the present rather rapid *rate* of inflation.

Unless Harvard and other institutions and individuals recognize this and prepare for it as Harvard has done in the past, the results in the future can indeed be disastrous. If one spends capital, obviously, there will be less in the future to earn money on. It really amounts to robbing the future to take care of the present. Of course, this procedure is tempting to any present incumbent. He'll probably be dead or out of the picture long before the inevitable fallacy of such a policy comes home to roost.

Your two predecessors as President of Harvard, with whom I served, always backed me one hundred percent in refusal to spend capital. Indeed, the income we "availed" ourselves of was, in fact, less by a few million every year than the income earned.

As of June 30, 1948, the market value of Harvard's General and Special Investments exceeded Yale's by approximately $100 million. At the end of fiscal 1971, the approximate market value of these funds were: Harvard, $1.3 billion and Yale, $547 million. Harvard's investments were three-quarters of a billion larger than Yale's! What caused this? Capital gifts to Harvard were bigger during this period but not enough so to account for this wide difference. Investment policy had most to do with it, but very important was the fact that Harvard saved money *every* year whereas, in many years, Yale dipped into principal. Yale now has a *policy* of doing so regularly. This unfortunate policy is disguised and made unclear by a formula of mathematical hieroglyphics. The simple fact is: it is Yale's policy to spend principal. . . .

There are other important reasons not to rob the future to make life easier now. The effect on donors and bequests could be very bad. Most givers of endowment funds assume and expect (and indeed sometimes legally specify) that the principal they give shall be maintained, not dissipated.

I realize that all colleges and universities have come on hard financial times—Harvard maybe less so for past wise preservation and growth of capital.

But let's face the facts and not go down the primrose path of capital spending but *cut expenses*. There are innumerable areas in this field. . . .

Finally, I beg you and the other members of Harvard's governing boards not to be a party to the slow strangulation of Harvard's goose that has laid so many golden eggs over past years.

I am giving this letter as much publicity as I can in the hope that it will induce alumni and friends of Harvard and Yale to beg the former not to go down this dangerous and probably disastrous road and the latter to return from it.

Sincerely,
Paul C. Cabot

Cabot won that battle. Common sense and tough experience again prevailed. The Harvard–Boston tradition has not only won out over the Yale–New York tradition, but has assured its superiority for the rest of the century. There's no way now that Yale can catch up financially for at least a generation or two. That means better-endowed chairs for Harvard, more scholarships, bigger libraries, a brighter collection of talent, more useful impact on America and the world. But beware complacency, Harvard!

The record of State Street Investment Corporation, the largest mutual fund run by Cabot's firm, provides a much longer continuous illustration of the skills of a few men. Cabot and his partners—all in their twenties—started it in the summer of 1924. The initial capital was $100,000, with 32,000 shares, giving a net asset value per share of $3.12½. By the end of 1928 the value had bubbled up sevenfold to $23.95 a share, and the fund had grown to $12 million. By the end of 1929 the value per share had declined to $21.80, but the size of the fund was up to $17 million. In the Great Crash, by the end of 1932, the value of a share was down to $10.68½—not a bad record at all for those times—and the fund had shrunk to $7 million. That was the low point. Not until 1943 did the value per share (including capital gains distributions taken in shares) climb back to the level of 1928, by which time the fund had reached $47 million.

From the fund's inception to the mid-1970s, assuming reinvestment of capital gains, an original investor would have made about a hundred times his money, including dividends, but before taxes, in just over fifty years. If one takes the not unreasonable position that the jump from $3.12½ a share in 1924 to $23.95 in 1928 was a freak—since the times were extraordinary and the fund so small—and starts the performance calculation at an arbitrary median of eight or nine dollars, then the total gain over a period of about fifty years, including dividends, and assuming capital gains taken in shares, would be fifty times the original money. If one skips to the late 1930s or early 1940s, then a rough figure for the gain becomes twenty times in forty years.

Over more recent periods the results are much less dramatic but still impressive. For the fifteen years ending December 31, 1975, the value per share advanced 94 percent, as compared to 55 percent for the S&P Index.

Clearly, when contemplating such a panorama, involving many thousands of investment decisions over a great sweep of time, no one transaction or group of transactions assumes much importance. Rather, the whole point of view and general approach is being tested and displayed.

What, then, is the cardinal point of Paul Cabot's approach?

As often as one asks him the question one always gets the same answer in a different way: realism and care; care and realism.

"First, you've got to get *all* the facts," he says, "and then you've got to *face* the facts." Characteristically, he goes on to mutter, "Not pipe dreams."

He always observes that there's no way to *be* a realist unless you've experienced the many facets of reality, which means having attained a certain age. With age, he's become more cautious.

Young people are optimistic. They come up with fantastic earnings estimates and are sure everything's going to be rosy. The younger you are the more chances you'll take. The older you get the more you've had a chance to see how often there's a slip between the cup and the lip. "I've only got confidence in older men, who've been through depressions, recessions, wars, and all the rest of it."

If you ask around among the old-timers in the Boston investment community what the essence is of Paul Cabot's investment technique you usually get the same answer: "He's so careful," they say; "he's so fantastically *thorough*."

Paul Cabot can be found at State Street Management, now housed in light, modern offices near the top of a Boston skyscraper. A handsome receptionist inters one's coat in a recessed closet. Everything suggests glossy efficiency, the twentieth century—maybe even the twenty-first.

Mr. Cabot's own office, however, is another story. Suddenly I was back in my Harvard tutor's study in 1948. There's an old pencil sharpener screwed to the inside of the door, a covey of simple wooden chairs, a wooden coat rack supporting one gray coat and one Boston hat (Boston hats are seasoned for several years inside tennis court rollers before being inaugurated), a glass-fronted bookcase containing business volumes and, behind a large plain desk, Mr. Cabot himself, a compact, rubicund man in his upper seventies. He wears the New England uniform of grayish tweedy suit with vest.

I asked him how well he had really done with the Harvard portfolio. Did the performance fully take account of capital additions and withdrawals?

"Well," said Cabot, "I took over in . . ." He hesitated, and leaned across his desk to inspect a huge gold-embossed red leather box, apparently the usual retirement token, ". . . Nineteen forty-eight. About all the goddamn thing's good for," he muttered, nodding at the box. "Can't remember dates. When I left in 1965 it had grown 500 percent. Harvard writes off a building in the year it's finished, which is right, because financially they're a liability. It just happens that gifts worked out to about as much as the construction came to, so five times is about how much the endowment really grew. Of course, those were damn good times. Wouldn't happen again."

I asked him about his even earlier days. What was it like in the twenties and thirties?

Cabot described some of his earliest transactions with wry amusement.

"I'll tell you what our idea of research was then. One of my two partners when I started out was my cousin Dick Paine. His father, my uncle, was a founder of General Electric, and a hell of an able investor: both of them, Paine and his father, had an amazing nose for what was good. The old man did his brokerage through Jackson & Curtis. Our idea of 'research' was that we had a friend in J&C who'd tell us what Paine's father—my uncle—was doing. Say he was buying American Gas and Electric. Our friend would tell us. So I'd study up on the company. Then I'd go to the old man and say, 'You know, Uncle, I've found an interesting stock. It's American Gas and Electric.' 'Is that so?' my uncle would say. 'Yes, I like it too. In fact, I like it a lot. I don't think it'll just go up 20 percent or something like that: I think it's going to double, and here's why.' So we'd know the goddamn thing was okay. That's what we meant by 'research'!

"One of our first big buys was Kraft—you know, cheese. Old man Kraft had started the whole thing at home, in Chicago. He used to go around in a horse and buggy selling the stuff. Later they found a way of pasteurizing the cheese . . . it ruins it. Makes it taste like some sort of goddamn toothpaste. I like natural cheese myself. Anyway, when we bought the stock it had sales of two or three million. Now it's two billion! We didn't like to go on the board of a company at that time. Now we do. So we asked a friend of ours called Jim Trimble to go on the board of Kraftco to represent us. He was a hell of a hard-boiled character.

"Mr. Kraft was a pious Baptist—never smoked or drank. One time we'd gone out to Chicago and were all in a room in the

Drake Hotel. Jim Trimble was on the bed with his feet up. We were all drinking bourbon and smoking cigars. Then Mr. Kraft came in. He told us he'd just borrowed $2 million from Halsey, Stuart. Trimble popped up like a jackknife coming together. 'Those sons of bitches?' he said. But that wasn't the worst of it. Mr. Kraft explained that Halsey, Stuart had gotten options on half the company as part of the deal. Trimble and I told him he was crazy as a coot. We figured Halsey, Stuart would sell the bonds they got for the $2 million and keep the options, which would have given them half the company. Not so. They gave half the options to whoever bought the bonds. So in a few weeks the bonds went up to 160 percent of par! We really got fed up with Kraft. He was a good merchant but didn't know a goddamn thing about financial management.

"That was how it was in those days. Years later, as a matter of fact, I went on the board myself. By that time they were selling two-thirds of all the cheese in the United States! Anyway, I found myself sitting next to Mr. Kraft at the board table.

" 'What does Mr. Trimble think of me now? Am I still crazy as a coot?' the old man asked me.

" 'I don't think he's changed his opinion, Mr. Kraft,' I told him. . . ."

"When I started out in this business nobody believed in common stocks, you know. People thought they were risky and exotic, unsuitable for a conservative investor. Bonds were the thing. The first serious discussion I ever heard of that presented stocks as a desirable holding was by a guy called Edgar Laurence Smith. It was called *Common Stocks as a Long-Term Investment*. That was the very first. Strangely enough, Edgar Laurence Smith never did it for himself. He died busted."

I told Cabot that it seemed to me that the ultimate in successful investment was to recognize real value, yes, but particularly when nobody else recognized it, such as common stocks back after World War II. What, I asked him, was around today that had the same characteristic of unrecognized quality? Probably nothing, he answered. As for State Street, they were seeking safety now at least as much as profit, and weren't trying for surprising coups.

Specific stocks, then? Was there another potential IBM among the secondary stocks in the portfolio?

"Most unlikely. IBM's a unique animal. The stock we have in State Street cost us $6 million. Now it's worth $27.5 million. We can't buy anymore.

"I like Dome Petroleum," Cabot continued. He reached into his desk and produced a huge computer printout in a stiff binding and spread it over his knees. "Dome's got a very steady pattern of income growth—$3.20 in 1975 and $4.75 in 1976. What particularly appeals to me about it is their enterprise in being the first people to get up into the Beaufort Sea, up in the Arctic, off the North Slope. They built these giant vessels to operate there and finally got them up in 1975, in August I think it was. I don't know how they drill the holes, but anyway they did. Of the first two they've drilled, one was dry but the other hit a hell of a big gas field. It begins to look as though the delta of the Mackenzie River is more productive than the area on shore.

"That's the speculative potential of Dome. Meanwhile you've got a good, steady rising stream of earnings from their regular operations."

What were to his mind the characteristics of a very desirable stock?

"The most important quality is management that's able and *honest*. A hell of an easy way to get taken to the cleaners is by some goddamn crook like Ivar Kreuger." He added a few contemporary names.

"Then, you want an industry that's prosperous and that's really needed. Jim Walter is a good one," he said, referring to the home building company. "We have $3 million, now worth $9.5 million. It's damn well run, and it's undervalued."

We talked about George Putnam, an exceptional man, who had succeeded Cabot as treasurer of Harvard, and I asked Cabot what he thought of Marsh & McLennan, the largest insurance brokers in the country, of which Putnam's firm, Putnam Management, is now a division. To me "Marsh and Mac" seemed very attractive: well run, extremely well placed in its industry, and requiring little capital to operate. So did Alexander & Alexander and some of the other insurance brokers.

Cabot shrugged. "I learned my lesson about service companies, companies with no assets, years ago. A friend of mine, McComber Framingham, was head of First of Boston at the time. One day he announced that they were cutting the dividend—or even skipping it entirely, I forget which. Then I heard that they'd raised salaries across the board. So I said to him, 'What the hell do you mean, raising your boys' salaries at the same time you're cutting our dividends? If you've got to cut the dividend, the salaries should come down too—or at least you shouldn't *raise* them!'

"And you know what the sonofabitch said to me? He said, 'We haven't *got* anything except our boys.' "

I pointed out the remarkable persistence of insurance premium income and the increasing computerization of this type of business. The computer doesn't ask for a raise—in fact, it gets cheaper.

I asked Cabot about insurance, now America's largest industry in sales volume.

"I've never understood one goddamn thing about insurance," he said, "except that I don't want to have any for myself.

"Now, a stock I like a lot is Hewlett-Packard. My partner George Bennett knows Hewlett himself. He thinks Hewlett's the best goddamn businessman he ever met. We've got a lot of it. It's okay."

Since Hewlett and Packard are approaching retirement, I brought up the problem of succession; you never know if someone can be replaced.

"A businessman who's that good worries about his successor along with everything else," said Cabot. "Anyway, they've got a lot of stock themselves. They're very interested in the successor management."

"About a billion dollars' worth at present market," I said. "Still, all of history tells us never to take a successor on faith. Not much grows in the shadow of an oak. Let's hope for the best."

As an example of an industry he liked, Cabot cited pharmaceuticals. Smithkline was his company's largest drug holding. They'd bought it recently and had had a double in it. I observed that they must have a good drug analyst to have caught the turnaround. "We do," said Cabot. "There was a change in the company's management, and we thought we could bet on the new guys."

He mentioned that State Street had doubled its money in ABC. "It's a hell of a well run outfit. The whole goddamn thing's based on Nielsen. There's this big pot of money for TV advertising, and it's split between CBS, NBC, and ABC, depending on the ratings. ABC's been getting a lot less per unit of time—it's two minutes, or something—than the others. But NBC's dropped to a poor third, and ABC's number one. So we figure ABC's got to get more per unit.

"Now, Continental Can—there's a good outfit. I used to be a director. The big problem's the can business itself—all that goddamn litter. They're not expanding in cans, though. A year ago they bought into the paper business—maybe that'll be the tail that wags the dog someday."

What was the greatest danger to investments?

"Inflation. It's the biggest problem in the world. I don't think we can do a goddamn thing about it. We'll probably go the way of England and Italy. Look at all these government budget deficits—frightening! I'm pessimistic as hell on that. I remember when I was treasurer of Harvard we had a bookkeeper who'd got the same salary for twenty years. He was doing the same work. He didn't *expect* a raise. You got *promoted*, sure; but not just a raise on general principles. After all, if you have a raise every year and the cost of living goes up the same amount you aren't *really* getting a raise. But you've sure built inflation into the system. How are you going to change that?"

I answered that it seemed to take a fearful shock to change people's point of view, such as losing a war, or a social upheaval. What sort of shock would do that here? The bankruptcy of the Social Security System, I suggested. It's actuarially bankrupt now, and sooner or later the pyramid has to collapse.

"They'll just print more money," said Cabot.

I noted that this would result in constructive bankruptcy, as had happened in some foreign countries.

"The majority of the people are so goddamn dumb they won't wake up until they starve to death," said Cabot.

What can one do to offset inflation?

"I'm goddamned if I know," Cabot replied.

In such an environment, how do you preserve capital?

In the future, Cabot said, the investor probably won't be able to preserve his capital in real terms, after inflation. I told him that one of the Rothschilds had declared that if he could be sure of transmitting one-quarter of his fortune in real terms to his posterity he'd take it as a bargain.

"How do you invest for yourself?"

"I have a big slug of good-grade municipals. Not New York . . . smaller towns, with a sense of responsibility. Needham [Massachusetts], where I live . . . Newton [Massachusetts]. I keep short and roll them over."

I pointed out that since inflation usually runs ahead of the return on municipals, that means living off one's capital in real terms.

"Sure, but that's true of a lot of stock dividends too."

Indeed it is, I agreed. Many dividends are essentially declared out of capital, to get the investor to buy the stock. In fact that's true of any stock whose earnings aren't rising as fast as inflation. To the extent that they aren't, your dividends are just a taxable return of capital.

Cabot has a friend who knows art and has invested in it, and seems to have done well. But, he said, "I don't know one goddamn picture from another."

I noted that contrary to general belief most works of art decline steadily in real terms from the time they were first sold. Looking around with hindsight at some works of art that have risen faster than inflation is like looking around and seeing a few people that live to be a hundred. It doesn't follow that most people do.

I asked him which were his favorites from the State Street list.

The ones with a small labor component, he answered. "But I don't know. The way I see it, there'll be a bust. And you know what they say, when the cops raid a whorehouse they take away *all* the girls. You can't believe a panic until you've lived through it. In the Depression, for instance, Deere went from 142 to 7. My partner Paine wanted to sell at 7 because he said it was going to go out of business. I tried to dissuade him but I couldn't, so he sold out. And do you know what happened? He changed his mind overnight, but the goddamn thing opened way up, and he repurchased the position the next morning at 10! There aren't many investors who'd be that flexible."

I asked Cabot if State Street tried to catch market swings—to buy low and sell high.

"No," he said. "It's luck. If you're lucky, you win. If you aren't, you lose. What the hell good is that? I'll tell you a story, though," he added. "In 1929 the stock market reached its peak. Then there was a hell of a bust. Then the market made quite a good recovery. During the rise we were about 60 percent cash and 40 percent stocks. Then all of a sudden the U.S. quit the gold standard. I was down in Florida. They called me up. I said, 'Buy all you can.' Paine agreed. So in one day we went from 40 percent in stocks to 90 percent in stocks. The market doubled in the next two or three months. It took us almost a year, though, to figure out exactly what we had bought in that one day."

I asked him about the moral aspect of investment management. "I don't think morals have a goddamn thing to do with it. One time we owned some of the liquor stocks: Schenley, National Distillers, and so on. Sometimes we got letters from shareholders objecting to them. We used to answer that State Street was in business to make money for our shareholders in a legal way, and that liquor was a legal business. If a shareholder wanted to assert a moral principle beyond the legal one, then all he had to do was sell his State Street stock. Only one ever did: an old lady in Vermont with a hundred shares or so."

I asked if as treasurer of Harvard he had been influenced by the sociological overtones of investment and if today there would be any problem in Harvard owning South African gold stocks, for example. "Not in the least," he replied.

"I remember when I was treasurer some editor of the *Crimson* called me up at night. He asked me if Harvard owned Middle South Utilities or Mississippi Power and Light. I told him we did. He said that they wanted me to sell them, that they were unfair to Negroes. I told him that he was a goddamn little squirt. I had a partner on the board and happened to know that they'd been better than almost anybody else down there. 'Go jump in the lake . . . to hell with you,' I said."

I asked Cabot what his point of view would be if a company he had stock in did have a poor record on minority employment, or whatever.

"It would be bad business for them. We'd try to persuade them to mend their ways." He thought for a while. "On the whole, business is pretty goddamn moral."

I observed that business seemed to me to be at least as moral as government, and more intellectually honest.

"It's a hell of a lot more moral than government," said Cabot, emphatically.

But what were his favorites, all the same . . . IBM? A company that can help you make 200,000 computations for one cent is helping you cope with inflation, after all.

"Well, I suppose that's it," Cabot replied. "A company's probably okay if it makes some goddamn thing a little cheaper or a little better than anybody else."

It was the end of the day. Cabot got up from his plain desk, went over to the coat rack, and put on his gray coat and his gray Boston hat. We left his Harvard tutor's study with the pencil sharpener screwed to the inside of the door and entered the long, airy corridor of State Street's modern offices. A group of handsome, intelligent-looking executives saluted him as we passed.

"G'night, boys," said Cabot.

3

Philip Fisher

Investment Engineer

Philip Fisher is the most famous of the older generation of investment counselors in San Francisco, although he has always kept
the number of his clients to a minimum. "Oh yes, *Common Stocks
and Uncommon Profits*," people will say, referring to his first
book. His experience and thoroughness give him the confidence
to be original and, above all, patient. If you tell an experienced
investor that Fisher took a major position for his accounts in the
original private placement of Texas Instruments, and has kept
the stock ever since, he will be awestruck.

Fisher is a friendly man with an easy, courteous manner. Of
medium height, he is sparely built and slightly stooped. His thin,
scholarly face, with dark brown eyes behind rimless glasses, is
topped with a high forehead and receding hairline. He has a
humorous mouth and large, pointed ears. He was always tallish
and slim. Since his hair has never turned gray, he looks much
younger than his seventy-plus years.

His father, who was a surgeon, provided his early schooling,
and apparently did a good job: Fisher entered college at fifteen.
Because his father believed that one should have something hot
for breakfast, Fisher, who doesn't like tea or coffee, starts the
day with a bowl of soup, accompanied by an orange and a piece
of toast. Once a week, year in, year out, he brews up his soup

supply for the next seven days, always using the same formula: two cans of Campbell's pea soup, two cans of tomato, and one can of . . . he couldn't remember what. "My wife buys it for me," he explained.

For lunch he sends his secretary out for some French bread; he used to spread peanut butter on it from a jar kept in a drawer but found that procedure messy. Now, instead, he takes it with a bite of chocolate, like a French schoolchild. He has a weakness for cookies, but drinks little. He has no hobbies, favorite games, or strong outside interests, except science and some weekend gardening. When he comes home he changes into an old blue sport shirt and trousers and settles down to read murder mysteries.

He set up shop as an investment counselor almost fifty years ago, and has spent thirty-five years in his present office building. During that time neither he nor his office has changed much. His reputation as an original, profound, and remorselessly thorough investment thinker has continued to grow, as has the value of the handful of portfolios he manages.

His small, unmarked office on the eighteenth floor of the Mills Building in San Francisco contains the simplest steel and plastic furniture. On his plain, worn desk is a white leatherette pen and pencil holder—nothing else. A beige wall-to-wall carpet is underfoot. The walls are embellished by a watercolor of Chinatown painted by a friend, another of a bright red pagoda, and a pseudo-mosaic depicting a bonsai tree and a Japanese lantern assembled by his wife. No equipment is visible except for a telephone and a digital clock (set seven minutes fast)—no files, no calculator, no In and Out boxes, no photographs, memorabilia, or knicknacks. It is believed in some investment circles that Fisher's office has no windows, but that's not so: he looks out on San Francisco's business district.

Fisher doesn't like expensive things. For years he wore an overcoat from decades earlier and drove a 1966 Oldsmobile-6 without a radio or frills. It's not that he particularly liked the car, he just didn't see the need for a newer one. Utterly logical in this, as in all else, he is often highly original.

He met his wife, who is from a small town in the South, during the war. She is a clever and perceptive woman with a remarkable green thumb.

When he married, Fisher bought a house after inspecting it for approximately twenty minutes. With the birth of his children, he needed a bigger one, which he also bought almost at first sight. Both he and his wife fell in love with its most unusual feature: although its front faces a city street, the house has terraced grounds behind with a view up to the foothills of the Coastal Range.

Alas, they soon discovered that in summer they had to pull the curtains across the picture windows to keep out the heat of the sun, cutting off their view of the mountains. Rather than alter the house or sell it, Fisher simply obliterated it with bulldozers and built an entirely new residence on the site, with the living areas above and the bedrooms below. This maneuver occasioned some comment in San Mateo.

Fisher's life revolves around home and office: his work, his wife, his children and grandchildren. (Fisher's son, Ken, has followed his father into the investment counsel profession, but has his own firm. He finds his father as puzzlingly original as others do.) He gets up at six in the morning, has his daily soup, starts telephoning when the New York Stock Exchange opens, then heads for the office. His friends on the commuter train are accustomed to seeing him reading the *Wall Street Journal* and business publications instead of talking to them.

He does enjoy holding forth on almost any subject, though, and is sensitive and responsive. He has common-sense views on politics, as on most matters. He feels that with the draft no longer a threat, the young are becoming more and more conservative. Though he sometimes supports candidates who promise to reduce waste in government he's usually disappointed by their subsequent performance. Once he hired a secretary who was not up to the job. In his usual kindly way he told her he'd keep her until she could find another position. The agency that had placed her announced that it had several openings, so he let her depart.

He was chagrined when, instead of taking another job, she went on unemployment relief for six months.

Philip Fisher first hung up his shingle as an investment counselor on March 1, 1931. After a year at Stanford Business School he had gone to work in the security analysis department (then called the statistical department) of a San Francisco bank. Shortly after Hoover's announcement that prosperity was just around the corner Fisher switched to a stock exchange firm. Unfortunately, the firm could not wait for Hoover's prediction to come true, and Fisher found himself once again on the street. For some time he had thought that he would like to be independent and so seized this occasion to start his own firm.

He found two unexpected advantages in beginning his career when he did. First, he talked to businessmen, and since they often had so little to do, they were delighted to chat. One executive he called on said he had finished the sports page and didn't want to go home yet, and so had asked himself, "Why don't I just let this monkey in to see me?" He became a long-time client, and later confided that a year later he couldn't have seen Fisher: he'd become too busy.

The other advantage of starting in 1931 was that almost every potential client was dissatisfied with his existing advisor—if he had any capital left at all.

In one of his Stanford courses Fisher had made weekly trips with his professor to visit companies in the Bay area whose executives were willing to talk seriously about their operations. This professor had helped correct operating weaknesses in a number of companies. Fisher offered to drive since he had a car and his professor didn't and, driving home, they talked about each company. That hour each week, Fisher says, was the most useful training he ever received.

Among the companies they looked at were the Anderson-Barngrover Manufacturing Co., which made fruit canning machinery, and the John Bean Manufacturing Co., which made pumps to spray pesticides for orchards and farms. Fisher told his professor that to him these two seemed to have the best prospects of any they had seen. In 1928 the two merged with a third, a manufacturer of vegetable canning machinery in Illinois, to become Food Machinery Corporation. The stock ran up in the 1929 boom, but in the Depression collapsed again along with everything else.

When that brand-new investment advisor, Philip Fisher, started calling on potential clients in 1931 he took the opportunity to tell them of his enthusiasm for FMC. For several years the stock afforded him and them no satisfaction whatever, and indeed it performed less well than the market as a whole. By the end of 1934, however, it caught fire again and became one of the darlings of the bull market that peaked in 1937. As it started to become a market leader, the people he had talked to about it became impressed, and bit by bit began to give him more and more money to handle.

(Fisher held his Food Machinery until the 1960s, when the company started to flounder. The management no longer seemed outstanding, and a number of acquisitions appeared ill-advised. Fisher first sold a quarter of his stock, and then a little more— perhaps 40 percent in all; not enough, he readily admits.

Early in 1973, however, a new president was appointed, Bob Malott. Because of his long-standing ties with FMC Fisher was able to spend a full afternoon with him after he had been in office only a few weeks. In vivid language Fisher told Malott about the many things in FMC that he thought needed to be changed. Malott agreed with many of Fisher's ideas, but argued strongly against the rest of them. Fisher liked that. It made him feel he wasn't being soft-soaped. Malott also said that bringing FMC back would be like turning a battleship around: it could only be done slowly—over a period of years, in fact. Under Malott and Raymond Tower the company was indeed turned around, slowly but very successfully. Fisher bought back all his stock and more.)

Fisher's first office, which he rented for $25 with the telephone thrown in, had no outside windows, only a glass partition separating it from the people he leased it from. In 1932 he earned an

average of $2.99 a month. In 1933 he averaged about $30 a
month—still not quite as well as he could have done if he had
been selling newspapers. In 1934 he was already doing better,
and by 1935 he was on his way.

Fisher likes to say that he spent World War II in every red-
tape job in the Army Air Corps, defending America in Texas,
Arkansas, Nebraska, and Kansas, usually in the northern states
in winter and the southern states in summer. He became a "bird-
balancer," as he says. During the war, places to live were extremely hard to find around military posts, and many officers
never did get satisfactory housing for their families. One never
needed to advertise a house in those days: the house owner simply
took his pick from the "house wanted" ads. Aside from everything
else, householders were reluctant to rent first-class properties to
the military, who sometimes left them in less than perfect condition and then disappeared beyond reach.

Fisher solved this problem in a singular way. For some reason,
in Arkansas and environs, there was considerable prestige in coming from California. So each time he arrived in a new area Fisher
took an advertisement in the local paper: "California army couple
desires adequate home for which they can guarantee first-class
care. They are used to handling fine things in their own home
in California. Only those with thoroughly attractive places need
apply." This invariably worked like a charm.

Fisher's Air Force job alternated between inactivity and over-
work. During his slack periods he had a chance to think about
what he would do after the war ended, and he resolved that
when he went back to his professional practice his first order of
business would be to identify the best chemical company in the
United States.

After he was discharged he spent nine months looking them
all over, finally winnowing the list down to three. In the end
he decided that Dow Chemical was the pick of the lot, and he
bought some stock in 1946.

In the spring of 1947 he was introduced to Dow itself through
one of its important customers. After meeting with the manage-

ment he decided that these people were among the most remarkable he'd ever encountered, and, he says, he has never had occasion to change his view. For approximately seven years in the 1950s the company did not perform outstandingly, but Fisher did not lose confidence or patience, or sell any stock. Since then the company's success has been legendary, and it long remained one of Fisher's important holdings.

Stephen Horton, a field analyst for Standard & Poor's, first mentioned Texas Instruments to Fisher in 1954, after which Fisher talked to many people about the company, becoming increasingly interested in it. One day he was talking to Emmett Solomon, later president of San Francisco's Crocker National Bank and at that time manager of the Provident Securities Company, a Crocker family holding company. He told Solomon that while he didn't know enough about this small Dallas company to invest in it, still, what he had learned so far was very exciting. Solomon was struck by this, since he and his wife had just met Erik Jonsson, the head of the company, on a cruise to Hawaii, where they'd had adjacent cabins. Solomon had been intrigued enough to resolve to visit Jonsson's company, and invited Fisher to go with him.

Morgan, Stanley had just advised the four founders of Texas Instruments to sell a small amount of their stock for estate planning purposes. After Solomon and Fisher's visit, the Provident Securities Company and Fisher's clients became two of the three purchasers of that placement. With additions bought near the bottom of three market breaks, it has since become one of Fisher's largest holdings.

Fisher discovered Motorola in a similar way. An investment man passing through San Francisco mentioned to him that Motorola seemed most remarkable. Fisher visited the company, representing both himself and friends in Fireman's Fund Insurance. Very much impressed, Fisher and Fireman's Fund both bought Motorola stock. A year or so later Fireman's Fund told Fisher that they had hired a New York bank to go over their portfolio. The bank ranked all their holdings as "very attractive," "attractive," or "unattractive"—all except Motorola, which was not ranked since, said the bank, it was not the kind of company worth spending time on. Later still, however, Fireman's Fund told Fisher that Motorola had been their best-acting stock.

These stocks—FMC, Dow, Texas Instruments, and Motorola—have been big holdings in Fisher's portfolios, which decline about as fast as the averages in a bear market, but have done much better in static or rising markets.

Fisher the investor is quite a different figure from Fisher the investment writer, who sets forth criteria by which one can judge almost any company and determine if it is worth investing in. Expressing one of his key principles, Fisher the investor says, "I don't want a lot of good investments; I want a few outstanding ones." He focuses his attention on a narrow range of enterprises and is unwilling even to consider most companies. He wants above all not to try to be a jack-of-all-trades and master of none.

I found this out when talking to him about a series of companies that I thought might fit his criteria: American Express, A. C. Nielsen, and U.S. Tobacco.

Fisher's general feeling about investments that are of interest to him is that the company in question should combine outstanding business management with a strong technological lead in most of what it does. He won't invest in companies that depend on the taste of the mass consumer, influenced by advertising; though he agrees that there is a technology of influencing the consumer, he does not feel he understands it.

His tastes quite frequently differ from the public's, which disqualifies him from picking outstanding consumer companies. He has found that when he and his wife, who like to plan their television watching, particularly enjoy some TV series, it is frequently discontinued by the network because of its lack of popularity. When I heard that, I explained that it seemed to me very much in the nature of things that a notable investor should disagree with popular thinking. The whole point is to differ from the mass: to be right when the crowd is wrong—if possible, to be the *only* one who is right. I mentioned a melancholy little maxim I had formulated as editor of the *Harvard Lampoon:* "If we like it, the subscribers won't."

He avoids insurance or other financial companies for two reasons. First, there is enough "cross linking" between some technological areas and others so that his contacts in one technology company help in appraising another in a different area. Second, he understands manufacturing. He feels the areas he covers differ enough in the economic factors that influence them so that he can achieve diversification without venturing into lines of business he feels less sure about.

Examples of the technological lead that Fisher insists on for his investments can, however, occur in companies one does not think of as being technology-oriented. For instance, in the sixties he bought into a coal company when the coal industry was shunned by the investment fraternity. He felt the company had developed a notable superiority in both extraction and transportation, such as in the use of barges and unitized trains.

He has, of course, seen other investors make successful commitments, based on his own principles, in fields he would never enter; for example, his son has done very well investing in retail enterprises.

I asked him how he was able to assess technology in spite of not being a technician.

He said that as in any other field, sources and knowledge slowly build up: one piece of technological information leads to another. The same is true in the consumer world, finance, or any specialty, but nobody can do justice to several of them.

As to the market as a whole, he points out that there are many investors, and indeed investment managers, who had never seen a real bull market. The Dow first touched 1,000 in 1966; until 1982 there had been no massive general advance. Quite the contrary; there have been three major declines: the two washouts in the Dow and the collapse of the first-tier stocks.

To illustrate both the possibilities and the pitfalls of a runaway bull market, Fisher tells a tale. In 1932 he realized that common stocks were cheap, and started buying, even though he had not fully worked out his investment philosophy.

One of his acquisitions was RCA 7 percent preferreds, at about $15 a share. At that price the investment would return 50 percent a year on the investor's money if the company really could pay the preferred dividend. When business picked up, the market turned too, and the stock doubled. Fisher sold his holding between 32 and 33, and became quite a hero to his clients. However, three months later the stock went into the low 90s! In other words, it was now worth three times the price he'd sold it at. For a while his status as a hero had its bittersweet aspect.

Fisher's key idea is that *you can make a lot of money by investing in an outstanding enterprise and holding it for years and years as it becomes bigger and better*. At the end your share in the enterprise is worth a great deal more than at the beginning. *Almost certainly the market price of your share will rise to reflect its higher intrinsic worth*. And, certainly, you should concentrate on growth in intrinsic worth: without that there's no reason for the stock to go up rather than down.

He ridicules short-term thinking. Throughout his life, he says, he's only known one in-and-out trader who made money consistently. (Many professional investors don't know any). Pursuing short-term goals Fisher regards as the worst possible mistake, both for the investor and for the company he has a stake in. He therefore insists that *management must first and foremost be working to build the company over the long term.* Growth only happens because management is profoundly dedicated to bringing it about and directs all its activities to that objective.

Fisher redefines the word *conservative* around this concept. To him, a conservative investor is one who makes his capital grow in a practical, realizable way, not in a way that can't succeed. People often describe large, well-known companies as conservative investments. But for Fisher, old and famous companies that have passed their prime and are losing ground in the jungle of international business are by no means conservative holdings. Rather, the conservative investor is one who owns winners—dynamic, well-managed enterprises, that because they are well situated and do almost everything right continue to prosper, grow, and build value year after year.

The owners of such companies don't have to worry about market values, since the assets are building: things are going the right way. Market recognition will follow.

Scuttlebutt

Strangely enough, Fisher's first substantive (as against introductory) chapter in *Common Stocks and Uncommon Profits* dwells on the importance of scuttlebutt—which he also calls "the business grapevine"—in investing. The theme recurs throughout his writing. In fact, Fisher suggests no other source of information for a number of the points he says a prudent investor must consider.

For instance, an investor should check on the effectiveness of the research and the quality of the sales organization of any company he's interested in—two features hard to determine from published figures.

Of the former he notes that "it is surprising what the 'scuttlebutt' method will produce. Until the average investor tries it, he probably will not believe how complete a picture will emerge if he asks intelligent questions about a company's research activities of a diversified group of research people. . . ."

And of sales he says, "Because sales effort does not lend itself to financial ratios many investors fail to appraise it at all in spite of its basic importance in determining real investment worth. Again, the way out of this dilemma is the use of the 'scuttlebutt' technique. . . . Both competitors and customers know the answers. Equally important, they are seldom hesitant to express their views. The time spent by the careful investor . . . is usually richly rewarded."

Scuttlebutt recurs in Fisher's discussion of cost controls, special business characteristics, long-range outlook, and management integrity:

(Point 10): "In this sphere the 'scuttlebutt' method will sometimes reveal companies that are really deficient."

(Point 11): "In both these matters our old friend the 'scuttlebutt' method will usually furnish the investor with a pretty clear picture."

(Point 12): "The 'scuttlebutt' method usually reflects these differences in policies quite clearly."

(Point 15): "This is a point concerning which the 'scuttlebutt' method can be very helpful."

Fisher is essentially talking about a corporate background check. "The business grapevine," he writes, "is a remarkable thing . . . most people, particularly if they feel sure there is no danger of their being quoted, like to talk about the field of work in which they are engaged, and will talk rather freely about their competition. Go to five companies in an industry, ask each of them intelligent questions about the points of strength and weakness of the other four, and nine times out of ten a surprisingly detailed and accurate picture of all five will emerge."

One of the richest sources of scuttlebutt is easy to reach and would not be thought of by most investors: trade shows. Their charm for the information-seeker is that many potential sources are assembled for him in one place, and everyone is there to talk, and indeed to contradict each other. They, not you, have made the appointment and paid the air fare. Far from interrupting the salesman or executive, you are why he's there. Further, the salesmen pushing their companies' products are bound to explain how they differ from the competition.

Another unexpected but convenient source is industry association executives. Here, of course, you must swear eternal secrecy, like a newspaperman, or they could get into hot water. The same is true of university and government researchers. People or companies who buy a company's products will also tell you a lot, as will the company's suppliers and purchasers, if you can get hold of them. And former employees will often give you an earful—not always unbiased.

A source Fisher doesn't mention but that I like for consumer durables (because it's factual and easy to reach) is repairmen. Any master mechanic or electrician will give you his ideas on which cars or TV sets last longer and have the vulnerable parts placed where they are easy (or impossible) to get at. *Consumer Reports* also often gives this information in a systematic way.

Fisher mentions in passing that getting introductions to all these sources can take as much time as one spends actually talking to them; for the ordinary small investor it may be impossible to get introductions at all. Further, the professional investor has another advantage over the layman: he can exchange facts and ideas—or stories—with the interviewee, so that the conversation becomes a two-way street; as the French say, he sends back the elevator.

What Makes a Good Stock

Fisher essentially espouses what is often called in Wall Street a "point system." One lists a number of characteristics that a company should have, such as outstanding management, proprietary products or new discoveries, financial strength, and excellent research. Depending on the results of this checklist (and what is sought), one pronounces it suitable or not suitable for investment, at a price.

Fisher describes fifteen of these desirable features in his first book, and in his second touches on several more. I think one can discern about twenty in all, though depending on what is considered a separate category the number may vary. While he doubtless has many others that he uses but hasn't cited, these twenty-odd must be overwhelmingly the most important.

The criteria that make a stock attractive comprise a yes-or-no checklist: the company either qualifies or it doesn't.

Most practitioners grade a company on a scale of one to five for these desirable qualities, then add up the total, perhaps with some system of weighting. Most "point system" analysts are rating a hundred or more companies. Fisher, I suspect, has already winnowed his list down to twenty or thirty standouts, so his final selection can be exceedingly rigorous.

Though not presented consistently in Fisher's two books, his criteria can be grouped under two main categories: qualities of management and characteristics of the business itself.

Characteristics of an attractive *business* include *growth* from existing products and from new ones; a high *profit margin* and *return on capital*, together with favorable trends for both; effective *research;* a superior *sales* organization; a *leading industry position* giving advantages of scale; and a valid *"franchise"*—proprietary products or services.

Management characteristics include *integrity,* implying *conservative accounting; accessibility;* an orientation toward *long-range* results (if necessary at the expense of this quarter's bottom line) without equity dilution; a *recognition of the pervasiveness of change;* excellent *financial controls; multidisciplinary skills* (where appropriate); the *special skills* associated with particular industries; and good *personnel policies,* including management training.

Fisher's discussion of personnel policy is particularly illuminating. He insists that a company must consciously and continuously try to become a better place to work, from the executive level to union relations, and to be so perceived by its employees. He cites IBM's extraordinary training programs, under which a third of a salesman's entire career is spent in IBM schools; Motorola's Executive Institute in Arizona, which readies promising executives for higher responsibilities; and Texas Instruments' policy of letting worker teams assign their own goals and communicate directly with top management, sharing in profits according to their performance.

In discussing profit margins Fisher makes a point that investors sometimes forget: exceptionally high profit margins can be a honeypot to attract hungry competitors. The safest position may be to have a small edge on the competition in profit margins and a higher turnover. (He doesn't mention that the greatest Japanese companies typically shave their margins to undercut competition. They make their exceptional returns on equity through a high turnover on top of a leveraged capital structure, a small equity base, and a lot of borrowed money!)

Fisher points out that it may be better to be established as the most efficient company in a competitive industry, rather than have a virtual monopoly in a very high-margin business, because there's little incentive for new competition to move in on you. Such a competitive advantage is likely to be secured by the largest company in an industry—the industry leader, hard to displace as long as management remains alert. Fisher ridicules the notion, sometimes put forward by brokerage reports, that a statistically cheaper number two company may be a more attractive investment because it has greater possibilities. A fully-installed dominant company—a Campbell Soup, GM, GE, or IBM—is rarely displaced.

Fisher insists on integrity in management. Insiders have any number of opportunities to benefit themselves at their shareholders' expense, both in material terms and by deceiving them about the prospects for the company.

A greedy management's most common abuse is issuing itself overly generous stock options when the company's stock happens to be at a low point—selling below book value, say. Time passes, the stock returns to a normal level, and through no merit of its own, management has taken millions of dollars of value from the shareholders.

Another unsound practice follows in a way from the shareholders' own laziness, when management is allowed to pursue short-range goals while talking long-term language. As an example, Fisher observes that many companies that suffer from poor labor relations describe themselves as "people-oriented"; as another, when a company uses "creative accounting" it is deceiving the shareholders into thinking things are better than they are, and is probably borrowing from the future for short-range results. However, the shareholders, particularly financial institutions, are usually aware of this practice. So really all a company that uses imaginative accounting can expect to achieve is a possible temporary boost for its stock, together with a long-term cap on it arising from the investment community's suspicions about management's integrity. Investment managers who buy the stock of such companies with their clients' money—the Tsais, the Mateses, the Cornfelds—reveal a lot about themselves as well. The prudent investor belongs elsewhere.

In passing, Fisher laments the Fourth of July tone of so many annual reports, which, he says, may "reflect little more than the skill of the company's public relations department in creating an impression about the company in the public mind. . . . They seldom present balanced and complete discussions of the real problems and difficulties of the business. Often they are too optimistic.

"If a vice-president reported to the president the way the president reported to the owners, that vice-president would last exactly ten minutes. The officers of a company often seem to feel that they should treat annual reports as a form of advertising. That's completely wrong."

Not in his books but in conversation, Fisher makes another point: management must have a continuous and effective program of cost-cutting. There must be a plan, it must be articulated, it must be understood, and it must work.

The Surest Thing in Investment

Fisher's fundamental idea is that if a company enjoys a favorable situation and is well run, the shareholders are best served when the company constantly reinvests a substantial part of today's profits for continued growth. This assumes, of course, that the return on this investment is greater than that which the shareholders would be able to get for themselves if the money was distributed as dividends. If the return on reinvested cash is inadequate, then the company should give the money back to its shareholders as dividends or through a stock repurchase program.

If a company can successfully put its profits back to work to build the business for bigger profits later, then its earnings and book value per share will in due course rise, dividends can be increased, the investment community will perceive that both are likely to go on rising, and the stock price will advance, although one cannot know exactly when.

"It's a good deal easier to know *what's* going to happen than *when* it's going to happen," says Fisher.

Heresies

Fisher reiterates that the investor who attempts the impossible abandons his only hope of doing well.

Above all, he excoriates the "performance game" hustlers who pretend that one can build capital by guessing what is going to happen in the market a year—or indeed a few months—from now. "I remember my sense of shock some half-dozen years ago when I read a recommendation from the sizable trust department of a theretofore highly conservative bank. The recommendation was to sell the shares of a company which was a customer of that bank and one about which the bank should have had considerable knowledge. However, the recommendation was not based on any long-term fundamentals. Rather, it was that *over the next six months* the funds could be employed more profitably elsewhere. Indoctrinated in the customs of an older and perhaps saner era, I remember my amazement at this pronouncement. Was a trust department either entitled or equipped to act as a short-term trader with funds it was attempting to manage?"

A similar folly sometimes grips the corporate manager. Instead of building for the future, sacrificing some of the present for better things later, he, too, plays a quarter-by-quarter earnings performance game, fattening the bottom line by cutting back on planned growth in future years. Tough treatment of suppliers and customers loses their goodwill. Skimping on long-term research may result in declining competitiveness.

How Fisher Does It

Most readers of this book would have great difficulty investing the way Fisher does. The first question to settle would be whether in the time you have available you could hope to develop a business grapevine or scuttlebutt machine like the one he draws on so heavily: good company contacts in most major industries, informants in government and industry associations, investing confreres who will exchange opinions. If not, you may have trouble with his method, since it depends heavily on qualitative factors that—unlike the figures needed in Benjamin Graham's approach—you can never hope to elicit solely from the publicly available material. In this event, says Fisher, you should use a professional advisor, either directly or by putting your money in a well-run fund.

Fisher proposes three successive phases in analyzing a company properly: absorbing the available printed material, triangulating through business sources, and finally visits to management.

1. *The printed material.* This includes the annual and interim reports, a recent prospectus, any proxy material, and the 10-K: the supplementary material filed with the SEC and available to the public. From these you should try to establish the characteristics of the company's accounting, how much is being spent on research and development and what the company means by those terms, management background and compensation, and profit margin trends.

You should review the available Wall Street literature, primarily for the investment community's perception of the company, since the difference between that perception and reality is what creates the investment opportunity.

2. *Additional information from business sources.* This is where good scuttlebutt is indispensable; the very point where the nonprofessional investor may be shaken off the scent.

You can gather more than facts about a company from secondary sources. You can also learn the key questions to ask of management. If a formerly excellent top executive is showing signs of alcoholism, the company will scarcely volunteer the fact; you can at least try to find out tactfully what the company is doing about the problem. Again, advance appraisals of the company officers you are going to see will give you some allowance for such traits as overoptimism.

3. *Company visits.* Fisher hopes to evaluate three things through calls on management: its stated business policies, whether those policies are being carried out, and the men themselves.

Policies to investigate are the balance between long-term and short-term objectives, sales force training programs, where the research is going, what the company is doing to build employee loyalty, and what sort of permanent cost-cutting program it has. Since talk is easy, the interviewer should then look for hard evidence that the company's policies are being achieved. Finally, an able and experienced person can often form a true impression of the company's officers by meeting them. You can try to size up whether the person you are talking to is honest and intelligent, sees things in a rounded way, and can make the hard decision to persist in a policy or pull back when circumstances change.

When to Buy

Fisher offers three valuable hints for timing stock purchases.

First, *buy when the start-up period of a substantial new plant—* which sometimes lasts for months and includes a special sales effort for the new product involved—*has depressed earnings* and discouraged investors.

Often the news of a successful pilot plant and the decision to go to full commercial-scale operations will attract weak buyers, uninformed speculators who will drop out if the stock doesn't rise promptly. Fisher reminds us of an old saying that compares a pilot plant to driving at 10 miles an hour over a poor road, and a commercial plant to doing it at 100 miles an hour. The public may forget that, and let itself be shaken out of the stock as month after month the engineers can't get the bugs eliminated.

As the stock sags, brokers will hint at more serious problems. This, says Fisher, may create a great buying opportunity, since after the first plant is on stream the company may be able to launch a second, third, fourth, and fifth much more easily.

The second time to buy is on *bad corporate news:* a strike, a marketing error, or some other temporary misfortune.

A third opportunity to buy on favorable terms arises in a capital-intensive industry, such as chemicals, where an unusually large investment in plant is required. Sometimes after a product has been in production for a while engineers figure out how to *increase their output substantially by spending a relatively modest amount* of additional capital. This may produce a significant improvement in the company's profits. Until the stock advances to reflect this prospect there should be a buying opportunity.

Fisher also mentions that one should not hesitate to *buy because of a war scare.* During this century, every time American forces have become engaged somewhere in the world, or there has been a serious danger that they would, the stock market has fallen, and every time it has recovered.

The reason to buy is not that war is good for business and therefore for stocks. It isn't. The reason is that governments plunge into debt to pay for a war, debasing the currency. So the prices of things go up, including stocks, which represent ownership of things. To sell stocks on a war scare in exchange for depreciating cash is lunacy. *"War is always bearish on money,"* Fisher observes.

Fisher argues that the usual way investors buy is silly. They sift through masses of economic data, conclude that the business outlook is favorable, and invest. Almost all investment letters from brokers start out this way: the economic outlook is good (or bad), so one should buy stocks (or hold off "until the outlook clarifies"). While this may sound persuasive in theory, it's impossible to apply in practice. Economic forecasting is not yet far enough advanced to permit long-range predictions. Fisher compares it to chemistry during the days of alchemy: "In chemistry then, as in business forecasting now, basic principles were just beginning to emerge from a mysterious mass of mumbo jumbo. However, chemistry had not reached a point where such principles could be safely used as a basis for choosing a course of action."

Fisher wistfully speculates on how much might be accomplished if the investment community, unlike the alchemists and theologians in the Middle Ages, could apply all the time spent turning out contradictory economic forecasts to something useful.

I would go one step further than Fisher: not only are the forecasts fatuous in themselves, but they usually echo each other and produce a consensus. The investor who holds off until there's a wave of optimism among the prophets, particularly the banks, is buying with the crowd and thus paying higher prices. Further, bull markets end and bear markets begin in good times, when everybody's optimistic. The bottom comes in bad times, when everybody's desperate. The Crash, after all, started amid universal euphoria in 1929, and the greatest buying point in history was when the banks closed in 1932: the market doubled in two months.

So really, the investor is safest doing the opposite of what any Wall Street consensus indicates: far from waiting to invest until the bank's "long-term economic overview" has turned favorable, he should try to hold off until a full-scale recession is in progress and the banks and economists say that all is lost. Then he can get solid assets for fifty cents on the dollar and outstanding growth stocks at prices that do not reflect their uniqueness.

What Creates an Investment Opportunity

To use my language rather than his, Fisher is always looking for the "double play": a company's earnings rise; the market gives a higher price-earnings multiple to those higher earnings; the stock soars.

The investor must therefore be aware of the facts and the perceptions. If the facts are more favorable than the perceptions, sooner or later the investment community will catch on, the perception will change, and the stock will rise.

When to Sell

One of Fisher's most famous utterances is on this subject: *"If the job has been correctly done when a common stock is purchased, the time to sell it is—almost never."*

He gives two exceptions: first, if it turns out that *you made a mistake* in your original appraisal; second, if the company *ceases to qualify under the same appraisal method.* The old management may lose its drive or newer management may not be as able. Alternatively, a company may get so big in its own market that it cannot do much better than its industry or indeed the economy as a whole. (On the other hand, Fisher, unlike T. Rowe Price, has no objection to holding a mature company that remains the low-cost producer in its industry, that continues to innovate, and that keeps cutting costs.)

A third exception, which Fisher considers rarely valid, is that *you discover a particularly attractive new opportunity*—such as a company with great promise of a sustained 20% annual earnings gain—and, to buy it, you decide to cut back on a holding with lesser growth prospects. However, you probably know less about the new company than the old one, about which you have been learning more and more for years, so there is a risk of making a mistake. You cannot, after all, know almost everything that could be important about more than a few companies. Those years of increasing familiarity, Fisher urges, should not be thrown away.

He also denies that you should sell because you think that a stock is too high-priced—has "gotten ahead of itself"—or because the whole market is due for a slide.

Selling for either reason implies that you are clever enough to buy the stock back more cheaply later. But in practice, you almost always miss the stock when it recovers. And in addition you have the capital gains tax to pay. After all, if you have chosen the company properly in the first place, with a reasonable prospect that in ten years, say, the stock will have tripled or quadrupled, is it so important that it's 35 percent overpriced today? And there's always *the possibility that the stock's price reflects good news you don't know about yet.*

Silliest of all, says Fisher, *is selling out just because a stock has gone up a lot.* The truly great company—the only kind he is interested in buying—will grow on and on, and its stock likewise. That it has advanced substantially since you bought it only means that everything is going just as it should.

Capital-Intensive Companies

While service companies and others without realizable values in solid assets were once viewed with suspicion by the market, today it's the other way around. Investors now worry that every plant may be a potential buggy-whip factory, which will earn money for the workers and the government but not for its owners. (Further, in an inflationary period the real cost of replacing plant as it wears out is likely to be much higher than the depreciation permitted for tax purposes, so the effective corporate tax rate can well become 75 percent of real profits.)

Fisher disagrees. He points to earlier instances, such as the cement industry after World War II. From overcapacity before the war the U.S. moved to a shortage after it. Inflation had enormously increased the cost of new plant, so once shortages began to develop the price of cement rose enough to justify new plant construction, which in turn meant spectacular profits for the older, prewar plants.

It all depends on the particular case. If there is a high rate of technological obsolescence, then the old plant may become unprofitable. Or if there isn't enough of a shortage to require new plant, then prices may not rise and the existing plant may not become a bonanza.

Fisher considers that some parts of the chemical, paper, and metals industries may now go through the same improvement in their fortunes that cement did after World War II.

Dividends

Fisher has pronounced views on dividends—so pronounced that "All the Hullabaloo about Dividends," his chapter on the subject in *Common Stocks and Uncommon Profits*, published in 1958, was reprinted word for word seventeen years later in his *Conservative Investors Sleep Well.*

One of Fisher's most interesting points is that a conventional piece of Wall Street wisdom on this subject—that reinvesting profits for growth favors larger investors with higher tax brackets at the expense of smaller ones who need the income—is mistaken.

Whether a given investor needs a higher dividend depends on what stage he is in in managing his affairs. If the investor habitually puts aside some of his earnings each year in the form of savings, it is more efficient for him to have the company plow back its cash to build the business—and the value of the investor's share in it—than to pay out the same money as a taxable dividend.

And on the contrary, a high-bracket investor who happens to be in need of funds—"a contingency not entirely unknown to those in high tax brackets"—may have to take money out of the business, and thus need the higher dividend.

So, says Fisher, *a company can best serve its investors by following a consistent, predictable dividend policy;* in fact, it is management's primary obligation to do so. He himself will be looking for long-term growth, which implies lots of reinvestment of profits at a high rate of return to build the business, and consequently a low dividend. Another investor may prefer to have a high dividend, which should in any event be the policy followed by a company without attractive opportunities to reinvest its profits internally. It is indeed a gross abuse of management's role to reinvest shareholders' money at a lower return than they could get for themselves.

Fisher produces an admirable analogy to illustrate his thesis about the need for consistency in dividend policy: Suppose you started a restaurant. A good operator can hope to build up a steady clientele with any of a number of different approaches: low prices and good value; expensive luxury; Chinese or Italian cuisine. There are customers for any of these at a fair price. The word will spread and a following will develop. What couldn't possibly work would be a policy that shifted unpredictably: high quality and prices one day, cafeteria-style the next, and so on. People wouldn't know what they could expect and would stay away. The same holds for dividend policy.

In passing, Fisher refutes a pervasive Wall Street myth about dividends—that a high dividend can improve one's safety by providing a cushion for the stock in bear markets.

Not so, says Fisher. *"Every study seen on this subject indicates that far more of those stocks giving a bad performance price-wise have come from the high dividend-paying rather than the low dividend-paying group.* An otherwise good management that increases dividends and thereby sacrifices worthwhile opportunities for reinvesting increased earnings in the business is like the manager of a farm who rushes his magnificent livestock to market the minute he can sell them rather than raising them to the point where he can get the maximum price above his costs. He has produced a little more cash right now but at a frightful cost."

All this follows from Fisher's basic belief that the attractive holding grows and grows and grows, almost always from advantageously reinvested profits. So high dividends mean lower reinvestment, which usually precludes the long-term building of value that investment is all about.

4

Benjamin Graham

The Navigator

Benjamin Graham ranks as this century's (and perhaps history's)
most important thinker on applied portfolio investment, taking
it from an art, based on impressions, inside information, and flair,
to a proto-science, an orderly discipline. He applied great astute-
ness, hard experience, and infinitely detailed labor to a field full
of superstition, tips, and guesswork, one in which most people
who have something to say also have an incentive to deceive
the listener. Employing analysis of published records, Graham
explained and demolished fallacy after fallacy—often as neatly
as if opening a letter.

Graham's *summa*, after almost fifty years still the basic text
of the profession, is his *Security Analysis*. More useful for most
readers, however, and indeed the best book ever written for the
stockholder, is *The Intelligent Investor*. One is ill advised to the
point of folly to buy a bond or a share of stock without having
read its three hundred pages. Many people, including experienced businessmen and professionals, have been financially ship-
wrecked because they trustingly set forth in a leaky craft cap-
tained by an incompetent. Someone who spent the few hours
necessary to understand *The Intelligent Investor* would be unlikely to suffer this fate. Yet, alas, few stockbrokers, let alone investors, have done it.

Graham can give a feeling for investment reality. Most of what you hear in Wall Street is blather; Graham helps you see it all in perspective and sense where to look for objective truth.

Benjamin Graham (who died while I was writing this chapter) came to New York from England with his parents in 1895 when he was a year old. His father represented the family chinaware firm, Grossbaum & Sons. (The family name was changed to Graham during World War I.) He grew up in Manhattan and Brooklyn, the youngest of three boys. After the death of his father, when Ben was nine, the family was greatly reduced in circumstances. His mother never adjusted to the change, and her anxieties undoubtedly contributed to Ben's subsequent preoccupation with achieving financial security.

He was an industrious student, and almost too good a boy. In his high-school years, when he took jobs to help support the family, he studied Greek and Latin, which became a lasting joy to him. After graduating from Columbia in the class of 1914, Ben was offered teaching fellowships in English and mathematics; instead he went to work as a messenger in Wall Street for Newburger, Henderson & Loeb. He soon progressed to doing write-ups and analyses, and during this period he married the first of three wives. By 1917 he was earning respect as an analyst, and started publishing in financial magazines. He became a partner of the firm in 1920.

Graham was a small, stocky man who became thinner as he aged. He had an odd round face, with heavy lips and light blue eyes. A complex person of boundless energy, he loved literature—Proust, Virgil, Chateaubriand, Victor Hugo, the German poets—and was a fountain of apposite quotations.

By Wall Street standards he had unusually wide interests: the Greek and Latin classics, philosophy, languages. He translated a book from the Portugese, wrote several books himself, admired Marcus Aurelius, and identified himself with Tennyson's free spirit, Ulysses, a wily and thoughtful adventurer who traveled far, leaving his wife lonely.

Once at a family gathering for his birthday he delivered this remarkable and revealing piece of self-analysis:

"One of the great heroes of my childhood reading was Ulysses, or Odysseus. In spite of the great praise heaped on the *Iliad* as the world's foremost poem, I must confess that I have never been able to read it through—although some passages, such as Hector's farewell to Andromache, have long been my favorites. But the *Odyssey* has fascinated me from the beginning, nor has that fascination diminished through the years. The wiliness and the courage, the sufferings and the triumphs, of its protagonist carried an appeal which I never could quite understand. At first I thought it was the attraction of opposites—Ulysses enthralled me because both his character and his fate were so different from my own. Only after I had long passed my maturity did I begin to realize that there was quite a bit of the typically Odyssean faults and virtues in my own makeup.

"As a youngster I rejoiced to think that Ulysses' wanderings and trials had ended in his triumphant reunion with Penelope, and they both were now to 'live happily forever after.' But a few years later Tennyson's great poem was to introduce me to the real Ulysses, for whom his island home and his wife's bed could never be more than a port of call. The concluding passage rang through my brain like a fiery challenge to a kind of life that seemed the very antithesis of my own values, ambitions, and expectations. How often did I repeat to myself:

> For my purpose holds
> To sail beyond the sunset, and the baths
> Of all the western stars, until I die.
> It may be that the gulfs will wash us down:
> It may be we shall touch the Happy Isles,
> And see the great Achilles, whom we knew.

"Then, much later again, I made the acquaintance of Dante's version of the dauntless expedition and the stormy death of Odysseus, as he is made to recount it in that brief and unforgettable passage in the *Inferno*. And, finally, I now hold in my hands a tremendous epic on the same theme, newly written by the modern Kazantzakis. Perhaps Ulysses is about my own age as again he leaves his wife and his now married son. Perhaps he is ageless, as at times I feel myself. In any case, in his mind of many turns *(polytropon)*, in the restless heart, in the dauntless body, all under his peaked sailor cap, I sense an iconoclastic ideal which has attracted me like an unseen magnetic pole throughout my life, with a force of ever-growing intensity that at last became too strong to resist."

While Graham sought women, he was not suited to marriage. His second wife was a secretary, and his third, Estelle, worked for him. The French mistress with whom he spent his final years he took over from one of his own sons. He developed a passion for dancing and signed up for several thousand dollars' worth of lessons, eventually giving it up and offering the unused time to his brother, Victor.

His interest in his own children only really started when they became concerned with ideas; then he became their walking encyclopedia. A born teacher, he liked to invent stories for them and answer their questions on any subject.

Generous and kind (he endowed a black church in New Haven), he was liked by the people he came in contact with, but had few intimate friends. In a self-description he quoted Estelle's judgment that he was "humane, but not human." Although an agnostic who held for no organized faith, he was interested in religious philosophy. He became a skier when that was an unusual skill, and a keen tennis player. As a friend says, he had no *minor* faults: he didn't smoke or drink, and ate sparingly. He was absent-minded and did not like to drive a car. He lived modestly but comfortably, and after he achieved financial security he was little concerned with money. Late in life he moved from New York to La Jolla, California, but in his very last years preferred the south of France.

Graham loved mathematics, and his approach to investment is mathematical, quantitative. In fact, he may well have been concerned with security analysis primarily as a branch of mathematics. Certainly no earlier investment thinker approached the subject solely through figures, without concern for the quality of the business or the character of management.

In 1926 he formed a pool, the Benjamin Graham Joint Account, which grew to $2.5 million within three years and which he managed in return for a share of the profits. During the first year he was joined by Jerome Newman, with whom he remained associated throughout his business career.

During this period Graham encountered Bernard Baruch, and was instrumental in his making a number of investments. A person close to the situation adds, "Baruch was lavish with praise privately but that was all; the relationship was all take and no give on the part of Baruch." Baruch is believed to have offered Graham a profit-sharing association, but not on a basis that Graham found attractive.

When the market collapsed in 1929 and 1930, the Joint Account sustained severe losses; from 1929 to 1932 it declined 70 percent as compared to 74 percent for the Dow Jones Industrials and 64 percent for the Standard & Poor's 500. But since the Joint Account had been using substantial margin at the beginning of the period Graham's stock-picking record was better than it seemed. Nevertheless, he personally was wiped out in the Crash. Having ducked the 1929 cataclysm, he was enticed back into the market before the final bottom.

From 1928 to 1956 Graham taught a popular evening course at Columbia Business School. In 1934, with Professor David L. Dodd, he published the monumental *Security Analysis,* the basic text for all serious students of investing, which has sold over 100,000 copies so far and seems likely to sell forever. (As a curiosity, and an indication of Graham's skill, the value of the list of undervalued special situations in the 1940 edition advanced over 250 percent in the next eight years, compared to a one-third increase in the Standard & Poor's Industrials.)

In 1944, Graham published *Storage and Stability,* offering a plan to stabilize food surpluses, world commodities, and world currencies. *The Interpretation of Financial Statements* appeared in 1947, and in 1949 *The Intelligent Investor.*

Graham's greatness as an investor may well have consisted in knowing how to say no. One of his assistants in Graham-Newman has described to me ruefully what it was like proposing a list of carefully selected and researched opportunities for Graham's consideration, only to have him find something substantive to object to in every one. He felt no compulsion to invest at all unless everything was in his favor.

When he finally did buy he was sure of what he was doing. His idea of a good, safe investment was simply buying a dollar for fifty cents over and over again. In any specific case something may go wrong, but if you do it dozens of times the procedure is virtually infallible. Diversification—a multiplicity of transactions—is thus a key to the method, just as in insurance.

And even as he bought, Graham always kept one foot out the door, ready to run if his calculations went awry. But this intrinsic caution robbed him of the flair necessary to catch major market moves. Besides reentering the market too soon in the thirties and getting cleaned out, he missed the great bull move beginning in 1950, even advising one of his protégés not to go to work in Wall Street in 1951 because the market was so high.

However, in the 1973 edition of *The Intelligent Investor* he was right: "We think the investor must be prepared for difficult times ahead—perhaps in the form of a fairly quick replay of the 1969–70 decline, or perhaps in the form of another bull market fling, to be followed by a more catastrophic collapse." And indeed, the 1973–74 collapse was the most severe since the great crash of 1929–32—creating the best buying opportunity since that time.

"Just Show Me the Balance Sheet"

All his professional life Graham sought explainable, specific techniques that he could teach to others to enable them to select safe and profitable investments. He wanted a method that was entirely *quantitative*, that did not depend on things one couldn't be sure about, such as social trends, a company's future success in bringing out new products, or quality of management.

He also wanted a method that could be used by anybody, and which therefore depended entirely on readily available published material, particularly the company's own reports.

He and his associates, after working for years, finally, in that prodigious compendium, *Security Analysis*, did give the investor the tools he needed. However, the methodology employed was so elaborate that although in theory the book offered the ordinary investor, as well as the professional, the keys to investment success, few of the tens of millions of nonprofessional American shareholders have used it.

Analyzing a number of industries, one after another, Graham explains the financial characteristics of each, and shows how, by comparing key operating and financial ratios, the analyst can determine which of a group of similar companies are successful and which unsuccessful, which financially sound and which weak, which overpriced and which bargains. He also discusses the evaluation of bonds and other securities. The analyst who has really mastered *Security Analysis* understands a lot.

Eventually, however, Graham did develop a simple investment touchstone that can be used by everybody: his definition of the Bargain Issue. It's not a general theory, like "growth" or "management" or "innovation" or "lowest-cost producer," just a measure of undervaluation. And toward the end of his career he developed two additional criteria of a bargain stock. He finally concluded that the availability of these three tools rendered his elaborate earlier technique less necessary.

Investment and Speculation

Graham constantly underlines the distinction between "investment" and "speculation." Investment must be based upon *thorough analysis*, and must promise *safety of principal* and a *satisfactory return*. A holding may fail to be an investment, and thus be a mere speculation, because the analysis, the safety or the return is lacking.

The first pitfall, risk-taking without adequate study, is mere guessing, and constitutes most of what passes for investment in the stock market. By his willingness to accept bets at the wrong odds the speculator gives the investor his opportunities. In this brief summary of Graham's ideas it is not possible to set forth in detail the analytic methods he proposes to establish safety of principal and adequacy of return: they take up hundreds of pages of his *Security Analysis.* He does not, of course, claim that every security can be so analyzed. The outlook for many companies is indeterminable. What he does say is that if you buy under those conditions you are not truly investing but rather gambling, and all too possibly buying at a price set by experts and insiders who are better informed than you are.

Real and Illusory Earnings

One of Graham's principles takes on cardinal importance every four years or so when the speculative pot again starts to boil over, and speculatively-minded buyers make the customary two ghastly blunders in examining a company's earnings record: comparing a year's earnings with those of the previous year retroactively adjusted downward, which gives a delusive impression of endless improvement; and accepting reported earnings without determing whether the company's position really has improved by that amount.

Graham's simple rule is that real earnings consist of dividends paid plus the increase in the net assets per share—which usually appears as the change in earned surplus, including voluntary reserves.

As a grim example of fake earnings he takes the reported earnings of Dynamics Corporation of America for the ten years ending in 1960, which were $13,502,000, or fifty cents a share. According to Graham's rule, they were only $6,846,000, or twenty-five cents a share. There proved to be $6,655,000 of charges against earned surplus, almost all of which should have been charged instead against earnings.

Graham ruefully points out that the market pays no attention whatever to the underlying reality during periods of speculative enthusiasm.

The Bargain Issue

Graham loved the Standard & Poor's *Stock Guide*, which appears monthly and gives the basic financial facts on thousands of stocks, including every stock listed on any exchange.

He describes with enthusiasm the pleasures an investment man can know by burrowing into this extraordinary "class album" of all the principal companies in America, companies that have multiplied their market values hundreds or indeed thousands of times, companies with century-long dividend records nestling by a company selling for two times latest earnings, or a stock that went from ⅜ to 68 and back to 3. (In a footnote he demurely admits to having at one time been an officer of that one.)

He then sets forth a series of criteria available in the *Stock Guide* that he applied to a number of companies to find out what stocks were likely to do best over a period of years. These criteria include minimum net current assets and maximum debt-equity ratios; earnings stability; dividend record; earnings growth; price in relation to net tangible assets; and quality ranking.

A further criterion, the relationship of price to book value, is not derivable from the *Stock Guide*.

Graham describes testing these criteria, singly or in combination, and finding in the end that the best by far is simply buying Bargain Issues, companies selling in the market for less than their net current asset value.

"It always seemed, and still seems, ridiculously simple to say that if one can acquire a diversified group of common stocks at a price less than the applicable net current assets alone—after deducting all prior claims, and counting as *zero* the fixed and other assets—the results should be quite satisfactory. They were so, in our experience, for more than thirty years."

As to these issues, you can make money without serious risk

"*if* you can find enough of them to make a diversified group, and *if* you don't lose patience if they fail to advance soon after you buy them. Sometimes the patience needed may appear quite considerable." The 1964 edition of *The Intelligent Investor* had observed that Burton-Dixie sold at 20, with net current assets of 30 and a book value of 50. It took until August 1967 before all the shareholders were offered 53¾, approximately book value, for this stock. Graham sounded almost apologetic over this three-and-a-half-year wait until his readers got a profit of 165%.

One of the by-products of Graham's simplified Bargain Issue approach is that it provides the easiest of thermometers for the overall temperature of the market. If a great many companies are selling in the market for less than their net current assets, then the market is depressed. If there are hundreds and hundreds of such issues, it's time to plunge heavily. If only a handful, then one should be very cautious or stay out entirely. (Of course, when the market is bubbling, the few remaining bargains are all the more likely to be snapped up before too long, so in that sense one is fairly safe with Graham's method even in high markets.)

Diversification

Graham's approach to investment leads him to favor a higher degree of diversification among different issues than has been popular in recent years, when the cry has been the familiar "Put all your eggs in one basket and watch that basket." Graham says that it makes sense to put a lot of money in one enterprise that you are directly involved in yourself, as an executive or member of a controlling group, and observes that for an outsider to concentrate his investments as though he were an insider doesn't usually succeed because he is usually so nervous about his holding that he sells out prematurely and misses the great sweep—lasting many years—of a long-term advance.

At a time when you can invest with safety—that is, when good companies are being sold below their intrinsic worth—you can usually find bargains in many different industries. We all make mistakes: the only way to be safe is to spread your bets around widely enough to let the law of averages operate.

Obviously, you must in theory work a bit harder to find several good opportunities instead of one, but in reality, as any practicing security analyst knows, in times of general gloom you always have many opportunities and are hard put to choose among them.

Growth Stocks

Many of the approximately ten thousand trained securities analysts practicing in America today had the early editions of Graham's *Security Analysis* as their textbook. It will surprise some of them who remember his intense and correct suspicion of the growth stock slogans of the late twenties—"No price is too high to pay for RCA"—to learn that in his latest edition he changes his tune quite strikingly.

He begins by pointing out the extreme difficulty of deciding what a growth stock really is. Experience shows that on this subject analysts are usually wrong and further, that when they are right they do not have the confidence to take advantage of it. The great time to own IBM was in the early fifties, when it was already a firmly established company and yet had the next twenty-five years of prodigious growth ahead of it. Today IBM is usually the largest holding in any mutual fund, even though its growth is slowing. In 1952, however, 118 funds studied by the SEC averaged only one-half of one percent of their holdings in IBM!

Graham gives several examples of the difficulty of being right in predicting the future action of a supposed growth stock.

"The Investment Performance of Selected Growth Stocks," an article in the May 1957 issue of *Financial Analysts Journal*, gives the actual result over different periods of investing in a series of growth stock portfolios listed in another financial magazine.

As another example Graham cites Wiesenberger Services, Inc.'s *Investment Companies 1961*. There, the mean ten-year performance results of all growth funds, assuming reinvestment of distributions, was 289 percent. The similar figure for the S&P 500-stock average was 322 percent.

Overall Gains, Including Dividends Received

Holding Period	Recommended Portfolios	DJIA
3 years	26%	22%
5 years	65	60
10 years	153	165

Graham concludes from this that one should distrust elaborate calculations of growth stock values.

I must confess, however, that from the same data I conclude simply that most "growth" funds don't do their job well, not that none does. After all, most "value" funds don't, either. Some stocks have rising earnings for many years, and their market prices rise accordingly. Some of the best funds invest in those stocks and have outstanding long-term records.

Funds as a class, however, are destined to do worse than an unmanaged list of securities—the funds have to pay for management, brokerage, custody, and the like. Also, most "growth" funds buy *official* growth stocks whose price is high but whose growth is slowing, or speculative ones whose growth never happens.

Everyone is looking for stocks whose earnings should rise over many years; so such stocks, if recognized, sell for too much. To make money at this game one must both correctly identify them and have enough confidence to buy them before they are generally recognized. Particularly, one must not pay high prices for mere speculations. The safe time to buy quality growth stocks is when their price-earnings ratios are little more than that of the rest of the market.

Curiously enough Graham, for all his deprecation of overpaying for growth, considered far higher prices justifiable than those prevailing in the market in early 1979. Based on a number of different lines of reasoning he suggests reasonable price-earnings multiples of over thirty for a stock with a sustainable growth rate of 14.3 percent, whereas the current market multiples are about half that (see table below).

Technology Stocks

In an appendix to *The Intelligent Investor* Graham offers a pleasant statistic. The Standard & Poor's *Stock Guide* for December 1968 listed forty-five companies with names starting with Compu-, Data-, Electro-, Scien-, or Techno-. Examining the September 1971 *Stock Guide* he found that two of the forty-five companies had advanced in price, thirty-one had declined (twenty-three of them by more than half), and twelve had been dropped from the guide.*

"It is virtually certain," observes Graham, "that the many technological companies not included in the *Guide* in 1968 had a poorer subsequent record than those that were included. . . . The phenomenal success of IBM and a few other companies was bound to produce a spate of public offerings of new issues in their fields, for which large losses were virtually guaranteed."

Expected Growth Rate (in percent)	10	14.3	20
Multipliers by:			
Molodowsky's method	23	31.2	46.9
Tatham's table	25		
"8.6T + 2.1" formula	24.4	36.5	55.3
"8.5 + 2G" formula	28.5	37.1	48.5
"Our preferred method"			
(7-year projection)	23.5	31	41.5

From Graham, Dodd, Cottle, and Tatham, *Security Analysis,* 4th ed. (New York: McGraw-Hill, 1962), p. 538.

* I am prepared to carry this subject slightly further by offering the following three rules on names:

1. A company that changes its name to reflect a current stock market fad will probably decline.
2. A stock group that is attracting such name-changes will probably decline.
3. You can with confidence buy an industry that managements are changing their names *away* from: e.g., the cigarette companies when they became Reynolds *Industries* and the like.

New Issues and Convertibles

Graham disapproves of certain types of issues intrinsically: for instance, he finds that new stock issues of companies that previously were privately held are rarely suitable for the true investor. Such new issues tend to be brought to market when the speculative pot is boiling, and are typically priced at several times book value or indeed any reasonable valuation.

Graham is also suspicious of exotic securities, including convertible issues and warrants. His reasons for avoiding convertibles are interesting and well reasoned, and rather than recapitulate them in detail, I refer the reader to the chapter on "Privileged Issues" in *Security Analysis*. Convertibles turn out to be mathematically attractive far less often than one would expect, just as one can rarely get mathematically fair odds at a racetrack. Their speculative appeal results in consistent market overpricing.

About the only approach to buying convertibles that he finds reasonable is as a better way of buying common stock that one wants to own anyway, when the convertible is selling close to parity. Elsewhere he reaffirms the Wall Street maxim, "Never convert a convertible."

"Mr. Market"

Obviously, what creates undervaluation and overvaluation is the passion of the crowd. Graham, like a doctor working over a patient who has fallen to the ground in a riot, rarely lifts his head to contemplate the madness around him, but in his books you can always hear that madness howling in the background.

What a fantastic commentary on human nature, for example, is this table (p. 96), adapted from *The Intelligent Investor*.

Bankers Securities was an investment trust floated in 1928, the last great age of miracles before the hedge fund–conglomerate madness of the 1960s. At the time it was sold, a rapturous public invented fantastic reasons to think that for one dollar of value

Bankers Securities Corporation

	Year-End Asset Value of Common Stock	Price During Year
1928	$65	$218
1932	$424	$140

it should pay more than three; some years later the inevitable hangover was so severe that for the same dollar the same public, now convinced that the world was coming to an end any day, would only pay thirty cents.

In discussing warrants in *The Intelligent Investor*, Graham becomes vehement. He considers the development of stock-option warrants close to fraud, an existing menace, and a potential disaster. Such warrants have created huge aggregate dollar "values" out of thin air and exist to mislead speculators and investors. They should be prohibited by law, or at least strictly limited to a minor part of the total capitalization of any company.* He mentions the American and Foreign Power warrants, which attained a market capitalization of a billion dollars in 1929, fell to $8 million in 1932, and, in 1952, when the company was reorganized (while still solvent!), were simply wiped out.

Privileged issues—notably convertibles—are to Graham "fair-weather investments." In good times they do well, but not as well as common stocks, and in bad times they do worse. Part of the problem is that like new stock issues of unseasoned companies they are often brought to market during times of market enthusiasm, just before significant declines in stock prices.

Preferred stocks issued at par are usually bastard issues, offering neither the security of a bond nor the growth potential of a stock.

Obviously, companies only sell cheaply when the market is worried about them, often for good reason. In Graham's own words, someone using his methods would ordinarily buy "when

---

* Graham would, I am sure, have felt the same about today's frenetic traffic in stock options.

the current situation is unfavorable, the near-term prospects are poor, and the low price fully reflects the current pessimism."

Graham at one point produces an admirable parable of the true investor's attitude toward a fluctuating market.

Let us imagine that we own an interest in a business in which we have a genially insane partner called Mr. Market. Every day Mr. Market, depending on which side of the bed he got out of and the dreams or fears that possess him at the moment, sets a price at which he will either buy out our interest or sell us some more. Most of the time we need pay no attention. Only if our sober study of the facts—of which we know as much as Mr. Market—convinces us that his price is absurdly high or low need we take notice of his offer. We need never act except to make an advantageous trade. "At other times," says Graham, the true investor "will do better if he forgets about the stock market and pays attention to his dividend returns and to the operating results of his companies."

Graham adds that one should never buy a stock because it has gone up or sell it because it has declined. Quite to the contrary, he suggests this motto; "Never buy a stock immediately after a substantial rise or sell one immediately after a substantial drop."

Predictive Formulas

In *The Intelligent Investor* Graham examines and rejects many approaches to market forecasting—buying or selling stocks in general according to a formula, whether the Dow Theory, his own "central value theory" propounded in *Security Analysis,* or any other.

He demonstrates that such formulas lose their utility just when a "playback" shows them to have worked well retrospectively. For instance, "the quality of the results shown by the Dow Theory changed radically after 1938—a few years after the theory had begun to be taken seriously in Wall Street. . . : For nearly thirty years thereafter one would have done appreciably better by just buying and holding the DJIA."

point he refers with gentle derision to an article in *˃me Journal*, "Everybody Ought to be Rich," by John J. Raskob—"a most important figure nationally as well as on Wall Street."

Raskob held that if one invested $15 a month in good common stocks, in twenty years it would grow, including reinvested dividends, to $80,000, from a total investment of $3,600.

"If the General Motors tycoon was right, this was indeed a simple road to riches," observes Graham, and then asks, "How nearly right was he?" Graham calculates that in the event (1929 to 1976) the sum grew not to $80,000 but only to $8,500. That, however, worked out to better than 8 percent compounded—a respectable result, considering that the market was considerably lower at the end of the period than at the beginning.

Graham in Practice

The success of Graham-Newman Corporation can be gauged by its average annual distribution. Roughly speaking, if one invested $10,000 in 1936, one received an average of $2,100 a year for the next twenty years, and recovered one's original $10,000 at the end.

The company simultaneously employed six different investment techniques:

1. Buying stocks for two-thirds or less of their net current assets—usually over 100 different issues at a time.

2. Buying companies in liquidation, where there seems an 80 percent or better chance of making at least a 20 percent annual return.

3. Risk arbitrage: buying the stock of one company and simultaneously selling the stock of another that it is merging with.

4. The "convertible hedge": buying a convertible bond or preferred stock, and at the same time selling short the common it converts into. The convert should be bought close to conversion parity, so that if the position is closed out by converting little is lost. The further the common and the convertible pull apart, the more the profit.

5. Buying control of a company selling for less than it is worth, to force realization of the assets.

6. "Hedged" investing: being long one security and short another that has no relation to the first—balancing out, so to speak. If one chooses rightly, the issues one has bought will improve and those one has sold short decline, so one prospers from their relative movement without regard to the general market.

By 1939 Graham-Newman had established that only the first five techniques worked out well enough to justify being continued.

Since then, the second, third, and fourth techniques—participating in takeovers and liquidations, and the convertible hedge—have become so professionalized as to be out of the question for most investors, and certainly the fifth, buying control of entire companies, is not a technique that can ever be generally available. So we are left with the first—buying "bargain issues" at less than their net current asset value—as that part of the Graham-Newman technique that is particularly appropriate for most investors today, along with two further ones Graham developed later.

Graham's coup in Northern Pipeline illustrates his methods. Going through the Interstate Commerce Commission forms that pipeline companies had to file, Graham noticed that Northern Pipeline held $95 per share of quick assets, although it was selling at only $65, at which price it yielded 9 percent. Graham's partnership bought a substantial interest in the company, with the thought of encouraging it to distribute the unneeded assets to its shareholders. At the 1928 annual meeting he arrived with proxies for 38 percent of the shares and went on the board of directors. In due course he was instrumental in persuading the company to pay out $50 per share. What was left was still worth more than $50 a share, bringing the total value to $100, or a substantial profit over his cost of $65. This transaction typifies Graham's approach. He didn't care what the company did or if management was capable; he was only interested in undervalued assets. For Graham's game it's actually better if the company can't make a go of things and has to sell out or liquidate, thus giving the investor his reward sooner rather than later.

In 1948 Graham-Newman Corporation and Newman & Graham, a companion partnership, put $720,000, one-quarter of their assets, into buying a half-interest in Government Employees Insurance Company. GEICO, as described in Chapter 1, sells automobile insurance to government employees, but always directly, by mail. It has no agency force. It can offer unusually attractive rates, since its costs are low, and experience shows that this class of driver has relatively few accidents.

Although, for SEC reasons, most of this investment had to be spun off to the Graham-Newman Corporation shareholders, the value in GEICO stock received by Graham's group eventually reached half a billion dollars! GEICO then fell on very hard times, and at the dead low in 1977 lost 95 percent of its value; but it has made a considerable recovery since.

Excluding the GEICO stock received by his investors, Graham was never managing more than $20 million at any one time—an inconsiderable sum by today's institutional investment standards, since there are now hundreds of portfolios worth over $1 billion. By distributing to his shareholders the cash received from holdings that were liquidated, he kept his company from growing. That was because he was not confident of being able to discover more than $20 million of grossly undervalued situations at a time. If he had allowed the money to build up in the company, it would have grown to a very considerable sum—on the order of $100 million—and the results would probably have been affected.

Graham's explicit followers have always managed a limited amount of money. I would guess that even today it amounts to less than $100 million, and quite possibly much less. With the availability of computer readouts on demand, the game will become much easier to play, and thus more competitive and less profitable.

Graham's Own Cultural Revolution

At the very end of his life Graham reversed some of his ideas on how in practice an investor may hope to achieve satisfactory results, to an extent that will startle the analysts trained in his original techniques.

His *Security Analysis* gave any investor of reasonably studious bent an instrument for digging out the values. It contains extensive tables and formulas for such key elements as inventory turnover, working capital ratios, the ratio of sales to plant, operating margins and the like, set forth industry by industry.

Essentially "Graham and Dodd" created a system, where before, except for industry specialists and operating management, investors had tended to rely on impressions. The book went through edition after edition, and formed a whole generation— or even two—of Wall Street professionals.

After forty years of this process, however, Ben Graham's truth became everybody's truth, and there was little hope of outsmarting the pack with his techniques. Investment resembles another competitive game, war. From time to time a new technique appears—the short sword, the longbow, the machine gun, the tank, radar—and sweeps the field. Then the other side adopts it and parity returns. Similarly, Graham's techniques had been adopted by the entire investment industry by the early 1970s, and to enjoy superiority a different weapon was needed.

In *Dance of the Money Bees* (later reissued as *Preserving Capital and Making It Grow*), I drew attention to this.

As recently as the 1950s the public was in the market in a big way, in almost every possible stock. The public does not know very much, and is highly emotional. As a result the market was full of distortions. . . . The result was an imperfect market, in which the professionals could make a lot of money.

Now things have changed drastically. The public has withdrawn from the market and is represented by large institutions, bristling with computers, statistical studies, the latest facts, eternal memories, retrieval and display systems, armaments of every sort. The pilot is no more skilled than the World War I ace, but instead of a Spad he has a Phantom:

ten times the speed, a hundred times the firepower, black boxes, radar—the works. I suppose that one of today's fighter planes could wipe out all the air forces of World War I, and today's analyst can cover so much territory with his memory banks and real-time displays that an army of Ben Graham–style statisticians cannot keep up with him.

Do you know how many more or less qualified American security analysts there are? Roughly ten thousand—and *with* computers! The next time a broker calls and says that maybe it's time to "look at housing stocks," just remember that many hundreds of those analysts and their computers and the billions of dollars they represent have the entire pattern in their radar, second by second. You are no longer trying to outsmart Farmer Joe, a manageable assignment; you *are* Farmer Joe.

I went on to suggest some simple touchstones for the nonprofessional investor to use instead of the full Graham–style analysis:

In recent years the Dow has tended to fluctuate between seven and twenty times earnings. A reasonable investment range might be ten to twelve times.

Those few stocks that have outstandingly high profit margins and year after year enjoy consistently high growth are, of course, in a special category. On average, such stocks rarely sell below fifteen times earnings. They will probably fall back after running up over thirty-five times earnings.

Tangible value is a useful measure. The Dow Jones Industrial Average often comes back to about 150 percent of its own book value. A much higher valuation is probably unsustainable, and a significantly lower one is probably a bargain.

Finally, when many stocks are selling below their working capital value you can usually afford to take a constructive attitude toward the market.*

The editor of that book, the late Virginia Hilu, was a friend of

---

*Dance of the Money Bees, Harper & Row, 1974. (*Preserving Capital and Making It Grow*, Clarkson Potter, 1983.)

Graham's, and sent a copy to him, which made me a bit apprehensive, like a seminarian having a paper graded by the Pope.

To my relief and pleasure Graham wrote very generously about the volume, even though it scarcely agreed with his published views.

I only really understood why two years later, when I read the posthumously published transcript of a seminar he conducted in 1976.

"I am no longer an advocate of elaborate techniques of security analysis in order to find superior value opportunities," said Graham at that time. "This was a rewarding activity, say, forty years ago, when our textbook 'Graham and Dodd' was first published; but the situation has changed a good deal since then. In the old days any well-trained security analyst could do a good professional job of selecting undervalued issues through detailed studies; but in the light of the enormous amount of research now being carried on, I doubt whether in most cases such extensive efforts will generate sufficiently superior selections to justify their cost. To that very limited extent I'm on the side of the 'efficient market' school of thought now generally accepted by the professors."

Graham then suggested a highly simplified approach, based on two criteria, to identify bargain issues:

"My first, more limited, technique confines itself to the purchase of common stocks at less than their working-capital value, or net-current-asset value, giving no weight to the plant and other fixed assets, and deducting all liabilities in full from the current assets. We used this approach extensively in managing investment funds, and over a thirty-odd-year period we must have earned an average of some 20 percent per year from this source. For a while, however, after the mid-1950s, this brand of buying opportunity became very scarce because of the pervasive bull market. But it has returned in quantity since the 1973–1974 decline. In January 1976 we counted over 100 such issues in the Standard & Poor's *Stock Guide*—about 10 percent of the total. I consider it a foolproof method of systematic investment—once again, not on the basis of individual results but in terms of the expectable group outcome."

His second approach was, he said, "similar to the first in its underlying philosophy. It consists of buying groups of stocks at less than their current or intrinsic value as indicated by one or more simple criteria. The criterion I prefer is seven times the reported earnings for the past twelve months. You can use others—such as a current dividend return above 7 percent, or book value more than 120 percent of price, etc. We are just finishing a performance study of these approaches over the past half-century—1925–75. They consistently show results of 15 percent or better per annum, or twice the record of the DJIA for this long period. I have every confidence in the threefold merit of this general method based on (a) sound logic, (b) simplicity of application, and (c) an excellent supporting record. At bottom it is a technique by which true investors can exploit the recurrent excessive optimism and excessive apprehension of the speculative public."

In 1976, Graham and his collaborators finished calculating the application of his simplified criteria of a bargain stock over the fifty years since 1925. They established that besides his traditional criterion number one, *A stock should be bought for less than two-thirds of its net quick assets* (working capital minus all debt) and sold at 100 percent of net current assets, either of the following gave excellent results:

CRITERION #2

2a. *The company should owe less than it is worth.* That is, the debt-to-tangible-equity ratio should be less than one, counting preferred stock as debt; *and*

2b. The *"earnings yield"* (that is, the reciprocal of the price/earnings ratio) *should be twice the prevailing AAA bond yield.* Thus, if a stock sells for ten times earnings it has a 10 percent earnings yield. If it sells for five times earnings it has a 20 percent earnings yield, and so on. So if AAA bonds yield 5 percent you can afford to buy a stock at a 10 percent earnings yield (or ten times earnings). If AAA bonds yield 10 percent, a stock must have an earnings yield of twice that, 20 percent, or no more than five times earnings.

CRITERION #3

3a. *The company should owe less than it is worth; and*

3b. *The dividend yield should be no less than two-thirds of the AAA bond yield.* Thus, if AAA bonds yield 6 percent then a stock should yield at least 4 percent. If AAA bonds yield 9 percent, then the stock should yield at least 6 percent.

Graham and his associates established that stocks conforming to the first two of these three criteria had provided an average annual appreciation rate of about 19 percent over the fifty-year period, excluding dividends and commissions, as compared to 3.5 percent for the Dow (7.5 percent including dividends).

Combining the second and third criteria gave much the same result: 18.5 percent compounded.

Graham had spent his life establishing his basic criterion (here number one) and knew its validity, so the appreciation rate was not recalculated in his 1975–76 work.

The rules for selling were simplified:

1. *Sell after your stock has gone up 50 percent;* or
2. *Sell after two years, whichever comes first.*
3. *Sell if the dividend is omitted.*
4. *Sell when earnings decline so far that the current market price is 50 percent over the new target buying price.* (In other words selling-rule number one applied to a hypothetical new purchase.)

The buying criteria assume that all qualifying stocks listed in Moody's and Standard & Poor's guides are bought. An investor today using Graham's simplified principles would want to buy several dozen issues at least—the more the better, even if this means buying odd lots. One's own preferences and subjective considerations must not enter into this sort of operation. It would do no harm and would probably even be for the best if, except for the figures, the investor knew nothing about the companies he bought—if he put the company's head in a bag, so to speak, assuming he had enough diversification so that occasional blunders would not be disastrous.

Applying Graham's Methods

Can the ordinary investor hope to apply Graham's methods successfully, as Graham hoped? I believe that he can, if he has common sense, a mathematical bent, and patience. He doesn't even have to do his own work. If he casts about among his connections in the brokerage business he will eventually come upon a qualified practitioner who will offer suggestions based on whichever of Graham's approaches the investor wants to use. Since it's so easy, the investor should undoubtedly check his advisor's arithmetic by consulting standard reference books and company reports, and insist on a large number of holdings. One problem is that brokers have to live, which means they must generate commissions, while the Graham technique is so flat and unexciting, so lacking in appeal, that it rarely pays a broker to make it the basis of his approach to customers. He will want to combine it with a good "story," which entails compromising the method.

The Grahamite who enjoys this type of study—and it is quite enjoyable—is therefore well advised to do his own work, starting out with the services that perform the basic sifting by computer. He must, however, bring a modicum of wisdom, experience, and training to the task, enough to understand the reality behind the simple formula, and, when the formula wears out, to move on.

Standard & Poor's *Outlook* occasionally carries lists of stocks selling below net working capital, and at discounts from book value. An example is included as Appendix VI.

The Value Line Investment Survey regularly carries lists of stocks selling below net working value (or liquidating value). An example is included as Appendix VII.

Forbes magazine annually publishes a list of "Loaded Laggards," or companies selling well below their stated book value. An example is included as Appendix VIII.

A service run by James Rea in Los Angeles provides computer-generated lists of stocks that qualify under neo-Graham criteria. An example is included as Appendix IX on page 264.

To the end of his life Graham continued to experiment with new approaches to investing, further simplifications of his original ideas. He would test, retrospectively, how these techniques would have worked out.

Some of his former collaborators are now managing money using formulas based on this work. I am, however, somewhat skeptical of their prospects. One can at any time, using computer playbacks, derive formulas that with hindsight would have enabled one to manage money with great success until yesterday. But such methods need not work for the future. Any formula is likely to be rendered obsolete by events. Its own success will eventually be its undoing, as more and more imitators plunge in and muddy the waters.

It would not surprise me if this turnabout occurred sooner than most neo-Grahamites now expect. There are few sure things in the world. A simple, mechanical, and safe way of making money using information available as of the moment—without the "leap of faith" required in most investing, which involves guessing what the future may bring—is bound to find adherents in due course. At that point the Grahamites will have to compromise their methods: instead of buying at two-thirds of net quick they will, as the opportunities dry up, have to be content with 80 percent of net quick; instead of 7 times earnings, 8; and so on. Then all the obvious opportunities will be snapped up—a limited "efficient market" will have been created. Then the old-style laborious analyst, trained, for instance, on that formidable work, *Security Analysis*, will come into his own again, aided by the computer. Such an analyst will be able to find values that the neo-Grahamites with their much cruder methods cannot perceive, as a mariner with radar can venture forth when the one without is held in port. Within the Graham school the full-scale old-fashioned orthodox Graham analyst will have an advantage over the simplistic neo-Grahamites, and within the market the "value" approach will be overdone, so that growth will be where opportunity lies.

The wheel will have come full circle.

Footnote to Graham:
Tweedy, Browne

The Pawnbrokers

What do you do if you own a large collection of pictures which have greatly appreciated since purchase and would like to sell a considerable number of them? The solution, which the extraordinary Dr. Armand Hammer of Occidental Petroleum and Baron Leon Lambert, the Belgian banker, among others, have adopted, is to buy a gallery. That way instead of paying a dealer or an auction house 30 percent or 40 percent on each transaction, you trade net with your customer, or indeed charge *him* a hefty commission; and if you choose a good location you will attract many customers to whom you'd otherwise not have access. Of course, out of the savings you have to pay for the additional overhead.

In addition to using the gallery to move the inventory, by having it there you can hope to make money trading: replacing the inventory you sell high with new pieces that you buy low.

The same principle goes for the stock trader. There are two situations in which the buyer of stocks will be offered outstanding bargains: during periodic market shakeouts, when everybody decides that all is lost, so he's almost the only buyer;* and if he's available when the owner of an illiquid stock wants to sell a few shares.

One investment company that capitalizes systematically on this

---

* In a curious way, John Templeton plays the same game of being the only bidder, but based on geography: there aren't many buyers of little Australian or western Canadian property companies. Buffett does it by plunging in during panics.

principle is Tweedy, Browne & Co., in New York. Like a thrift shop they stand ready to buy small amounts of a large range of different items at a price, and are then happy to reoffer them at leisure to anyone who wants to buy—at a higher price. The original Mr. Browne called them pawnbrokers. For years they've made a nice living filling this useful function. Prepared to handle an exceedingly wide range of securities merchandise (literally thousands of different stocks) on short notice, some of which appear on their counter rarely or never, they must have simple and trustworthy valuation methods. As it happens, they have found over the years that Benjamin Graham's value criteria are by far the safest and easiest to apply. So we have here, in a way, the ultimate elaboration of the Graham idea in practice.

They claim, in fact, to be the only absolutely pure followers of Graham's original doctrine operating on any significant scale. Basically, they are prepared at all times to buy the stock of companies selling at two-thirds of net current assets, reduced by every conceivable charge, including future lease obligations, and then sell them again at 100 percent of net current assets. They will also buy and sell according to other Graham criteria, but almost never do they perform a conventional security analysis beyond the simple Graham rules. They don't really even care what the company does. They just want to see the numbers in the handbook.

In the 1920s Forrest ("Bill") Tweedy used to go to the annual meetings of small companies—with, perhaps, a few dozen shareholders. To drum up business he would obtain a shareholders list, and then send postcards offering to buy or sell 50 or 100 shares. Since inactive securities tend to be very cheap, when he was offered stock and had no seller he would sometimes put the holdings into the investment account of the firm. Then he broadened his scope to cover somewhat larger companies.

When Ben Graham began to have a following, his disciples would sometimes identify a company that was grossly undervalued, and then notice Tweedy, Browne's name in the "pink sheets," which list potential buyers and sellers of quoted securities.

Other than that, the firm was virtually unknown for about fifty years.

In 1980 they managed about $850 million and usually tended to have an inventory of more than a thousand items; that is, stock in that number of companies. Their average holding period is about three years, which implies that in any year about 300 stocks are bought and about 300 disposed of. Approximately 10 percent of their holdings are taken over every year by merger or acquisition.

Their holdings run in a smooth curve between $50 and $3 million to $4 million, with the median around $1 million. They have a few investments in the low millions, generally where they have acquired effective control of a company. (Ben Graham occasionally got into control positions too: besides GEICO there were Philadelphia & Reading and Atlantic, Gulf and West Indies Steamship.)

Hooks in the Water

Tweedy, Browne's principal vehicle, TBK partners, is listed in the *National Stock Summary,* which features inactive securities, as a potential buyer or seller of 2,500 to 3,000 different stocks, and in the "pink sheets," which covers larger and more active issues, as potentially interested in 70 or 80 more. They maintain files on these companies, and if they get a call from someone— the executor of an estate, say—who wants to dispose of a few thousand dollars worth of some obscure and illiquid situation, they can in a short time update their calculations and make a bid. They describe their machinery as "hooks in the water," through which they keep turning over their inventory. Continuing my gallery analogy I would call these listings their showroom, or perhaps their catalogue.

The company's portfolio is usually distributed about 70 percent in classic Graham intrinsic value investments; 10 percent in situations where it has acquired control of entire companies; and 10 percent in completely inactive stocks; with a smattering of "hidden asset" situations: coal, timber, and underutilized business assets.

TBK has enjoyed a twenty-year compound growth rate of well over 15 percent, deducting all expenses, but before tax. That makes it a very successful investing operation, or a good but not prodigious business, depending how you think of it. Considering the minimal risks involved in this approach I would call it a very convincing demonstration of Graham's methods in action.

Trying to Improve on Graham

With the aid of one of their partners who has a Ph.D. in statistics, Tweedy, Browne tried to improve on Benjamin Graham's net current assets criterion—for example, by specifying that the companies had to be dividend-paying, that they had to have low price/earnings ratios, that they had to be making money, losing money, or whatever. They found that there was no difference between companies that were making and losing money or paying dividends or not paying dividends. It did work out better to buy companies with price/earnings ratios in the 6 or 7 area, as against those that were selling for one to two times earnings. The reason for this seems to be that the higher market multiple reflects the better business franchise. A price/earnings ratio of 2 or 3 implies something seriously wrong. The investor is not at a disadvantage if a company is losing money, since management tends to sell out the whole company that much faster. Since one has bought the company for a fraction of its current assets, getting all its plant and equipment for nothing, the sooner the assets are liquidated—or redeployed effectively—the better.

By definition the stocks that Tweedy, Browne buy tend not to have brilliant management, since well-managed companies do not sell at such a discount. They feel, however, that mediocre management usually sells for a bigger discount than it should.

Tweedy, Browne has made one necessary adaptation of Graham, which is to factor in the cost of money. In Graham's day interest rates were low. Now that interest costs are 8 percent or higher, one must find correspondingly better bargains.

They have not taken much interest in companies with hidden assets, since they find that the discount-from-current-assets game is much easier to play. Nor will they buy a company because it has an attractive "business franchise"; however, they are encouraged when one turns up in their discount situations.

They have not found many attractive situations in the *Forbes* list of "Loaded Laggards," even after close study. And they do not believe in the neo-Grahamite approaches that are springing up, which they find too simplified.

Chris Browne, son of the original Mr. Browne, liked Gray Communications, then selling for $22, and worth, he says, $70 in a breakup. They own newspapers and television and will eventually have to sell out.

In 1980, he also liked Storer, selling at $32 as we talked, "a sleeping giant" with a breakup value of $90. He expressed great enthusiasm for Investors Insurance Holding Company, which the firm started buying in 1973, now holding 80,000 shares, or 10 percent. They made a tender for 25 percent of the company at $4, as compared to a book value of $6.50, and got about 265,000 shares. In 1980 it had a book value of $11. Browne described this as a beautifully run little company, writing about $18 million of premiums a year. Tweedy, Browne themselves run its investment portfolio.

Among timber companies one of his favorites was Simpson Timber, 99 percent of which is held by the Simpson family. It owns about 10,000 acres of redwood forest, which at recent prices of timberland worked out to about $500,000 per share of Simpson Timber, as compared with the stock market price of $13,000 to $15,000 per share.

Tweedy, Browne once decided that the most they could manage on strict Graham lines would be about $10 million, but now they have reached $850 million and have begun hearing of other groups in the field—a million here, a million there. They wonder —as Graham followers have wondered for decades—how long the opportunities will continue to be available.

Some years ago the partnership took over a mutual fund called Assets Investors Fund, whose portfolio they invested entirely in net current assets plays. It was worth about $6 million, distributed among some fifty stocks. A closed-end fund, it sold at a substantial discount from the values of the companies themselves. The portfolio of this fund, which the principals of Tweedy, Browne had been putting their own spare cash into, is shown as Appendix X. This fund was liquidated in 1980 because of adverse tax considerations.

5

Stanley Kroll

"We Who Are About to Die . . ."

After having spent thirteen years as a commodity broker, during which time he had approximately a thousand customers and wrote a book on commodity trading, Stanley Kroll started trading for his own account, in company with a handful of discretionary clients, and made himself and them a fortune.

Happily Ever After

About noon on December 9, 1974, Stanley Kroll, from his office at 25 Broad Street in New York, telephoned his wife, who was taking a course in spoken French at the Alliance Française on Sixtieth Street.

"I'm coming uptown to take you out for lunch," he told her. From a professional commodity trader, who spends his working hours glued to a battery of direct lines to the trading pit in Chicago, the commodity exchanges in New York, and other exchanges all over the country, an invitation to lunch is a command performance, so Jarrett Kroll automatically accepted, and started framing her excuses to her teacher: "Je regrette mais mon mari . . ."

When Kroll arrived to pick up his wife she asked where they were going. "To Seventy-third Street," he told her. She was puzzled.

"I don't know any restaurants on Seventy-third Street," she said. Kroll, a heavy, dark-haired man of forty, smiled mysteriously. And indeed, when they finally got out of the taxi Jarrett Kroll found herself in an automobile showroom.

"Here it is!" Her husband smiled triumphantly, pointing at a light brown four-door Rolls Royce.

As they glided majestically away in the noble vehicle—whose clock was completely inaudible (the engineers having finally coped with that embarrassment)—Kroll said, "Well, I'm out."

"You mean you closed out the wheat?" asked his wife. For months Kroll—and his wife—had been sweating out an immense and terrifying long position in wheat: 2.5 million contracts, or $12 million worth, which he had bought earlier that year for himself and his discretionary accounts. Every cent that wheat went down had cost $25,000. A ten-cent decline would have cost $250,000 and a decline of eighty cents would have put Kroll into bankruptcy. From May to November wheat had slowly, with many a sickening lurch backwards, worked its way from $3.60 a bushel to over $5.00, making Kroll's group a million dollars in the process. For some time now Kroll had thought the market's action looked sick, and he had been agonizing over whether to sell.

"No," said Stanley Kroll to his wife. "Out of everything. I'm closing the office. We've got enough. The car is for you. We're going away to live in Europe."

And so they did. They bought a house overlooking the Lake of Geneva, about forty minutes from the city. In winter they cruise in the Caribbean, and in summer they ply the canals of Europe in a barge. They're building a canal barge for the charter trade, and are bringing out an illustrated book on European canal cruising.

That morning, a Monday, Stanley Kroll had come to the office worried. It was no unfamiliar feeling, since he had been worried each Sunday, Monday, Tuesday, Wednesday, and every other morning—and indeed evening—for many months, ever since he had put on his huge wheat position; but this time he was even more jittery than usual.

Over the weekend he had taken out his boat and gone sailing on Long Island Sound in the hope of getting the wheat off his mind, but he couldn't. There had been bullish news for wheat— a drought somewhere, or a new Russian purchase—and as the market opened on Monday Kroll hung on the line to his clearing broker. He guessed that under normal circumstances the news would have been good for about two cents at the opening.

"Give me the Marches!" He spoke anxiously into the telephone, referring to the March future. "Have you got the Marches?"

"Down four cents to $4.88," said his trader.

Kroll hung up. No good. In fact, terrible. Time to get off the train. He buzzed his chief clerk. "Get me a complete list of all the wheat we have in the house," he said. "I want it in ten minutes." While he waited March wheat advanced a cent, wavered, and fell back again. No good. When his clerk came running in with the positions on a piece of paper, Kroll knew what he had to do. He barely glanced at the list.

"Get me the total," he said. The clerk went over to a calculator and began tapping in the figures. Wheat rallied again, then fell most of the way back once more. In another minute the clerk appeared with the same sheet plus a number on the bottom with a double underline.

"That's it?" asked Kroll.

"That's it."

"You're quite sure?"

"I'm sure."

Kroll picked up the telephone and spoke softly and slowly, but urgently. "Mike?" he said, "I want to sell one million bushels of March wheat. Got that? One million."

"Wow," said the trader. "One million."

"Right," said Kroll. "Now, do it carefully, Mike. Wait for them to take it."

"Don't worry, Stanley," said the trader. "Thanks." In the next three-quarters of an hour Kroll gave two more orders for three-quarters of a million bushels each. Two and a half million bushels meant more than two thousand railcars of grain, or a line of railcars twenty-five miles long. The commission alone on the trade was $15,000. Kroll then called the head margin clerk of his clearing broker, who also kept a record of all his positions on their computer. "I want to know what you showed us as holding in wheat as of Friday's close," he said. "I need it now." In a few minutes he got the confirmation: two and a half million bushels.

Meanwhile on the floor of the exchange his broker was at work. Without revealing the size of his order, he was waiting for wheat to strengthen, and then selling heavily into the market. Sometimes he would withdraw his offer, to allow wheat to run up and attract further buying interest. Other traders would see that Kroll's broker had suspended operations and be encouraged. Then, as the volume and prices picked up, the broker would drop off another series of contracts.

From time to time he used the direct line to report to Kroll on his progress. After about an hour and a half the broker's clerk called Kroll and said, "Well, that's it. Here are the last trades." He read off a series of transactions which Kroll noted on his pad and handed to his chief clerk. "Great work, Mike," said Kroll. "Well, I guess I'll call it a day."

It was then that he telephoned his wife, made the date to meet her, bought the Rolls, closed up shop, and headed for Europe.

Kroll had acually bought his wheat in May and June, several months earlier. All the signs had seemed right. Wheat had bottomed out the previous December and thrust upward strongly for three months, moving right up past its previous intermediate high price on good volume. Then it stalled, faltered, and slid off again. Over several weeks it made its way down until it had retraced most of its gain since November. Volume gradually dried up.

At that point, Kroll's years of experience in commodities told him that a strategic moment had come. He started to buy for himself and his customers. He bought more and more, until he had all that he and they could possibly afford. Wheat rallied on heavy volume. The action strengthened his convinction that the main trend was up.

However, he owned so much wheat that it made him nervous day and night. Rather than risk being panicked into selling when the market declined, he decided to go abroad and try to decrease the psychological pressure. Flying with his wife to Switzerland for August and September, he moved into a rented chalet above Nyon, avoiding the telephone and reading the commodity prices in the papers once a day. Sometimes wheat was up, sometimes it was down, but while he was in Switzerland it made him several hundred thousand dollars.

Then he came back to New York for two weeks, to get the feeling of the market, and started getting nervous all over again. He took his sailboat out for a two-week cruise to Block Island and Newport, but when he got back the market didn't feel right. After several weeks of increasing tension he finally had his great morning, and in a couple of hours sold all the wheat that he and his accounts possessed.

He had made them and himself $1.3 million on the transaction. Had he held on any longer, they would have lost $1.5 million in the next six weeks.

This last coup of Kroll's career was the culmination of a phenomenal three-year run during which he had turned $18,000 of his own into over a million, and the capital of some thirty-seven quasi-partners who joined him at various points during the period from $646,000 into more than $2.5 million.

In his thirteen years as a customer's man, first at Merrill Lynch and then at other commodity brokerage houses, including his own, Kroll had always let his clients call the shots—and lose their money. After Merrill Lynch he moved from one house to another, handling customers (about a thousand of them, although he has lost count), organizing commodities departments for several firms, and getting more and more knowledgeable. In 1967 he started his own firm, Kroll, Dallon and Company. Mr. Dallon left, but

Kroll felt that two names sounded more memorable.

Kroll says that during this time he created a number of variations of commodity contracts that have since become standard, including a contract for silver coins, but after a while imitators appeared and he had to develop new ones.

While he was making a substantial income, and, through observation and trial and error, had evolved many ideas on speculation in commodities, he had never accumulated any capital. Finally he resolved to change course, to put his conclusions into practice by trading on his own. He decided that any account he ran would have to do exactly what he was doing, without discussion. Since most customers feel that in commodities you can easily be bankrupted by being too aggressive, he had very few takers. So essentially he left the retail side of the business for good . . . and started to make money.

Kroll's System

Over the years Kroll had developed a profoundly cynical attitude toward Wall Street, but he had also learned many things about trading commodities, the most important of which is the simplest: *Wait until a major trend is clearly established, and then do your buying or selling during periods of correction against that trend.* When the trend finally concludes, liquidate.

In other words, if soybeans establish a strong up trend and then undergo a major retracement, try to find what you think is a reasonable level within that retracement—often an earlier resistance point—and put in your buy orders at that level. If the beans advance to new highs—thus confirming the trend—and then fall back again with falling volume, this confirms your basic judgment: buy more, but not as much as before.

A typical mistake of the commodity speculator who is going to fail is that he increases the size of his orders as the main trend continues: he pyramids. As a result, when the trend finally reverses he loses money very fast, since most of his money has been invested near the end of the move. Kroll, on the contrary, *invests less and less on each correction,* so that when the turn finally comes he has a good hope of excellent profits, even should his last few trades prove unsuccessful.

To illustrate the dangers of pyramiding, Kroll describes a customer he had who correctly foresaw a move in cocoa from twelve cents to thirty cents. He bought two contracts at twelve cents and two at fourteen cents and when it got to twenty he was so convinced he was right that he bought twenty more contracts.

At the end of each day, wrung out, he used to go for relaxation to a bar frequented by cocoa people, who would regale him with exciting rumors and stories.

Having gotten over twenty, cocoa faltered, and Kroll's customer was so nervous at holding such a large position that he sold out at seventeen cents. He ended up losing $200,000 on the whole maneuver, even though he never wavered in his conviction that cocoa was going to the mid-thirties—as indeed it did.

When the major trend does change definitively, Kroll liquidates during favorable reactions against the new unfavorable trend. In other words, if he is long soybeans and the market tops and starts coming down, he avoids selling into weakness, only into rallies.

How do you recognize a major trend when it arrives?

The big grains are the easiest, says Kroll, since they get into a groove like an express train thundering down the track, and you can safely bet the trend will go on for a while even if it falls off the track later. Wheat and beans are the best of all, Kroll finds, because their markets are too broad to manipulate. Corn is somewhat less satisfactory, although it tends to follow beans, for which in many uses it is a substitute.

The broader the market, says Kroll, *the more likely it is to have an identifiable major trend.*

I observed that the same thing is true in the stock market: the stock trends of General Motors can usually be identified, and indeed are a good indicator of the market as a whole, just as the major oils have long sweeps up and down, while a small stock can jump around much more erratically.

Kroll characterizes the way potatoes are manipulated as "obscene": the investor or speculator who is in fact right on the economics of the supply and demand can still be wiped out by manipulators. He thinks it is scandalous that in potatoes you cannot substitute an Idaho contract for a Maine one. In corn, for instance, the quotation is in the basic grade of yellow corn, but you can satisfy the contract with a better or lower one at an appropriate premium or discount. Similarly, you can satisfy a cocoa contract with cocoa delivered from any country in the world.

Kroll insists that you should *never argue with the market*. If the trend turns against you to the point where you are asked for additional margin, *don't respond*. Sell out, walk away from the whole situation, and reconsider.

You should avoid averaging down in the way that can be so profitable in common stock investment. In commodities you don't dare: the margin can kill you. If copper costs sixty cents a pound to produce and the price gets down to fifty-five cents, you can buy for all cash and probably come out ahead sooner or later. A commodity trader operates on, say, 10 percent margin, however, so if copper gets down to forty-five cents before turning up, he can be cleaned out if he goes on putting up the additional margin required.

One problem in commodities is that if you trade on a large scale, you risk being caught by a series of "limit days," which make it impossible to buy or sell at all. For each commodity the exchange prescribes the largest price change that is permitted during any one day—five cents per bushel, say. After the commodity has moved that much, trading ends for the day, even though there may be a great number of unfilled orders. This rule is to prevent stampedes, to permit the market to reflect overnight and to react judiciously to sudden moves; but in that situation you can lose almost unlimited amounts and it's virtually impossible to protect yourself. You may have wanted to close out a dangerous short position but day after day be unable to do it as the price jumps the limit and trading stops.

Occasionally you can get out anyway, if you know how. For

instance, in sugar, if you can't move in the U.S. market, you may be able to take an opposite position in London. If that doesn't work, then you can try options. All this can be expensive, though. The only real protection is to be on top of the situation all the time, and get out *before* the rush starts.

In the late 1960s and early 1970s this limit-day phenomenon ruined many Wall Street houses that, in their eagerness to pick up business, had been negligent in establishing their customers' financial strength. When there was a series of limit days, and as sometimes happens a customer was unable to provide margin or simply evaporated, the brokerage firm itself got stuck with the losses. Many old and well-known names went bankrupt in just this way.

To recapitulate: Kroll thinks that the basic art of commodity investing can be summarized by these four rules:

1. *Identify a major trend, and decide to make a big move.*
2. *Put your position in place during reactions against the main trend.*
3. *Put on smaller additional positions in subsequent reactions.*
4. *When the trend runs out, reverse the procedure in order to liquidate.*

That is the beginning and the end of Stanley Kroll's system. "It's quite simple," he says. "I could turn almost anybody into a successful commodity speculator if he would stay with me for a few years and give it his undivided concentration." Perhaps; unfortunately, to me it seems simple in the same way walking on a narrow plank is simple—the problem is the penalty of falling off. It's easy enough to walk on a board laid on a sidewalk, but over Niagara! It might be easy to do what Kroll says if the penalty for being wrong were ten dollars, but if the penalty is a million and a half for overstaying a market by a few weeks—as would have happened if he had lingered in wheat—you need iron nerves and prodigious confidence in order to function.

His description of his simple system reminds me of Bill Tilden's book on tennis. Here again, it's all quite simple. You are born six feet four inches tall, with a marvelous physique—and incidentally wonderful looks. Smiling fatly you begin by cracking over a serve so powerful that a new term has to be coined for it, the "cannonball." It scours a furrow in the court out of reach of the wildly staring receiver. Should it inexplicably go astray, you whip over a second with so much spin it flies up out of reach of his backhand. If by throwing his racquet into the air or some other freak he dabs it back across the net, you've already bounded to the forecourt like a lion crushing an impala to flick away his return with a half-volley that grazes the baseline for an easy win. All very simple, to be sure. But try and do it if you aren't Bill Tilden!

In the same way, you haven't much hope of following Kroll's simple system unless you are yourself a Stanley Kroll, with the same experience, the same determination, the same temperament, and the same iron control over your fears and desires.

Kroll's idea of "undivided concentration" may not be so easy for most investors, either. When he is in his office he follows with minute attention every trade that takes place in any commodity he is interested in. He says that during trading hours he tells his office staff not to talk to him, and if he has to give them instructions he is likely to do so by gesture rather than words. He won't leave his office to go to fire drills and won't even tell the others to go downstairs; he just waves his hand.

Kroll says that to make money in commodity speculation you must have no other daytime interests, and do nothing else.

Junk!

Kroll has steeled himself to exclude from his mind any outside opinion and any information that is not completely certain to be true. Since little information meets that criterion, he's almost saying that he pays no attention to any facts, only to market action. I found that surprising when I first heard it, but after he explained, it made much more sense.

First, *a commodity "fact" is probably fiction.* The presumption has to be that information generally put about is intended to mislead.

Second, *one does not know if it is complete*—and half a story is often worse than nothing.

Third, even if it passes the first two tests, there's a presumption that *anything true is already reflected in the market.*

"Take cocoa, for instance," Kroll says. "It's almost all grown in Ghana and Nigeria. The information that comes out of those two countries is issued by their cocoa marketing boards, which are what they sound like—instruments for getting the best price they can for their cocoa growers—about as impartial and factual a source of information as Tass.

"The same for 'information' on other commodities. In recent years the big moves in wheat, for instance, have often been on purchases by Russia and other foreign governments. But are they going to announce ahead of time what they are doing? Far from it. They mask their transactions with deceptive rumors and false moves in various markets. The 'informed speculator' who laps it all up is buying into a sucker game. The market action, if you know what it means, will tell the true story.

"Another completely misleading type of 'information' in the commodity markets is the word that, for instance, Continental Grain is buying. When a broker calls me up and tells me something like that, I just hang up. In the first place, Continental may be executing an order for somebody else. Or it may be balancing a position in one month against something it is doing in the opposite side of the market in another month. Or indeed it may be buying and selling just to confuse the market."

To sum up, almost all of what one hears in the commodity newsletters and the like is misleading; the first step toward success is to exclude such stuff from one's consciousness. Kroll described a visit from one of his customers, a leading securities analyst in a famous Wall Street firm. Kroll had bought his discretionary accounts plywood futures, and the analyst, much agitated, came to the office to repeat that he'd just been at a Georgia Pacific meeting for securities people where management had predicted that plywood was heading down.

"And here's another thing," said the analyst. He produced a copy of *Time* with an article discussing the plywood industry, which showed conclusively that prices were due to fall.

"You take that away!" shouted Kroll. "Lock it up in your brief-case! You should know better than to put a thing like that on my desk—all that stuff is junk!"

Describing this episode, Kroll became indignant all over again, like a vegetarian bishop telling of having been offered a dish of human flesh by cannibals. Everything was wrong. First, the tale in *Time* was probably not true. Even worse, it was persuasively written. And whatever truth there might be in it would have been reflected in the market anyway.

Kroll mentioned that one day a nice-looking young man from a famous international banking house with Middle Eastern ante-cedents came in and said, "We understand that you're buying copper." Kroll doesn't ordinarily answer such questions, but in this instance replied, "Well, perhaps."

"Copper's coming out of our ears in London," the young man continued. "We have economic studies here from one of our banks and other authorities saying that there is much too much copper in the world. Why don't you wait a year before buying?"

"Because it's going up *now*," answered Kroll. The handsome youth departed, troubled, leaving with Kroll a collection of volu-minous studies. A few days later a Chinese trade delegation sur-faced in London, briskly buying up the world's entire floating copper supply, and the market took off like a rocket.

As an example of that exceedingly rare thing, a possibly useful fact, Kroll pointed out that while corn is harvested as late as November, the critical months are in the summer, and after sev-eral dry months an expert who is actually out in the fields in Indiana and Illinois can say that the drought's held on so long that rain can't help anymore. The crop has to be a bad one.

If corn has already advanced from $2 to $4, then it's not useful information, even if true, but if corn has only gone from $2 to

$2.20, say, then it may be a buy. The information may be known, but the market may be more interested in some other "fact," such as that Russia is supposedly having a big crop, and as a result may not pay enough attention to the midwestern drought.

I asked what would happen if one actually moved to Indiana and became a corn expert. That might work out well, Kroll replied, but would require superhuman patience. Kroll needs to follow about ten different commodities at all times in order to have enough to occupy his mind, and to have enough different price sequences going on so that from time to time one of them will manifest an obvious major trend that he can use as a basis for action. At night he lies in bed and replays every jiggle of the day until one of the charts starts talking to him. After a while he feels the pressure building up and goes in again. He'd die of boredom wandering through Indiana's alien cornfields, pining for the Street.

Going back to nonfacts, Kroll said that one can most easily purge oneself of the herd instinct if one simply does not know what the crowd is doing, and so he refuses to listen to "news." After a year or so of experience with him, the brokers on the floor don't dare try to give him news flashes.

Some time ago in Chicago, visiting a top executive of a leading grain trading firm, Kroll asked what use one could make of the information that such a firm was buying or selling. The executive said that there wasn't any, since his company might be selling through one broker but buying through three others. And yet, when Merrill Lynch flashes its offices that "Continental Grain is buying," in every office two or three customers run to put in buy orders to take advantage of this piece of wisdom.

Kroll tells another tale of a customer who was a radio operator in the merchant marine. Whenever he came ashore, he used to blow the nest egg he had accumulated on his voyages in commodity speculation. He'd sit at a desk in Kroll's office and plot on a chart the movements of the commodity he was interested in, using a complicated system of colored pencils. One day he sat down and for four days did not enter a single order.

"Maybe the guy's getting good after all," Kroll said to himself.

Then one morning Kroll's clerk announced in a loud voice, "Bunge (a large trading house) is buying wheat." The radio operator almost broke his leg getting across the room to the order clerk to enter a buy order. Wheat declined, and as usual the man lost his savings. Later on Kroll asked him, "Why did you do *that?*"

"I don't know," the operator answered. "Maybe I was bored?"

Kroll's Rules

Kroll set out his trading principles in *The Professional Commodity Trader,* and they do seem to be the essence of his approach. All his stories of success confirm them, and most of his worst experiences have been when he violated one.

Every evening he fills out a large card for each commodity he is interested in, showing the long-term trend, the short-term trend, the price objectives, and his present strategy. He will *not depart from the strategy* once written out on his card. *Inspiration and whims are almost always expensive.*

Nor will he enter the market in a commodity that is bouncing around too much. He insists on acting *only when the whole pattern seems obvious.* This means that in the eight or ten commodities he follows closely, there might at any moment be none or possibly one that seems to have a worthwhile investible trend.

One of the reasons that the big brokerage houses are so expensive for their customers is that they usually have an opinion at all times on every commodity. Further, specialists I have talked to point out that really good commodity men are exceedingly rare; a brokerage firm rarely has even one. Most of the registered reps the customers are talking to are losers themselves who happen to be plausible salesmen.

A Million and a Half Down

It's hard to establish good positions, and almost impossible to do it quickly. You need a number of weeks or a month or more. In Kroll's book he describes how hard it is.

He became convinced in November and December of 1971 that silver was going up, and bought a good position at $1.40. Early in 1972 he sold it again at $1.55, feeling it was going much higher but that he could buy it back at a lower price and catch the rest of the move. Alas, it moved right on up to $2.50. Still sure it was going to go much higher, he decided that he would wait for three things to happen before buying: first, a retracement of 40% or 50% of the advance; second, lower volume and general market discouragement; and third, a decline to a point that constituted a reasonable base, such as a previous area of market congestion.

Unfortunately, silver failed to react, and went all the way up to $2.70. Kroll says he gained about ten pounds during this period.

At last the minor trend did indeed reverse. On March 1 it rose the limit, on March 2 it opened on an upside gap, and after that final surge it went straight down, closing on the lows at $2.64. On March 5 it went down the limit again, and Kroll concluded that this was it.

He decided that a 50% retracement of the whole trip upward would take July silver down to about $2.20, and at the same time he thought he identified a support area at $2.05 to $2.10 for spot silver, which corresponded to $2.15 to $2.25 for July silver.

He decided that he would wait and wait and wait until silver came down to that price, regardless of what happened in the meanwhile. Fortunately it took only a fortnight for July silver to reach $2.20, and for more than a month it traded in that area while Kroll bought 125 contracts.

Misery! On April 17, July silver crashed down to $2.12, costing Kroll $125,000. He then bought another 40 contracts for July silver at about $2.13. For another three weeks silver stayed in that area, but with volume drying up and liquidation of long positions by speculators, which meant that stronger buyers were taking positions.

Encouraged by that, Kroll bought still another 35 July contracts, paying $2.15 to $2.19.

On May 3, July silver jumped from $2.14 to $2.22, by May 8

it was at $2.29, and on the next day July silver was $2.35. On May 15 it rallied to $2.55 but then tumbled to $2.36 at the end of the trading day. Kroll bought another 10 contracts.

Throughout the collapse the commission houses were selling frantically, while as usual the major trade and professional operators were coolly buying. After a series of gyrations, July silver finally reached $2.51 on May 25. After the close the Bureau of Mines announced that there had been a significant rise in industrial consumption of silver during the first three months of the year, coupled with a substantially lower inventory in the hands of industry than had been previously expected. This was new and bullish, and the market rose the limit the following day.

Kroll was now long 210 contracts, hoping for an advance to much higher levels, and also hoping that there would be reactions along the way so that he could get his total position up to at least 300 contracts. There was a reaction during the week of June 11, and he was able to buy another 70 contracts between $2.55 and $2.65. He switched his July contracts to March to avoid taking delivery.

To his horror, between August 1 and September 11 the March market declined from $3.13 to $2.61, which meant that Kroll and his customers had given back almost a million and a half of their paper profits! In early September, after another rally, the market again declined to $2.61 and even Kroll finally lost his nerve, selling off some 90 of his 280 contracts. Finally on September 14 at two o'clock he realized that the market was about to close on the high of the day and indeed of the whole week, so he concluded that the down trend had been reversed. He jumped back in and was able to repurchase 50 contracts at a somewhat higher rate than that at which he had recently sold his 90.

The market now rallied to $3.12 and declined all over again to the $2.86 area, which Kroll had concluded was the interim support level, and where he was able to buy another 70 contracts—310 in all. A series of bullish stories began circulating: Bunker Hunt was about to take delivery of 20 million ounces of silver, the Swiss banks were setting out to squeeze the shorts, various other operators were buying. Within a few days March silver had gone to $3.18, but dropped to $3.00 on December 5. This flushed out more brokerage house speculators, but the bulls absorbed their sales and on January 8, March silver reached $3.44.

Kroll put in orders to sell 160 contracts in the $3.42 area, about half his position.

For a while nothing happened. Finally Kroll decided that he couldn't stand it anymore, even though he projected still higher prices, and sold out completely.

After a while his back-office manager calculated that they had regained the million and a half lost during the crisis and had picked up an additional $300,000, meaning a total profit on this transaction of $1.3 million over a period of less than two years.

Some Tricks of the Trade

Kroll couldn't think of any brokerage or statistical service useful to him except Commodity Chart Service, which costs $240 a year. Once Kroll decides that a commodity is really getting interesting he orders the daily chart and monitors it continuously. He has tried point and figure charts, moving averages, and other presentations, but ended up with a simplistic approach based on conventional line charts. He finds that it doesn't help much to follow the volume and open interest on a daily basis, although they can be of value from time to time, particularly to indicate reversals. There are, however, individual brokers he respects in particular commodities.*

Kroll points out that there is a way of speculating on currency by the use of commodities, enabling anyone to hedge a currency even when direct currency hedging is for some reason impossible: Go long cocoa, for instance, in New York, and take a similar short position in London. If the relative values of the dollar and the pound do not change, the transactions cancel out. If, however,

*He gave me one specific name in a well-known house, but that broker has since lost all and indeed more than all the funds entrusted to him by a commodity pool I'm aware of.

as has occurred in recent years, the pound falls, you profit. This can be a very handy way of hedging, or indeed speculating, when banks will not accept final hedging orders except for identifiable business purposes.

Kroll imagines the floors of the commodity exchanges to be inhabited by dragons. Once he was on the floor of the Chicago exchange when there were a great many sellers and no buyer in the corn pit. A floor broker from Merrill Lynch appeared, clutching a large buy order, and was immediately pounced on by a howling pack of brokers. While Kroll watched in fascinated horror, they tore off both sleeves of the broker's coat in their eagerness for his business.

Another time he walked over to the commodity exchange, of which he was technically a member, and actually went down to the floor to execute a trade himself and save the floor commission, but he couldn't make head or tail of what was going on. Even more surprising, when he shouted out his order nobody would trade with him. Finally, feeling like a child ignored in a playground, he gathered up his marbles, went back to his office, and phoned one of the same men on the floor, who instantly executed his order.

Be Right, Sit Tight . . .

One of Kroll's favorite quotations is from a book he considers an indispensable guide to the commodity speculator, *Reminiscences of a Stock Operator*, by Edwin LeFevre—actually a fictionalized autobiography of Jesse Livermore.

The narrator describes how he woke up to the importance of trading only for major moves:

Studying my winning plays in Fullerton's office I discovered that although I often was 100 percent right on the market— I was not making as much money as my market "rightness" entitled me to. Why wasn't I?

First of all, I had been bullish from the very start of a

bull market, and I had backed my opinion by buying stocks. An advance followed, as I had clearly foreseen. So far, all very well. But, what else did I do? Why, I listened to the elder statesmen, and curbed my youthful impetuousness. I made up my mind to be wise and play carefully, conservatively. Everybody knows that the way to do that was to take profits and buy back your stocks on reactions. And that is precisely what I did, or rather what I tried to do; for I often took profits and waited for a reaction that never came. And I saw my stock go kiting up ten points more and I sitting there with my four-point profit safe in my conservative pocket. They say you never grow poor taking profits. No, you don't. But, neither do you grow rich taking a four-point profit in a bull market.

Where I should have made twenty thousand dollars, I made two thousand. That was what my conservatism did for me.

The more Kroll has gotten into trading on his own, the more he has tended to retire from the commodity clubs and the social side of that world. He plays a lone hand, feeling that the more lonely he is the better.

Another quotation from LeFevre is typed out on a card in his top desk drawer:

After spending many years in Wall Street and after making and losing millions of dollars, I want to tell you this: It never was my thinking that made the big money for me. It was always my sitting. Got that? My sitting tight. It is no trick at all to be right on the market. You always find lots of early bulls in bull markets and lots of early bears in bear markets. I have known many men who were right at exactly the right time, and began buying or selling stocks when prices were at the very level which should show the greatest profit. And their experience invariably matched mine; that is, they made no real money out of it. Men who can both be right and sit tight are uncommon. I found it one of the hardest things to learn. But it is only after a stock operator has firmly grasped this that he can make big money. It is literally true that millions come easier to a trader after he knows how to trade than hundreds did in the days of his ignorance.

Kroll says that if one is going to be successful, one cannot hold commodities positions for less than an average of three months or so, and even that's a minimum. Four or five months should be the length of the average holding, time—if you are right—to make seven or eight times your money. If you try to scalp small moves you will be devoured by the commissions and the spread between bid and asked prices.

You must have a massive long-term concept, such as that wheat will rise from $2 to $4. If the objective is only that it will go from $2 to $2.10, you'll be chafing to get out at $2.07, which will preclude staying in through all the jiggles and reactions of the major move.

Kroll once typed out an expression attributed to Jesse Livermore and put it in front of his telephone: *"Money is made by sitting, not trading."* He used to read this card several times a day.

If Kroll's target is $4 and wheat goes for $2.40, he will buy a little more on a reaction, rather than selling out. If it reacts from $2.40 to $2.30 and the volume dries up, he will buy still more.

One has to presume a major move, but have indices that will tell you it has ended. Then, if things do work out, you have the patience and courage to stay aboard even if you have already made a huge profit.

It's not easy to sit with a huge winning position, particularly if you started life as a poor man. Once, for instance, Kroll opened a trade with $200,000 to his name. Eventually the commodity moved in the right way and his fortune grew to $400,000. Jarrett, his wife, wondered if he shouldn't sell out.

"No," said Kroll, "I'm shooting for $600,000." Then the market reacted, and his net worth shrank to $250,000. He had a big discussion with Jarrett at that point: "If it goes back to $400,000," she asked, "won't you sell then?" Kroll said, "No, if that was my idea I'd sell out now. I'm going to buy more on the first reaction after I reach $450,000."

In *The Professional Commodity Trader* Kroll analyzed the trading record of several of his customers. One of them, for instance, had twice as many losing trades as profitable ones, and average losses per trade more than three times higher than average profits per trade. Kroll reconstructed the trading record of this customer to assume he had limited his losses to 45 percent of the margin on each losing position. In that case the average profit would have been about 25 percent more than the average loss. Applying the identical principle to another customer's account, the average loss would have been reduced to one-sixth of what it actually was. Both customers, it is apparent, tended to trade against the major trend, and failed to cut their losses.

Kroll compared their record with his own over an eighteen-month period: he had twice as many profitable trades as losing trades, and the average profit was twice the average loss.

. . . And Go Down with the Ship

On the other hand, you can easily see why adhering to the rules is so difficult. How many traders would experience a million-dollar loss without panicking? How many have a million to lose? What sort of man, indeed, wants to be subject to such risks?

And how much you have to know to be sure that you really are right! Can you know that much? If things are not working out, do you dare persist in your position when you can easily be wiped out if a reaction against the main trend lasts long enough?

After all, a million-dollar loss in a reaction against a winning trend may become the first of many millions if the reaction turns out instead to be a new major trend in the wrong direction.

Kroll once received a letter from a man who as a boy had asked his father how you made money in the futures market. His father answered, "You have to be bold and you have to be right."

Kroll's correspondent then asked his father, "What if you are bold and wrong?"

"You just go down with the ship."

"He did just that, unfortunately," added the correspondent.

Morituri Te Salutamus

The average life of a commodities account is about six months. Kroll says that when two retail commodity brokers get together to talk about things, it is always assumed that their customers will have lost all their money within a year or so. The only question is, will they have lost it to the market, or will they have lost it in commissions?

In contemplating this gloomy tableau—all the customers of all the commodity departments of all the brokerage firms in the United States betting steadily away, with almost none escaping from the game with any capital at all—I am reminded of that dreadful gladiatorial event, the *munus*.

When the emperor wanted to be particularly magnificent he would stage one of these displays. Initially, two hundred gladiators might fight to the death, a hundred against a hundred, with the dead then hauled away. Fifty survivors were then pitted against the other fifty. The victims were again dragged off. Twenty-five now faced twenty-five.

At last, a single gladiator survived, who, depending on the will of the emperor and the populace, could walk alive out of the arena.

Similarly, sooner or later virtually every speculator in commodities gets killed off. Almost no one can overcome the fearful annual handicap—easily 50 percent and often 100 percent on equity—imposed by the commissions. Margin, which is always used in commodity trading, means that the speculator controls ten or twenty times his actual capital. His $10,000 becomes $150,000, say. Turning over $150,000 every few weeks for a year will easily generate $5,000 in commissions. Even should he build up his stake from $10,000 to $1,000,000, if he keeps on trading the commission bite will apply to the higher amount.

Further, if his stake should grow, the speculator often starts trading in larger units, graduating from 20 contracts to 200, say, so when he finally loses, he declines at a much faster rate than he previously gained, and he gets wiped out as quickly as if he had never won anything.

All of Kroll's thousand or so customers, many of them wise and experienced men, lost money. Only if one happened to get ahead at some point and dropped out right there did he escape; if he went on trading regularly, sooner or later he lost all the capital he had invested.

What's more, Kroll and the other commodity specialists I've talked to agree that the retail commodity speculator will always sooner or later lose his money, as infallibly as if he cranked away day and night at a slot machine until the stake was exhausted, like those elderly ladies in Las Vegas who wear a glove on the hand that pulls the lever. It's only a question of time.

The commissions that spell sure disaster for the retail speculator also bring gorgeous profits to the brokers, whose cynical enthusiasm for this sinister trade resembles that of the famous trading houses who foisted opium on the Chinese a century ago.

Kroll says he has heard of individual floor brokers in particular commodities who make money consistently, but they have a big edge over the outside customer, because of their access to the trading "book." He doubts if there are more than a handful at best, and also doubts that even the men on the trading desks of the commodity companies make money regularly on their futures trading, although in putting together complex swaps in different markets for the physical commodity, quite a different business, they can make good profits.

The One Sure Way to Make Money in Commodities

Is it safe to invest in a commodity when the price gets down to much less than the cost of production, as it is generally safe to buy a stock for a fraction of its working capital? Kroll replies that the cost of production is worth knowing but is not a reliable guide for a margin trader, since if the trend is down it can go so far below the cost of production that he will be wiped out. Weak buyers may move in as the price falls and then be flushed out again in a panic if it plunges right on down.

For instance, in the early 1960s sugar got down to 3 cents a pound. The economists all pointed out that this was less than the cost of the bag and the labor of putting the sugar into it, so that one was getting the sugar itself for nothing. The commission house customers bought hand over fist. Then, however, sugar fell all the way to 1¼ cents and thousands were "tapped out," as Kroll says. He played that one himself by purchasing call options in London.

I asked him why one could not buy entirely for cash, as distinct from margin, when one wanted to speculate in a commodity that was selling below its production cost. He replied that commodity speculators always invest on margin, and that even he could not make a satisfactory living if he didn't.

That seems illogical: a sure thing is worth a lot more than something risky, however much the risky thing's profit can be amplified through margin. After all, most people are wrong most of the time. Thus, if a commodity slips substantially below its production cost and you buy some for cash, you know that it will climb back again eventually and you will come out all right, whatever its gyrations in between.

Kroll says that if a broker called him up on the Lake of Geneva and announced that copper was selling for thirty-six cents as against a production cost of forty-two cents, he would buy about $50,000 worth, using so little margin that it would amount to a cash transaction. Similarly, if copper went to $1.90 he would sell short, although a smaller amount. If a broker called and said that wheat had been up sixteen days in a row and Bunge and Continental (another large trading house) had just declared bankruptcy, he would sell short cautiously, but with a high cash reserve.

I asked him what would happen if one told a broker to call up only when the prices of major commodities got well below their production cost, with the intention of buying for cash only: no margin. Kroll replied that it would have to be profitable, but that it left little incentive for the broker, who requires constant activity to live. Indeed, the broker would probably not even know the cost of production, which varies constantly. One would have to retain an economist for that purpose, and for once he might well be worth it. There aren't that many sure things in the world.

6

T. Rowe Price

Fertile Fields for Growth

After Benjamin Graham, T. Rowe Price is the most eminent investor in this book and the only one who gave his name to an entire theory of investment. (Price died in 1983.) Over the years, the "T. Rowe Price approach" has been heard on Wall Street almost as often as "a real Ben Graham situation": both phrases are instantly understood. Price also created the largest pool of capital of any of our subjects; the firm he founded, T. Rowe Price Associates, Inc., in Baltimore, manages some $22 billion. Their principal mutual fund, the T. Rowe Price Growth Stock Fund, was started in 1950 and today is worth more than $1.4 billion. Five other funds add another billion dollars.

Price's thesis, briefly, was that the investor's best hope of doing well is by seeking the fertile fields for growth, and then holding growth stocks for long periods of time. He defined a growth company as one with "long-term growth of earnings, *reaching a new high level per share at the peak of each succeeding major business cycle* and which gives *indications of reaching new high earnings at the peak of future business cycles.*" It may, however, have declining earnings *within* a business cycle.

Price said that since industries and corporations both have life cycles, the most profitable and least risky time to own a share is *during the early stages of growth.* After a company reaches maturity, the investor's opportunity falls and his risk rises.

Successfully working out and applying this approach made him one of the most famous investment practitioners of his day.

A portly man with sad eyes and a dark moustache surmounting a knowing, tired, and somewhat grim smile, Price came from Glyndon, Maryland, then a summer resort for people from Baltimore. His father was a country doctor.

Investing was his life. Price liked to talk with exaggerated understatement about his own position and achievements: He might call someone in the investment business and open the conversation by saying, "This is Rowe Price . . ." If the respondent was silent, he'd continue, "Have you ever heard of me?" He also liked to describe mistakes he had made.

Like most of the greatest investors—or artists or professionals of any sort—Rowe Price lost himself in the task; his first interest was always in superior performance, not in making a killing for himself. He craved immortality in the record books and was thus a good professional: the client came first. "If we do well for the client, we'll be taken care of," he liked to say. To help shape his own monument, he kept a close eye on what the press said about him. And later, long after retiring from his firm, he started writing articles on his investment suggestions, hoping to create a new performance record.

Price, at eighty-two, still got up at 5:00 A.M. He was exceedingly disciplined and organized, with an agenda for each day, always executing the items in the order listed and never taking up unlisted ones. Similarly, when he bought a stock at 20 he also established that he would sell some at, for instance, 40, and did, even if everything had changed for the good. If he had determined to buy more stock at 13, so he would, even if the news from the company was discouraging.

An associate recalls him as being "amazingly able, irascible, and egotistical." He was "Mr. Price" to almost everyone: he wouldn't be aboard the ship at all unless he was the captain. He might have liked to say, "I make a lot of mistakes . . . I'm not very bright," but all the same, everybody who worked with him always had to do exactly as he specified. His former associates report that Price could be charming when he wanted to, just as long as they did what he said; when they didn't, he preferred not to see them at all. Since he hated to delegate responsibility, he would have made a bad industrial manager.

Nothing Grows in the Shadow of an Oak

To be a great investor, says one of Price's colleagues, one must be a loner, a crowd-opposer. But it's virtually impossible for loners to create a self-sufficient organization. Typically, the strong-willed loner has weak followers. He thus must either sell his company to outsiders to realize a capital value for his efforts (which leaves his clients prey to the acquisitor) or else, like Price, he must sell it with great trepidation to his own followers, openly concerned that they are not fit to succeed him.

The best hope for the organization is to have a talented successor still in his thirties when the sixty-five-year-old founder wants to retire. The latter may not be jealous of a much younger man— a psychological grandson.

When a member of Price's organization did better than he did in the market, Price's competitive juices would start flowing, and he'd begin to compete, to the point of seeking, usually with success, to humiliate the rival. According to company veterans, he would sometimes shatter the victim in the process, particularly if it was a former favorite. His was the problem of the outstanding salesman who becomes the sales manager: though he is supposed to train other salesmen and take an override, he all too often tries instead to compete with the men he is managing.

Price liked to start new things, but not to operate them. Once they were launched, he went on to something else. When the T. Rowe Price Growth Stock Fund became established and successful, Price pressed on to the New Horizons Fund. When that was thoroughly established, he went on to the New Era Fund. The same for his firm: after building it up, he sold it, and later started publicizing a series of independent portfolios to prove he was still the master. Each time he moved on after having made his point.

T. Rowe Price Associates had a relatively small volume of assets under management until late in Price's life. In the early 1950s the firm's portfolios totaled only a few hundred million dollars, and in 1966, when Price was in his late sixties, the firm ran approximately $1.5 billion while a number of investment counsel firms started at the same time were two or three times larger. Price himself did not believe that his firm could expand further after he retired. When he sold out to his associates, they offered him an arrangement under which he would participate in the firm's growth for five years, but he declined, only to see the portfolios under management expand fourfold during the following five years. The company had two extraordinary pieces of luck after Price retired:

First, smaller growth companies became extremely popular with investors, giving six years of glory to the Growth Stock Fund and even more to the New Horizons Fund, and the exploding market for pension fund management brought the managers of pension funds to the firms with the best recent records.

Then, Charles Shaeffer, who succeeded Price as president, was a supersalesman rather than an investment philosopher, and did not tamper with Price's approach. As a result, the firm gained an enormous amount of new business, riding the growth boom all the way up—and later down again—and made a great deal of money.

There was, one can see in retrospect, a possible conflict of interest between the firm and the clients who gave it their money to manage based on its record. Probably it should have announced—as Price, in retirement, did personally—that the growth mania was being overdone, then switched to a balanced approach, and refused to accept business from investors seeking all-out growth-oriented management.*

* (The management of New Horizons Fund, to its credit, twice—from October 1967 to June 1970, and from March 1972 to September 1974—when it was receiving about $1 million a day in new subscriptions, refused to take any more because it felt the market was dangerously high. Each time, when the fund closed, there was a frenzied clamor from investors who wanted to buy; the market collapsed, and when the fund reopened investor interest was minimal.

The Method in Action

Price made available the audited holdings and performance figures of a "model growth stock portfolio" consisting of the common stockholdings of two family accounts, one started in 1934 and one started in 1937, from inception through 1972. (See Appendix XI.)

The amounts involved were modest at the outset, and cash and bonds have been omitted. It is, in other words, a demonstration of stock-picking, not of portfolio management. That said, the performance is striking. One thousand dollars invested in stocks in 1934, with dividends reinvested, but not including tax, would have become $271,201 by December 31, 1972; the investment would have grown roughly only half as much if one had begun at the end of World War II. The market value, ignoring dividends, grew approximately twenty times from 1950 through 1972, and roughly four times from 1958 through 1972. If the account had been 50 percent in bonds during the period, the results would have been somewhat less than half as favorable.

Some of the individual stock purchases worked out amazingly. For instance, by the end of 1972 Black & Decker, held for thirty-five years, had risen from 1¼ to 108; Honeywell, held for thirty-four years, had gone from 3¾ to 138; MMM, for thirty-three years, from ½ to 85⅝; Square D, also for thirty-three years, from ¾ to 36⅞; Merck, held for thirty-two years, had advanced from ⅜ to 89⅛.

Obviously a taxpaying investor who finds stocks that he can hold for almost a lifetime enjoys a marked advantage over one who buys and sells at shorter intervals, since he postpones capital gains taxes indefinitely and thus has the use of the tax money he would otherwise have paid out, besides avoiding brokerage commissions. Because of compounding, his after-tax results in cash should exceed those of an equally skillful investor who must pay capital gains taxes and brokerage commissions as he goes along.

I became very conscious of this difference in the 1950s, when I was associated with the investment counsel firm that ran the best-performing mutual fund for that decade out of the 200-odd funds then in existence. It also had about the highest portfolio turnover. The runner-up by a narrow margin was T. Rowe Price's Growth Stock Fund. After a while, however, I realized that the Price Fund, which had one of the lowest portfolio turnovers, was doing a better job for most of its shareholders after taxes. Nor did the system need to be operated by a genius. Mr. Price was a sensible, astute and exceedingly experienced man of iron discipline and a strong will, but did not profess to be a prodigy. On the contrary, one of the merits he claimed for his approach was that a nonprofessional could carry it out successfully.

Considering all this, I concluded that in the real world an investment approach based on searching out the exceptional company with a view to holding it for long periods of time seemed likely to work out better for an experienced and able but not phenomenally well equipped investor than would a buy-and-sell approach. He wouldn't have to know as many different things or make as many difficult decisions.

"Even the amateur investor who lacks training and time to devote to managing his investments can be reasonably successful by selecting the best-managed companies in fertile fields for growth, buy[ing] their shares and retain[ing] them until it becomes obvious that they no longer meet the definition of a growth stock," said Price.

Can the amateur investor really do that? Consider some of Price's requirements for growth companies:

1. *Superior research* to develop products and markets.
2. A *lack of cutthroat competition.*
3. A *comparative immunity from government regulation.*
4. *Low total labor costs,* but *well-paid employees.*
5. Statistically, Price likes to see at least a *10 percent return on invested capital,* sustained *high profit margins,* and a *superior growth of earnings* per share.

To select such stocks, he said, the investor needs experience and judgment, and must take into account general social and political influences as well as economic ones. All this, I would judge, does indeed lie within the competence of a hardworking nonprofessional.

Price might be called a qualitative analyst of investments, whereas Benjamin Graham, finding that this approach leads to subjectivity and impressionism, always emphasized the quantitative, what can be measured in numbers. On the other hand, "Graham" investment does require training, while common sense, political savvy, and general wisdom will tell Price or the rest of us that, for instance, railroads can't do well over the long term in the face of regulation, featherbedding and consumerism; and that the semiconductor and the minicomputer are explosive growth industries. And toward the end of his career Price even stopped contacting companies firsthand in making his own investment decisions, relying entirely on company reports, his long experience, and a few secondhand sources.

Then again, how many investors will have Price's extraordinary discipline, which is the heart of his method? How many will be perfectly comfortable in bucking the crowd, sailing into the teeth of the gale?

Perhaps the answer is that while an experienced and patient businessman who masters Price's approach should be able to do well, he's most unlikely to be able to do as well as Price did. Strangely enough, though, a businessman, one with a professional experience of the real world, as distinct from stocks, could quite possibly have avoided the strategic blunder of Price's successors, described below.

What to Look for in a Growth Stock

Price maintained that there are two aspects of capitalizing on the "fertile fields for growth": identifying an industry that is *still enjoying its growth phase,* and settling on the *most promising company* or companies *within that industry.*

The two best indicators of a growth industry are *unit volume of sales* (not dollar volume) and *net earnings. Return on investment* must also be watched carefully. To be attractive, an industry should be improving in *both* unit volume and net earnings. Many studies are available on a regular basis showing which industries are experiencing the fastest growth. Investors are usually aware of the most exciting ones, but are often not aware that they are maturing.

Price pointed out that when an industry finally began to go downhill it might do so on "leverage": carrying profits down even faster than unit volume. Writing in the 1930s he correctly identified railroads as a maturing industry: in the late 1920s, railroad ton-miles had started to decline in the face of improving business; by the late 1930s ton-miles were substantially lower than in the previous decade. Since fixed charges did not decline equally, profits fell drastically.

Looking ahead, Price had no difficulty in perceiving that with the trend toward government domination, public utility companies were likely to become unsatisfactory investments. Similarly, even before World War II he readily identified the superior prospects of aviation, diesel engines, air conditioning, plastics, and television over, for example, the maturing automobile industry.

An old industry that is experiencing new growth, whether because of new products or new uses for old ones, may also become attractive for investment; new growth products have transformed the office equipment, specialty chemicals, and oil equipment industries, and given new life to their stocks.

Finally, there are specialty companies that go their own successful way, such as Coca-Cola and MMM.

How do you find the best companies within an attractive industry? Price looked at their records. They must have *demonstrated* their superior qualities, either by showing improving unit growth and profits right through the down phase of a business cycle ("stable growth") or by showing higher earnings from peak to peak and bottom to bottom through several cycles ("cyclical growth"). When one finds such companies one studies how they are doing, and tries to determine if they will be able to prolong their superiority.

Some of the qualities that may contribute to their superiority are:

1. *Superior management.*
2. *Outstanding research.*
3. *Patents.*
4. *Strong finances.*
5. *A favorable location.*

One wants to establish whether these factors will continue before deciding that a company is probably a growth stock.

When growth turns to decadence it can usually be attributed to the erosion of former advantages. For instance:

1. *Management may change* for the worse.
2. *Markets may become saturated.*
3. *Patents may expire* or new inventions render them less valuable.
4. *Competition may intensify.*
5. *The legislative and legal environment may deteriorate.*
6. *Labor and raw materials costs or taxes may rise.*

These adverse changes will be reflected in unfavorable comparisons in *unit sales, profit margins,* and *return on capital.* They warn the growth investor that it's time to move along.

Price did not believe in *specific predictions* of a company's future. "No one can see ahead three years, let alone five or ten," he has said. "Competition, new inventions, all kinds of things can change the situation in twelve months." As a result, the "valuation models" that are popular in Wall Street, which project future earnings, year by year, apply a discount factor, and give a theoretical price today which can be compared with the market price, are highly suspect if not worthless. According to Price, the right approach is just to stick with the best companies in the highest-growth industries as long as their progress continues. Do not try for a pinpointed mathematical approach that creates an illusory certainty out of an unknowable future.

Price never carried his argument to its logical conclusion by comparing countries, as he did industries and companies. In recent years the Japanese economy has offered many rewarding investment opportunities, both because of the extraordinary productivity of the Japanese themselves and because of foreign investors' neglect of the Japanese market. Some of the greatest companies in the world languished for years at three and four times earnings, even though they were becoming larger and stronger all the time.

Price reasoned that he was doing well enough, and had better stick to what he knew best.

Switching Between Cyclical Growth and Stable Growth

In his early writing Price proposed a more aggressive technique than just buying and holding the best companies in the highest growth industries, a technique one hears less about in his later work. He pointed out that within the growth category cyclical growth stocks are more volatile in both earnings and market action than stable growth stocks. That makes Coca-Cola, for instance, which maintained its dividends even during the Depression, more suitable for an endowment or trust fund requiring regular income than a stock that, in spite of long-term growth, has to cut or skip its dividends from time to time.

Market washouts also create greater opportunities in cyclical stocks than in stable ones. With various examples Price demonstrated that you make the most money, starting from the bottom of a bear market, by first buying a washed-out cyclical stock for the kick it has coming off the bottom, and then switching to a stable growth stock that never went down as much.

There are several things wrong with this strategy, which is perhaps why Price later didn't talk about it much. The first is taxes. If you can just buy and hold for very long periods you don't yield the bite to the tax collector (and the broker) that you do if you try to trade. So you don't have to be as clever and bold to achieve the same net result. Second, you can no more be right all the time than you can bat 1000. Your success is likely to improve as you limit the number of companies you have to study, thus increasing your focus and your hope of relative superiority. So if you can resist the temptation to do too much, such as attempting a program of cyclical-growth to steady-growth switches, you may end up better off.

A question Price liked to ask in contemplating an investment is, *what is the investor's own return on the money he has invested?* If you buy a stock at a high price-earnings multiple—forty times earnings, for instance—you are only getting an "earnings yield" of 2.5 percent on *your* money, whatever the company itself may be earning on *its* capital. Further, your dividend yield in such a situation will probably be less than 1 percent. Of course, you hope it will rise, but it will take a long, long time for those dividends to total as much as you would have received from bonds yielding, say, 9 percent.*

---

* In the growth-stock fever of the late sixties and early seventies, I devised a paradox that I used to try on my friends in the securities business who recommended high multiple growth stocks. Let us assume the perfect stock, whose earnings grow at 20 percent compounded forever, selling for fifty times earnings. Paradox: Assume that in year one you buy $1,000 of such a stock to yield $10, or 1 percent, and the dividends increase 20 percent a year. After ten years your dividends—which start out at 1 percent the first year, 1.2 percent the second, 1.44 percent the third, and so on, total some $260, which is much less than the 35 percent inflation one could then assume for a decade (and which is higher now). Over the period you have *lost* about $100 in real terms. You then start the next decade. This goes on decade after decade. The reader may enjoy working on this puzzle, which will help him understand the danger of paying very high multiples.

The low return on a growth stock bought at very high multiples becomes particularly serious in periods when bonds are offering attractive yields as an alternative, as Price pointed out in his *Principles of Growth Stock Valuation.*

How to Buy

Price proposed a specific plan for buying any stock, which one should *write out and then adhere to.* It has two parts: *fixing a price,* and then *buying (and selling) on a scale.*

A. *Valuation*

As one might expect, Price emphasized the price-earnings multiple approach to equity valuation, rather than the appraising of hard assets (although late in his career he became keenly interested in natural resources).

Several factors help determine the multiple of earnings one should be prepared to pay:

1. Above all, *a record of earnings growth.* But one shouldn't project the rapid increases of the dynamic phase of a growth stock too many years into the future.

2. The best time to buy is when growth stocks, especially those one is interested in, are *out of fashion.*

3. *"Blue chips"* with a record of rising dividends are worth a higher multiple than secondary stocks without dividend growth.

4. *Stable growth stocks are worth more than cyclical stocks* subject to the vagaries of the business cycles, and of course *cyclicals are worth a higher multiple of their recession earnings than of their boom earnings.*

5. *One should pay a lower multiple* of earnings for growth stocks when bonds are available at high yields.

6. Similarly, when the general level of stock prices is low enough so that they are yielding 5 percent or more, one should pay lower price-earnings multiples for growth stocks than when stocks in general are high enough to bring yields down to, say, 3 percent or less. Put differently, *the "total return" of growth*

stocks has to compete with that available from bonds or stocks in general.

In practice, Price seemed to fix the appropriate price-earnings ratio for a desirable growth stock by noting the high and low p/es of the last few market cycles and establishing a target p/e at something like *33 percent over the lowest p/e the stock touched during the period.*

B. *Scale Buying*

Price's examples indicate that *as a stock fell to his target buying range he started buying quite vigorously,* without "bottom fishing," which he clearly felt did not pay. If a stock went a lot below the initial price he paid, he would have done some buying near the lows, but most of his buying averaged out not too far below his initial target price.

How to Sell

Price emphasized that one has to be able to tell when a company's earnings growth is coming to an end. He didn't say how to do it, except to warn against some changes and pitfalls:

1. *Beware of a decline in the return on invested capital.* That's often a warning of the onset of maturity in a company.

2. *Business recessions create a confusing background* against which to study the performance of a particular company. Its earnings may decline because its growth is still intact but is being dragged down by general conditions, or on the contrary its growth may really have peaked and one may overlook it in the general business decline.

3. *Some industries,* such as real estate and fire and casualty insurance, *have their own cycles* that are separate from the business cycle, confusing things further.

Scale Selling

When he did decide to sell or cut back on a stock in a bull market, *Price waited until it has risen 30 percent over its then upper buying price limit.* At that point he sold 10 percent of the position, and thereafter an additional 10 percent each time it advanced another 10 percent.

However, he would sell out at the market a stock scheduled for scaled elimination *if the bull market peaked out,* or *if the stock itself seemed to be collapsing, or if there was bad news from the company.*

Price Changes Tack

By 1965 Price had spent thirty years as a growth stock advocate. Originally he had been almost alone in recognizing the investment merits of companies whose earnings rose from one business cycle to the next. Little by little he had attracted such a following and built such a large organization that not only was this method called the "T. Rowe Price approach" but many of his favorite stocks—Black & Decker, Emery Air Freight, Avon Products, Rollins and Fleetwood, for example—became known as "T. Rowe Price stocks." In the late sixties, however, Price finally announced that the time had come to change one's orientation and over several years published a series of bulletins which were summed up in a pamphlet, *The New Era for Investors,* which created a great stir in the investment community, not so much among those who read it, since its reasoning is most persuasive, as among those who merely heard about it. T. Rowe Price advising against the "T. Rowe Price stocks"! What next?

Price hadn't changed his spots, however; he'd just decided that there weren't many bargains left in the kind of stock he wanted to buy. His goal was that a stock should double income and market value over ten years (or less if inflation is very high), but that's far from easy if it's already at forty or fifty times earnings. What happens if something goes wrong? And what hope is there that such multiples will still be applied to those stocks at the end of the period?

In the late sixties Price not only decided the long bull market in growth stocks was over but also sold to his associates his controlling interests in the companies that managed the business he had built up, including the management of the Rowe Price funds and of institutional and private portfolios. He received some $2.3 million for the package, far less than if he had held on a while longer, but more than enough to make him comfortable.

Price decided about this time that in the excitement over growth that might never happen, investors were neglecting natural resources assets. He therefore formulated what he called his "new era" approach, which meant, in addition to growth stocks, buying assets that should be inflation-resistant: real estate, natural resources, gold and silver.

He cut back on his growth stock investments, and put a substantial part of his family assets, including what he got from the sale of his firm, about equally in bonds and stocks, the stocks being mostly in his "new era" selections, particularly gold stocks.

Ten years later these holdings were at a substantial profit, unlike the rest of the market, particularly the growth stocks.

Price v. Price

To Price's intense dismay his successors in his firm went right on playing the old game, putting the funds that came in to them for management into the same sort of stock, apparently almost indifferent to how much they were paying for a dollar of earnings or dividends. (I remember, in fact, an enthusiast close to the company telling me that it was if anything *better* to buy the stocks with the highest price-earnings ratios, because then when the earnings advanced—as they surely would, since that was why you'd bought them in the first place—those stocks were the most certain to rise, since they enjoyed the highest degree of institutional acceptance.)

We now recognize all this as the usual silly rationalization of the herd instinct, but anyway, it happened.

By 1974 what Price feared had come about. Growth stocks became a disaster, with many falling 75 percent to 80 percent from their old highs. A share of Price's pride and joy, his New

Horizons Fund, lost 42 percent of its asset value per share in 1973 and then 39 percent more in 1974; and the whole fund fell in size from $511 million to $203 million over the two years as redemptions followed the market decline.

It could almost be said that the Price organization had been fated to ride the 1972–74 bear market right over the waterfall. Price's successors would have needed the courage to quit a winning game in its most successful period. It was profoundly gratifying for the firm to have important clients asking to have it manage their money. Turning them away would scarcely have been in the nature of things and would have involved a repudiation of what the firm stood for—including the selling of many of its holdings, which might have risked breaking their prices. It would also have involved restructuring the firm's research department, which was dedicated to growth stock analysis—about like shutting down a highly successful French restaurant and reopening it as a Japanese sushi bar with new people in the kitchen: theoretically possible, but most unlikely. Finally, everybody was just too busy to worry about what lay ahead. Stocks like Avon were rising by 1 and 2 percent a month. Price Associates bought them, and Morgan Guaranty picked them up. The price rose. U.S. Trust and other banks and mutual funds piled aboard. That put the price up more. Private Swiss banks who were serviced by the same brokers got on the bandwagon. Other funds and hedge fund managers came in. This made the original purchase look very smart, so Price Associates bought more. The cycle continued. Even more delightful, the rising prices created wonderful performance figures, meaning more clients and higher fees.

When growth stocks fell from favor in 1974, the firm had picked up so much business and so many able people that although the growth stock equity accounts were gravely damaged, the firm itself never had a net shrinkage of managed assets. The reason was that the amount of business it lost from falling stock prices and clients who left was offset by new cash from existing pension funds remaining with the firm, and new fixed-income funds that were created and sold.

The very name "growth stock" became virtually taboo in Wall Street. The same institutions that had rapturously bought Avon in 1973 as a "one-decision" holding at $130, or fifty-five times earnings, then dumped it in 1974 at $25, or thirteen times earnings, until by late 1974 the wringing-out process had gone so far that Price himself decided it was safe to begin buying growth stocks once more, though not necessarily the same ones. While their market prices had come way down, many of them had moved that much further down their life cycle toward maturity, and thus offered less growth potential.

So in his personal portfolios, Price changed tack still again. He divided his interests into three categories of stocks: "growth stocks of the future"—companies that he felt were still at an early point in their life cycle; older, seasoned growth companies with less dynamic prospects but whose price had declined below what he felt they were worth; and a mixed grill of companies, notably natural resources—gold, silver, and others that had fallen to what he called "receivership prices."

Price considered a number of "emerging" growth stocks to be attractively priced in mid-1977: Alcon Lab (which later doubled and was replaced by Harris Corp.), American TV and Communications, Castle & Cooke, Dome Mines, Dome Petroleum, Jack Eckerd, E. G. & G., ESL, Flexi-Van, Hexcel, Houston Oil & Minerals, Lowe's Companies, Magma Power, McCormick, Payless Cashways, Perkin Elmer, Sabine Corp., Scientific-Atlanta, Thomas & Betts, and Viacom International. Later he decided Rite-Aid would have been a better bet than Sabine, and Waste Management than Flexi-Van.

Of his former "established" growth stock favorites, he considered only six attractively priced in late 1977: Black & Decker, Continental Oil, Dow, Newmont, Georgia Pacific, and Weyerhaeuser. At the right price he also considered as suitable candidates Burroughs, Digital Equipment, Walt Disney, Kodak, Emery Air Freight, GE, Hewlett-Packard, IBM, Johnson & Johnson, K mart, Merit Freight, 3M, Pepsico, Polaroid, Revlon, Schlumberger, Texas Instruments, and Xerox.

By late 1977 Price had grown so disturbed by the confusion in the public's mind between his personal investment philosophy, which although growth-oriented is keyed to buying only real values, and that of his old firm, which he felt had gotten locked into a simplification of his ideas, that he gave a number of interviews and statements to make clear that "Price Associates and Rowe Price are as different as day and night."

There's a certain melancholy humor in this spectacle of indignant older gentlemen excoriating their successors. I'm somehow reminded of another eminent southerner, Colonel "Kentucky Fried Chicken" Sanders denouncing the "goddam slop" that his specialty became after he sold the company.

Anyway, Mr. Price was justified in having been "appalled." His company had so much money under management when the growth stock balloon collapsed in 1973–74 that very possibly the firm (not Price himself) has lost more dollars for its clients than it previously made for them, since in its great period it was so much smaller. With hindsight it's hard to conceive of all those intelligent, trained, experienced money managers, not only in Price Associates but also in the Morgan Guaranty, the United States Trust Company, and many other distinguished establishments, happily holding on to and indeed buying more of the high-flying growth fad stocks at prices that could not possibly be justified even if the companies achieved all that one could dream they might and still more. Even worse, some of Price's followers who bought his stocks near the top sold out in desperation after the stocks had dropped by three-quarters, abandoning the growth idea just when it was about to pay off all over again. It isn't hard to understand why Price wanted to stand apart from all this, just as Marx once said, "Moi, je ne suis pas Marxiste," meaning that he was the real thing: he knew the grand principles behind the simplified formulations.

How could Price have avoided the catastrophe? Only in two ways, that I can see: having worked out his growth doctrine he could have imbued his firm with a basically flexible and pragmatic approach, always (like Paul Cabot and Larry Tisch) insisting on common sense, realism, and flexibility as the highest investing virtues; or he could have found and cultivated a worthy successor, another master investor to grow up at his side and eventually inherit his authority—someone with the wisdom and strength to alter course when it became necessary. But that, as we know, since Price's makeup didn't permit it, was not in the cards.

7

John Templeton

To Everything There Is a Season

One day in 1939, just after war had broken out in Europe, a young man named John Templeton called his broker at Fenner & Beane and gave one of the oddest and most annoying orders a broker could ever hope to receive.

"I want you to buy me a hundred dollars' worth of every single stock on both major exchanges that is selling for no more than one dollar a share."

The broker might have refused the order, which was a nightmare to execute and a most unsatisfactory way to earn a negligible commission, except that Templeton had worked for him as a trainee two years earlier.

After a while he reported that he had bought Templeton a hundred dollars' worth of every stock on either exchange that was not entirely bankrupt.

"No, no," said Templeton, "I want them *all*. Every last one, bankrupt or not." Grudgingly the broker went back to work and finally completed the order. When it was all over, Templeton had bought a junkpile of 104 companies in roughly $100 lots, of which 34 were bankrupt. He held each stock for an average of four years before selling. The result was no joke at all: he got over $40,000 for the kit—four times his cost.

Some of the transactions were startling. He bought Standard Gas $7 Preferred at $1 and sold it at $40. He bought 800 shares of Missouri Pacific Preferred—in bankruptcy—at twelve cents and eventually sold out at $5. (It eventually went over $100: had he sold at the top, that particular $100 would have turned not into $4,000 but $80,000!)

A singular aspect of this transaction was that Templeton didn't have $10,000 in cash. He was convinced that stocks were dirt cheap, and that of them all the neglected cats and dogs selling for less than $1 were the best values. When the war started in Europe he reasoned that that, if anything, was going to pull America out of its economic slump, and virtually all stocks would rise. So he had gone to his boss and borrowed the entire amount.

John Templeton was poor. He came from Winchester, Tennessee. During the Depression, while he was in his second year at Yale, his father told him that he couldn't give him any more money for his education. So Templeton worked his way through college, with the aid of scholarships. After that he won a Rhodes scholarship and went to Oxford for two years, seeing Europe during his vacations. Then he came back to Tennessee and eventually went to New York, first as a trainee at Fenner & Beane, one of the predecessors of Merrill Lynch, and after that in a seismic exploration company.

There he was when World War II began and he became convinced that the ten-year slump in stock prices was over and everything would boom—especially the Cinderellas that nobody considered as suitable investments.

That one extraordinary transaction set the pattern for Templeton's later ones.

First, *he insisted on buying only what was being thrown away.*

Second, *he held the stocks he had bought for an average of four years.*

That usually gives a bargain enough time to be recognized, so you can make the big revaluation when a stock moves to a higher multiple of higher earnings, the "double-play" profit. (Of course, you completely miss the twenty-year run of the great growth stock in its prime, which for most investors is their best hope of stock market profits. There are very few Templetons

who succeed in buying undiscovered values and selling them
again in a four-year cycle.)

After his coup Templeton had some money, so two years later,
when he learned that an elderly investment counselor wanted
to retire and sell his business, which had only eight clients, he
wrote him a check for $5,000 and took over the firm. The clients
stayed, but eight isn't many, so Templeton had a bad time of it
at first, and had to live off his savings. Then, however, word of
his abilities began to spread, and he has never lacked for clients—
or income—since.

His firm—Templeton, Dobbrow & Vance—eventually grew to
manage $300 million, including eight mutual funds. The trouble
was that having so many different clients left Templeton working
so hard that he didn't have time enough to think. Finally he
and his associates sold their firm to Piedmont Management, keeping only Templeton Growth Fund, which Piedmont didn't want
because it was based in Canada and couldn't be distributed in
the United States.

At fifty-six, John Templeton started all over again. He resolved
first that he would never let himself get so busy that he ran out
of time. Not only time to think about investments but also to
reflect on the larger world, particularly the various approaches
to religion. So he moved to Nassau, and on the grounds of the
Lyford Cay Club built a white house in the southern style, with
columns on all four sides. There he assembled his securities files
and started giving his attention to managing his one tiny remaining fund, of which he and some of his old clients owned most
of the shares. The record of this fund in the next years proved
that John Templeton is one of the great investors.

Over the twenty years ending December 31, 1978, a $1,000
investment in his fund became worth about $20,000, if all distri-
butions had been reinvested in more shares—which made it the
top performer of all funds.

Even more impressive, in each of the preceding seven years
his has been in the top quarter of all funds, and some computations
by *Fundscope* have put Templeton both among the top twenty

funds (out of more than four hundred) in making money in rising markets and the top five in not losing it in down markets. I am particularly impressed by the latter achievement, since the most decline-resistant funds include some that are permanently in bonds. To give an idea of the singularity of this record, the much larger T. Rowe Price New Horizons Fund, which also buys secondary companies and does spectacularly in rising markets, ranks more than two hundred places behind Templeton in down markets. In a word, Templeton's consistency can only be described as phenomenal.

To be fair, one should compare his results only with other small, international portfolios that are not concerned with owning "big names." The manager of a $1 billion domestic pension fund has a far tougher job than the manager of a small, uninhibited account. It is the *QE II* compared to an ocean racer.

In the first place, the small size of Templeton Growth Fund obviously gave him a flexibility not enjoyed by the managers of fifty to a hundred times as much money. A $100,000 commitment in the stock of a small company can substantially affect his fund's performance if it doubles. Also, he can and does sell stocks and raise cash when he gets edgy, which the largest funds almost never do. He sometimes moves 50 percent into reserves, although he says he has little ability to recognize tops and bottoms in the market—a trait he shares with most of the top stock-pickers.

Then, his investment selections range over many markets. He is quite as much at home in the Japanese and Canadian exchanges as in American exchanges, and knows those of Switzerland, Germany, Holland, Belgium, Australia, and South Africa.

Finally, and perhaps most important of all, he does not need to stick to large, familiar names: what trust companies wrongly call "quality." An established small specialty company with fat profit margins selling for a low price-earnings ratio is often a safer investment—if you are sure you have the facts right—than a huge, mediocre, heavily unionized and regulated standard industrial that sells at a high price because everybody knows about it. Templeton will go into dozens of little companies his clients have never heard of, and is prepared to buy almost all the stock available. Managers of large portfolios avoid smaller companies. They fear, rightly, on the whole, that they don't know enough about them. If they are dealing in big numbers, taking the time to master small situations won't pay.

Incidentally, the willingness to invest in many countries ties in with a willingness to buy "junior" stocks. Quite often the smaller, cheaper, faster-growing company is outside the U.S. For instance, Safeway sells at about eight times earnings, and will do well to maintain a 15 percent growth rate in the future. Within the food-chain sector, Templeton, instead, bought Ito Yokado, the best-managed and second largest supermarket chain in Japan, at ten times earnings, growing more than 30 percent a year. He points out that in Japan supermarkets, which are a direct bridge between the producer and the consumer, are still in their infancy, and have decades to grow before they are as common as they are here.

Real estate provides another example. Templeton considers it a field of perennial interest in an inflationary era. Having looked at real estate companies in Japan and England—where property companies enjoy great favor with investors—he discovered that the Canadian market offers better bargains than either. Once he had decided to invest in Canadian real estate, he chose a package of companies that almost no American investor—even a professional—would have heard of: Abbey Glen Property, Daon Development, S. B. McLaughlin Associates, and Nu-West Development, all bought at between two and four times cash flow per share; also Allarco, at five times earnings (which, however, he thinks will triple). A willingness to invest in smaller companies further implies great diversification among stocks. The fund's portfolio not long ago contained 220 different names.

Still, the advantages of internationalism, small size, and diversification into secondary names only set the stage for superior performance. They don't bring it about.

What is Templeton's technique? How does he do it?
His basic philosophy can be stated in one sentence:

Search among many markets for the companies selling for the smallest fraction of their true worth.

He is not content to buy a bargain. It must be the *best* bargain. Of course, many seeming bargains are nothing of the sort. So when he finds one, he studies it, restudies it, and only buys the stock when he is convinced the values are authentic. Even then, he ruefully admits, he makes constant mistakes. They are inevitable. But because he is heavily diversified, the damage is limited.

The best bargains will be in stocks that are completely neglected, that other investors are not even studying. That, of course, explains the proliferation of unfamiliar names in his portfolio.

"Look it over," he said to me, with his usual bland smile. "I'll bet you don't know more than a third of them." I did a bit better, but not much. And a number of the companies I was familiar with were on his list for reasons I didn't immediately think of.

For instance, Wells, Rich, Greene. Most people in the business world know about Mary Wells and her success in building up one of the "hot" advertising agencies of the sixties. But to *invest* in an ad agency—a collection of prima donnas in one of the most volatile and personal of all businesses? Very risky! When the agencies went public in the late sixties I thought it was a typical bull-market blowoff phenomenon: outsiders willing, in essence, to pay the insiders their peak salaries in advance for the next ten or fifteen years and still hoping to make something for themselves out of the investment. It can be remarkably tricky to invest in a people business. If things go well, the insiders will want to increase their take.

That's how it worked out with Wells, Rich, Greene. The insiders sold $14 million—690,000 shares out of 1.6 million outstanding—in two public issues at about 20 when things were booming. The stock eventually got up to 28. Then times got rough and the stock drifted down to 5. I observed all this with gloomy satisfaction. What you'd expect, I said to myself: never invest in a profession.

Then, however, came a twist. With the stock at 6, Mrs. Wells and her colleagues offered to buy it all back. They offered paper with a real value of about $9 a share, as against a book value of

$11 a share. They were able to buy back and retire 1,632,000 shares this way, leaving only 464,000 outstanding (plus 400,000 reserved for options). The original buyers at $20 who sold out again had parted with half their money.

At about this point the Templeton Fund bought 25,000 shares—almost all the "float" left in the market—at 8, which meant that on average it paid even less than the company itself did. Templeton feels that with the smaller number of shares and better conditions, earnings per share could well triple. If so, the fund's purchase would work out at less than twice earnings. Thanks to the reduced amount of stock, book value went back to $20 per share, which is what the fund sold it for.

At some time almost anything is likely to become a bargain, if you're in a position to evaluate the neglected factor that will change things for the better. To perceive this factor you have to wear glasses different from those worn by others who don't like what they see. Templeton thinks that the investor needs this ability to recognize unfamiliar values more than any other skill. He calls it flexibility.

A flexible viewpoint is the professional investor's greatest need, and will be increasingly needed in the future.

Templeton has several of the same concerns about the future of investments that I do.

He is always attentive to the tendency toward direct or disguised expropriation in a given country—what he calls socialism. Not only outright takeovers, but price controls* and other entanglements that inhibit business and destroy the investor's incentive.

Always ask yourself whether a company is in an industry that's a natural candidate to be socialized. The answer should be sought on a worldwide basis. For instance, in almost all countries banks are a natural target of government intervention. So are mining

---

* He agrees with "Train's Law"—*Price Controls Increase Prices* (by reducing production). How slow mankind has been to learn this simple truth, and how expensive it has been. Rent control has done as much as anything to wreck New York City.

companies. Otherwise, copper mines would be interesting, since the price of the metal is rising.

Templeton offered women's hats as a perfect regulation-proof industry. I replied that through the years the Romans and others tried to regulate the excesses of women's clothes through sumptuary laws—generally without success. Templeton was entertained by my observation that Tampax seemed an unlikely subject of regulation: one could scarcely conceive of Teddy Kennedy rising on the Senate floor to excoriate the profiteers behind this humble device: "I have here in my hand . . ." (Even Tampax has in fact been the subject of an attempt at price regulation in the U.K. There the government suggested that the margins were too high.)

Templeton cites Josten's, Inc. as a company that should not be a natural target of regulation. It is America's leading maker of high-school class rings, and has a strong position in academic diplomas, caps and gowns, and yearbooks. It has had steadily rising earnings for twenty-one years; sales have quadrupled and earnings per share almost tripled over the last ten years.

He points out that hotel-room prices are less subject to control than residential rents. Templeton has owned several hotel companies: Commonwealth Holiday Inns, Four Seasons Hotels and Skyline Hotels—all Canadian—and United Inns of Atlanta. In all real estate transactions the buyer looks at cash flow—earnings plus depreciation—rather than at plain earnings. United Inns is still only 3.5 times cash flow.

Newspaper chains, I observed, some of which are money machines and ideal monopolies, are regulation-resistant. Freedom of the press!

The other great problem is inflation, which Templeton expects to accelerate in the future. A company must be able to cope with inflation to be a sound investment. Advertising agencies have this ability, he observes: their income is a percentage of the customer's gross advertising outlay, so as prices go up their income rises accordingly. Eventually most countries will have to switch to inflation accounting, which shows what a company is doing in real terms, not just in nominal dollars; when that happens, the earnings of companies with high debt loads will at least double as they are seen to be repaying their bondholders with depreciating currency. Electric utility companies will be prime beneficiaries of this restatement of earnings, but are so heavily regulated as to be unattractive investments anyway.*

Debt-ridden real estate companies are, on the contrary, excellent speculations during an inflation. They are thoroughly unpopular: despised, in fact, except in England and Japan. The U.K. property companies, for no good reason, sell for more than twice their Canadian counterparts, and the Japanese companies for more than three times.

Another hedge against inflation that Templeton likes is shopping centers. Ordinarily the leases between the landlord and the operator are specifically drawn to offset inflation, and provide for escalation of payments according to a formula linked to turnover. If the supermarket's volume rises, so does the rent it pays to the owner of the center. While Templeton does not hold stock in shopping center companies at the moment, he mentioned General Growth Companies as a major owner, along with E. W. Hahn, a California-based operation.

Listening to Templeton emphasize the importance of trying to see the values that the public is overlooking I was reminded of Hemingway's advice that at the moment of climactic action a writer should take his attention from the main event—the torero going in over the horns, or the boxer flooring his opponent— and study the crowd, lost in its own emotion, unconscious of itself. Theodor Reik talks of the importance of listening with the "third ear": behind the self-centered babble of the patient there often emerges a quite different, simpler pattern—the real message, the essential truth of the situation, of which the speaker is unaware, and for which the therapist should always be listening. But how does the investor escape from the unending static of "news" and opinion, the surge and ebb of the passions of the crowd?

* Another possibility might be higher taxes on the restated profits, and thus even less cash for the companies.

One answer is experience. After thirty years of getting a bloody nose every time he jumps on a bandwagon, even the most enthusiastic investor attains some measure of detachment from the crowd's enthusiasms and desperations.

Templeton has gone a lot further, though, to make it as easy as possible for him to keep his perspective. The distance from his large, cool, porticoed white house on its little hill overlooking the grounds of Lyford Cay to the roar and shouting of the floor of the stock exchange is measured in psychological light-years. The house itself and everything in it are a silent reproach to excitement and hyperactivity.

Templeton himself, a spare, neat man, even in that warm climate carefully dressed in pale lime-colored trousers and a striped lemon-colored jacket with a neat striped tie, would be, one knows at once, the last man in Christendom to fall victim to some ephemeral enthusiasm. As he drives slowly in his blue Rolls from his house to the club to have a light lunch with a Canadian banker, is his soul full of passionate yearnings to catch a one-week move in some over-the-counter speculation—an above-ground swimming pool company, perhaps, or a highly-promoted mining venture? Scarcely.

Does he worry about the ambitions of his number four man, or whether his staff is getting lazy or the overhead is getting out of hand? Scarcely. He has a staff of one, plus two secretaries.

Does he spend feverish days on the telephone, getting the latest gossip from the brokers, the latest news off the broad tape, and the jokes going around the floor? Scarcely. The brokers are told to send him in writing what they think he'd like to see; not to call.

Does he worry about each week's sales of the fund, and have intense meetings with the sales manager? Scarcely. He lives in Nassau but the fund's office is in Canada and the sales organization is in St. Petersburg, Florida: one imagines they are not encouraged to call him day and night with small problems.

The whole *mise en scène* helps Templeton do his job.

Templeton has endowed a prize for progress in religion which is awarded annually in London. Its value, about £80,000, has enabled it to attract the interest and support of eminent people. Templeton hopes that the award will help focus attention on the life and work of the recipients, who have included Mother Teresa of Calcutta and Aleksandr Solzhenitsyn.

He compares spiritual growth to gardening. "If you find a weed," he says, "you go out and get rid of it. The same for a bad thought or a bad emotion."*

I asked him if good works and nonattachment to material things figured in spiritual development.

"Works *come* from spiritual development," he said. "If you start with the works you move to humanism, a very different thing."

As to nonattachment, he doesn't believe in it at all. He is attached to many things, including the stock market.

The Lyford Cay Club floats in space, financially speaking. Its 950 members are drawn from more than two dozen countries, and the tone is far more English than American. One has no predisposition to think automatically in terms of American stocks, as a portfolio manager in Minneapolis would, or of European stocks, as would one in Hamburg. The investment scene as viewed from Nassau resembles a coral reef perceived through a glass-bottomed boat: you float by and study what seems interesting, without being anchored to one spot or another. Templeton's remoteness certainly helps him reflect judiciously on the risks and rewards in the various countries he is prepared to invest in.

Another advantage to Lyford Cay, surprisingly enough, is Templeton's access to firsthand information. A portfolio manager in New York is likely to have contacts with other portfolio managers and with stockbrokers, who themselves have limited information and are always trying to sell him things. The population of Lyford Cay, on the other hand, is made up of successful industrialists from many parts of the world—they have to be, to pay the dues— and their guests. They have come to the sun on vacation to enjoy

---

* I tried on him the Buddhist paradox: "The mind of Buddha is steeped in corruption, sin, and death." The point is that to God no created thing is alien: our weed may be God's orchid. Templeton seemed unimpressed.

themselves. One can exchange opinions with them easily in that attractive ambience, much more easily than would be likely in an office visit on a tight schedule.

Templeton has far broader sources of information than this, of course. Almost thirty years ago he was a founder of the Young President's Organization, which now has thousands of members and former members around the world. He was also a president of the Chief Executives' Forum, a sort of YPO alumni association, which meets twice a year. Through his acquaintances in the YPO old-boy network he says he has access to about five hundred presidents and top managers of every sort of business.

These sources, added to the knowledge and contacts built up in forty years of investing, mean that Templeton can count on being able to develop primary sources of information on almost any company he finds interesting.

How does Templeton decide which are the countries to invest in and which are not?

Obviously, the ones to avoid are those which have conditions that make investment difficult or impossible: socialism and inflation. The two go together. Either stifles growth.

For years Templeton has favored Japan, and historically perhaps the most striking thing about his fund, after its interest in small "special situations," has been its concentration of investment in that country, which reached a peak of 60 percent in 1970, and has fallen to 10 percent in 1979, in response to the rise in the Tokyo stock market together with the fall in the U.S. market.

Even now, says Templeton, over the next ten years Japan should have much less tendency toward socialism than the United States and, perhaps for that very reason, about twice the growth rate.

In 1962, when Templeton first got interested in Japan, one could buy the leading companies at two or three times real earnings, with the benefit of extensive hidden assets that didn't appear on the balance sheet. American and European investors just couldn't believe their eyes, so the bargains persisted year after year: pharmaceutical companies growing 30 percent per year and selling for a third of the multiples of the comparable U.S. companies.

Today, the growth rates are slowing down in Japan, although they are still higher than here, but more important for the investor, the values have been recognized, so the prices are no longer the bargains that they were. Templeton says, therefore, that he is slowly cutting down his exposure to Japan and moving back to the U.S., which, he finds, is the other most profitable place to put his money.

We discussed some specific Japanese companies that Templeton finds attractive. Templeton says that of all the companies he owns, Ito Yokado, the supermarket chain, is the one he has most confidence in for the long term. It should maintain a 30 percent growth rate for a good ten years. Supermarkets are just getting started there. In 1980 it sold at over twenty times earnings, but with such brilliant prospects it's well worth it.

I asked him about Toto, which dominates the bathroom fixtures market in Japan—where few houses have bathrooms. Templeton said he preferred Takara Standard, in a similar line of business. The Japanese have traditionally had wooden kitchen installations, and are just catching on to the American style of Formica and metal counters, cabinets, and sinks, which are easier to build and keep clean. Takara Standard has 89 percent of this market. Like Toto, it has depots all over the country and so can make rapid and cheap deliveries to any point. A new company entering either field has trouble delivering these heavy installations to different cities rapidly and cheaply.

Templeton points out that when he first invested in Japan twenty years ago, Japanese investors liked the big names because they had heard of them, and so would pay more for a stranded whale—the Japanese equivalent of an Allied Chemical, Chrysler, or Westinghouse—than for a specialty growth company in its dynamic phase. They also give more weight to the six-month earnings outlook than to the six-year prospects. Now, however, the smaller companies sell at a substantial premium over the giants.

The entire Japanese stock market—which is measured by an

index called, in a spirit of flattering imitation, the Dow Jones Average—now stands at over twenty-seven times earnings. What bargains there are in the Japanese market are found among the growth stocks.

Thus Matsushita, says Templeton, has a 15 percent earnings growth prospect as far as the eye can see, and yet the Japanese will only pay nine times earnings for it because of shorter-term uncertainties. He says that Matsushita might be his second choice from his list of Japanese companies as a long-term holding.

Nissan Motors, makers of Datsun, he once found far more attractive than its American counterpart, Ford. Both companies are less vertically integrated than GM. Ford should continue to be highly profitable, but is unlikely to grow as fast as the average U.S. company. Nissan, on the contrary, should be the fastest-growing car company in the world—at a rate of perhaps 15 percent a year, unless the yen remains overpriced. It is the principal imported car in the U.S. Its competitor Toyota has a larger turnover in yen, but lower unit sales, and does not enjoy Nissan's greatest strength, outstandingly able management. On the other hand, in 1979, Templeton found Ford, at three times reported 1978 earnings, a much better buy than Nissan at fifteen times. Bridgestone Tire, Japanese in spite of its name, has sales of about $1 billion a year and controls most of the Japanese tire market, as though Goodyear, Firestone, and Goodrich had been able to beat down antitrust constraints and form one huge, dominant concern.

Among the Japanese stockbrokers he finds both Yamachi Securities and Daiwa Securities most helpful: penetrating, thorough, and still improving.

Besides Japan, the U.S., and Canada, Templeton considers only a few areas suitable for investment: Germany, Switzerland, the northern European countries, Spain, Australia, and New Zealand (the last two of which have at least for the moment shaken off the socialist virus), Hong Kong, and Singapore. South Africa's social tensions imply to Templeton that, to be attractive, a stock there should be twice as favorably priced as one in, say, Germany. He finds Brazil of great potential interest, once its present restrictions on foreign investments are removed.

He has a few outstanding sources of information for non-Japanese foreign securities, but since the true facts are not publicly available he still has to depend on industry scuttlebutt, insiders' tips, and bankers' indiscretions. He considers Harry G. A. Seggerman, of Fidelity Pacific Fund, to be a very skillful investor in foreign companies, apparently using methods similar to Templeton's own. I asked him if he made a practice of studying portfolios of other funds as a source of ideas. "I do indeed," he replied. "I follow about twenty of them, and every time the reports come out I go over them carefully to see what they've been able to think up."

While Templeton has tried venture capital investing, his experiences have been unsatisfactory; he was giving far more time to his stable of new ventures than their place in his portfolio justified.

Early in his career Templeton made hundreds of personal visits to companies, going through the plants and sizing everything up. In recent years, however, he has rarely found this necessary.

He has a standard list of questions he likes to ask management: One of the first is *"Do you have a long-range plan?"*

Then, *"What will be your average annual growth rate?"*

If the target growth rate is higher than the historical one, he asks, *"Why should the future be different from the past? What are your problems?"*

And then, a key point, *"Who is your ablest competitor?"* and the essential, *"Why?"*

Finally, a question that Templeton finds particularly enlightening, *"If you couldn't own stock in your own company, which of your competitors would you want to invest in . . . and why?"*

As you find out fast enough in security analysis, contact with a single company can mislead as much as it informs. Management is obviously going to blow its own trumpet. If you visit most of the companies in an industry over a period of many years, you eventually develop an informed concept of the entire group. You learn which sources are reliable, which managements achieve their objectives, which company officers tend to make exaggerated claims. Particularly, even a few minutes with a company's chief competitor or a major supplier may be vastly instructive. Your informant can tell what he knows about a competitor, while he is not permitted to divulge inside information about his own company. Even if he does, the investor can be punished for using it. Also, of course, he will propably speak more impartially about the outside company.

Templeton also makes extensive use of secondary sources, and indeed relies much more on the figures than on firsthand impressions. Perhaps his most important source is the great panorama of facts in *The Value Line Investment Survey* (not the opinions, which are half-baked). By working one's way through the fifteen-odd-year history of such elements as sales, profit margins, depreciation, working capital, and all the rest one can grasp most of what is essential about the life of an enterprise.

Templeton also finds the *Wall Street Transcript*—which reproduces dozens of brokers' reports on companies each week—a valuable aid. To maintain his files, which he keeps in an office in a tiny shopping center just outside the gates of the Lyford Cay Club, he used to need a librarian. Now, he says, he can find the answers to most questions by looking up the company in the index of the *Transcript*.

He makes wide use of brokers, but only for establishing facts, paying no attention to their buy and sell recommendations. Almost no brokers—less than 1 percent, he judges—think in his terms. (Similarly, he doubted that even one Swiss banker was considering the variations of real estate values between England and Canada that he found so interesting.) Over the years Templeton has learned what brokerage sources are likely to be useful to him for collecting facts. He instantly discards everything else.

A paradox of collecting for profit—whether stocks, works of art, real estate, or anything else—is that the best buy can never be what the dealer or gallery is pushing at the time. A notable book collector—Philip Hofer of the Houghton Library at Harvard—has told me that one of his most successful approaches in visiting a dealer is to ask, *"What do you have that you don't want?"* That volume will usually be covered with dust in the cellar, and if of real quality is likely to be a far better buy than the "special" in the window, which will perforce be marked up to what a dealer thinks a passerby will pay for it.

Similarly, if a stock is so out of favor that there are virtually no buyers—that is, it practically can't be sold—a broker who has to pay a lot of overhead and support his salesmen can't afford to get involved with it; least of all a stock with a small float. Thus the bargain-hunting investor will always tend to be on his own, unable to rely on others for ideas, as distinct from facts.

Templeton's portfolio represents what he thinks are the best buys in marketable securities anywhere in the world—giving full consideration to the safety of the countries where they are found.

Once a stock has moved up and no longer is a bargain, then if he finds a much better buy, out goes the first one.

He always uses this comparison-shopping approach to investments.

I asked him if he made any effort to buy stocks just as they emerge from the wilderness, as investment interest picks up.

He replied that he had only recently begun to give weight to that factor. Throughout his career he had always been able to be patient—perhaps too patient, he now thinks. So: *if one of two otherwise similar stocks is just starting to attract interest and the other is still in eclipse, then he gives preference to the one that is starting to move.*

In his analytical approach, Templeton starts by trying to determine the intrinsic value of a company. In the mid-1940s his investment counsel firm did as much as any to apply Graham's original, full-scale technique systematically—the analysis of companies through careful study of their significant financial ratios in the hope of establishing true values. The drudgery that this entailed has now been much alleviated by such services as *Value Line,*

where for $300 a year you have easily available most of the inform-
ation that an office full of analysts assembled for you in the old
days less promptly and less accurately.

So now, Templeton says, he almost never has to do basic financial analysis himself. For U.S., Canadian, and Japanese companies
it's available for a fee, and for other foreign companies it's almost
impossible, because the published figures aren't real. You have
to find out what you can by asking questions. There are a hundred
or so factors that can well be considered in making an appraisal,
although not all are appropriate to any given enterprise. Thus,
in studying a natural resources company you might omit perhaps
a quarter of the possible factors; for a manufacturing company,
a different quarter.

About six factors are crucial, and universally applicable to every
situation.

1. *The price-earnings ratio.*
2. *Operating profit margins.*
3. *Liquidating value.*
4. The company's *growth* rate gets a lot of weight, and particularly the *consistency* of earnings growth. If a company's growth
falters for one year, that may be all right. If it misses two years,
then it is suspect. Templeton parts company from Graham on
the question of growth. He is interested in financial strength and
hidden asset values—very interested.

Consistent growth is best of all. After all, in an inflationary
period just staying even in real terms means reporting growth
in nominal terms. On the other hand, *one should be suspicious
of hyperrapid growth. Ordinarily it is unsustainable.*

He cited Commerce Clearing House as a company with a steady
growth record. I asked him about one of my own favorite financial
service companies—far less established than Commerce Clearing
House, to be sure, but with an extraordinary earnings growth
record—H & R Block, then about fourteen. Templeton said that
he expected that eventually its growth—which has been phenomenal—would be interrupted. The overhead, he thought, might
eventually get out of control. I asked him about T. Rowe Price's

theory that the investor should seek out the "fertile fields for growth" in the economy—those destined to expand and flourish in the years ahead—and buy the leading companies in them. Templeton replied that at one time or another he had probably owned most of the stocks in the T. Rowe Price Growth Stock Fund, but such companies usually also have high price-earnings ratios. Quite often the specialty company is less expensive, because less understood. It takes neither training nor experience to go out and buy a highly visible premier growth stock without regard to price.

Everything has its season, which does not last forever. The world changes its spots, and the investor must change his. The T. Rowe Price big-growth stock philosophy, says Templeton, had a long day, but in the end that family of stocks became unreasonably priced. A prolongation of the earlier rate of gain could no longer be reasonably expected. The David Babson organization in Boston, which also favored top growth stocks, had a six-year span during which their fund almost always ran near the front of the pack. According to Templeton, by the end of that time they should have been eagerly looking for any good excuse to change their entire approach. And Morgan Guaranty, which produced such handsome results in the late sixties and early seventies by bidding its Avons, International Flavors, and the like to almost infinite prices—how much happier might they have been if their Mr. Samuel R. Calloway had retired and they had sold the lot in 1973—rather than in 1975, after a 50 percent decline.

5. *The cardinal rule is flexibility.* You must get ready to change when everything seems to be working particularly well. When the cycle is perfectly in gear with your expectations, prepare to jump.

6. *Don't trust rules and formulas.* Thirty years ago Templeton knew an officer in the trust department of the Chemical Bank who finally, after the market had puzzled so many people for countless generations, got it all together. All the numbers, all the cycles, all the psychological, financial, and fundamental data since the beginning of markets now trumpeted the same message: the Dow Jones Average was going straight down for three years.

He put his clients into cash. Alas! The first year, the market went up. The second, it went up more. And the third year, it went up more than ever.

Templeton's sometime partner Vance, then an elderly man, used to enjoy lecturing about investments. Part of his kit was a huge chart plotted on a roll of wrapping paper. It was so big that during his lectures he would have to get a volunteer from the audience to help him unroll it and put it on the wall. This chart plotted the market for the previous twenty years. Then there were different squiggly lines representing the various factors that influence it—industrial production, money supply, and so on. One squiggly line was best of all. It worked perfectly. Year after year if you had followed it you could have known where the market was headed and made a killing. When the audience, fascinated, demanded to know what it represented, Mr. Vance told them. It was the rate his hens were laying, in the chicken coop in back of his house.

Mr. Templeton's most remarkable change of tack has come about as this book goes to the publisher.

When I first visited him in Nassau, Templeton's fund had about $20 million in assets; both he and his holdings were unrecognized. As I wrote this in 1980, investors were jumping aboard the Templeton bandwagon: the fund was then over $200 million, and he started a second fund which had another $70 million. He was taking in $2 million a week. You have to put that kind of money to work in big chunks; you can't seek out only tiny undervalued situations. So, Templeton, obedient to his principle of flexibility, bought such huge names as Ford and Royal Dutch.

In this game, however, he is competing directly with the best brains in the business. Lots of people, to say the least, can figure out the investment merits of Ford and Royal Dutch. Many, on the contrary, were inhibited from following Templeton out onto the thin ice of little Canadian real estate companies and Japanese trading firms. Maybe, however, Ford and Royal Dutch really are the best bargains, regardless of the amount of money one is managing. Time will tell.

8

Larry Tisch

The Pragmatist

"I'm a businessman," said Larry Tisch, sprawling comfortably in his chair. "I think of stocks as businesses."

We were sitting in his pale tan modern office in the 666 Fifth Avenue Building, where Tisch, a smallish man with a ready smile, runs Loew's Corporation (which is in tobacco and insurance and owns movie theatres and hotels) and also looks after its stock portfolio, which is usually worth several hundred million dollars. A stock quotation machine next to his desk blinked ticker symbols and stock prices at us continuously as we talked.

"The different systems—Ben Graham, growth stocks, and the others—are fine, as long as you have the discipline to stick to them. Most people don't, though, so they have the worst of both worlds. Myself, I have no system. I'm a pragmatist, I just wait until the fourth year, when the business cycle bottoms, and buy whatever is offered, whatever I think will have the biggest bounce.

"Coming off the bottom, lots of things will double or triple before the next peak in the cycle, two or three years later. You never know what they'll be."

But doesn't he prefer one type of merchandise to another— the great long-term growth companies to the cyclical ones or companies with little growth?

"No, anything has its price. For instance, the last time around

U.S. Steel got down to 19 on the present stock. I don't like U.S. Steel very much, but at 19 it certainly is a gift. And what did it do then? It tripled!"

Still, if you're a long-term investor worried about capital gains taxes, you would want to buy a stock that you might not have to sell and pay taxes on for years—one that you could hold for a very long term. Would U.S. Steel be a good one in that situation?

"No, no. I wouldn't hold U.S. Steel for the long haul. But then again, if you're going to have to pay high capital gains taxes, I'm not sure that common stocks are attractive at all just now. With a 6½ percent yield available on municipals, why bother?

"And another point: an astute investor doesn't try to fight the market. In the third year of the cycle, with the Dow Jones at 950, you're in a very different position from where you are coming off the bottom with the Dow at 750 or 800."

Larry Tisch doesn't just buy stocks, he also buys whole companies. Using Loew's as a base, of which he and other insiders control about 40 percent, he acquired Lorillard, the fifth largest American cigarette company (producers of Kent, Newport, and True), and CBS and control of CNA Financial Corporation, which is in casualty insurance (Continental Casualty) and fund management. Loew's also has a 25 percent interest in Wheeling-Pittsburgh Steel and is a large-scale builder. Without CNA it has about $1 billion in revenues, and with it, $3 billion, up from $100-odd million in ten years. Earnings per share have risen more than ten times over that period.

As a businessman, what qualities does he look for in a company that he wants to buy, either for Loew's or its stock portfolio, or as a private investor?

"The one thing I look for most is *free cash flow* after all capital expenditures. Profits that have to be reinvested in more capital outlays may not really be profits at all.

"Most of the time you should *expense* capital outlays in the year they are incurred, not capitalize them and add them to the balance sheet. More and more, a big company has to go on spending money just to maintain its existing earnings stream.

Isn't that really an expense, rather than something that should be considered as a true increase in value?"

I mentioned that in the previous decade DuPont had borrowed a billion dollars long-term, but only paid $500 million in dividends, without increasing either earnings or dividends—and yet continued to sell at a high multiple.

"That's ridiculous," said Tisch, "the stock is overpriced."

Does it follow that a great many American companies are unattractive, since they are indeed reinvesting their cash just to maintain their earnings and dividends?

"They certainly are. In what we call 'smokestack America' there often isn't any accumulated free cash after capital outlays. The companies in many cases aren't really making money."

I noted that in England a parliamentary commission had decided that after honest depreciation—taking account of inflation—the United Kingdom's industry as a whole was not in fact making money at all, and that the UK corporate tax rate was not therefore 50 percent but infinity.

"Absolutely," said Tisch.

Knowing all this, if we had to select a portfolio of stocks to be held for twenty years—for a child, for instance—what stocks did he think would be more attractive than bonds—considering that after tax and inflation there is no true return on bonds?

That was a tough one.

"Well, I suppose you'd have to have one of the great insurance companies: Aetna, Traveler's or Chubb. They're all selling at five or six times earnings and nobody wants them. They're good value. Then, for a service company you might have Rollins. That's a real long-term growth situation, thanks to its Orkin Exterminating subsidiary. Then I suppose one of the great forest companies, such as Weyerhaeuser or International Paper, with an endlessly renewable tree crop. They ought to be able to beat inflation."

We talked about a number of other possibilities that did not quite make the grade, among them Procter & Gamble and the technology companies. After a while Tisch said, "Dow Chemical: now there's one of the greatest companies in America. At a price it ought to be on our list, just so long as they can maintain their advantage in research. Another good category that people don't want now is the savings and loans associations. The biggest and best is probably Great West Financial."

Suddenly he became enthusiastic. "Here's one that we have ourselves, Waldbaum. It's a series of supermarkets in New York, run by a wonderful manager, Ira Waldbaum. He's terrific—only forty years old. And it's only selling at three times earnings! There's twenty dollars of book value and the stock is at 8½.

"Most industries I don't understand, but one that I do follow is the department stores. I suppose Federated would be a good one for your twenty-year list. They have fine management in place, and they know what they're doing, although of course they could have trouble just because of the troubles of the big cities. Retailing is a very tough business anyway. Another one that we have in our own portfolio and that I like a lot is Oil Shale Corporation: 'TOSCO.' I have a funny feeling that we may all be living off oil shale after a while, but in TOSCO you aren't even paying for the oil shale part of it." *

"For a patient long-term investor, FNMA [Federal National Mortgage Association] looks good to me. They raise their dividend every year and every year they earn more. It's a 6½ percent yield selling for less than six times fully diluted earnings. The worst thing that could happen to it would be that the growth could slow a bit, but meanwhile you have a fine return and a completely safe situation."

Tisch mused for a time, and then brightened. "You know, a really fascinating speculation is Savin Business Machines. They have the best copier on the market by far. I have one right outside the door here. It's a fantastic machine. The growth rate is amazing, and it's only five times earnings. You can't go too far wrong on that one. And it's got a great man running it."

We talked about the whole class of medium-sized specialty companies, of which Rollins is an example. He liked the principle, but did not follow very many of them.

I asked him what he thought of land as an investment.

* The stock soared after we talked.

"Well, you know, there's a big problem now that you didn't used to have: the environmentalists and ecologists. You don't know anymore if you can actually use the land once you've got it, so it's a new ball game."

I observed that since there were more and more restrictions on new developments, it followed that an existing single-family house will become a more attractive holding because of the shortage value and increasing replacement costs.

I asked him how his pension funds were invested at the moment.

"Well, right now I think that we're late in the business cycle, and so our pension funds are 90 percent in bonds. It's a funny thing, there are lots of bonds of perfectly good companies yielding 10 percent to 10½ percent today. Many investors throw up their hands in horror if you talk about buying a BBB bond, and yet they're perfectly happy to go out and buy an unrated stock."

I asked if at the bottom of a business cycle a stock wouldn't often snap back more than a bond would.

"Well, yes," he said, "and yet at a market bottom you often get a good bond yielding 14 percent or 15 percent, and by the time the cycle peaks you've made a 40 percent move in the bond and you've been getting the 14 percent interest all along, so really you're almost as well off as if you had bought a depressed stock, and a good deal safer. Of course, for a corporation the dividend of a stock is much better after tax than bond interest, because it's 85 percent tax-free."

I asked him how a rich individual's portfolio should be positioned.

"He can get 6½ percent tax-free, and since if he lives in New York he'd pay about a 50 percent capital gains tax on the growth in value of a stock, even if he did make a profit in it, I'd say that today, late in the cycle, he's at least as well off in a municipal, and certainly safer. Why bother?"

I observed that since a municipal's 6½ percent yield, although tax-free, was no better than inflation, in real terms an investor in municipals was only holding his own.

"Yes, I know that," he replied, "but then, most investors don't make money in the stock market either."

In Loew's own portfolio he goes from as high as $400 million in stocks down to as low as $100 million, where he is now.

I asked him what he thought were the biggest mistakes of corporate managers, mistakes that made their stocks unattractive to an outside investor.

"The biggest problem is ego," he said, firmly. "A great many managers are basically on an obsessive ego trip. The manager wants the company to grow and grow even if it isn't making any more money as a result. He wants a bigger plane and a bigger office. That may not be at all the same thing that's best for his shareholders.

"The second biggest problem is a manager who surrounds himself with yes-men.

"The third biggest is a variation of the second: the manager who isolates himself.

"Another big problem in companies is that mediocre people eventually get to the top—the guy who waits the longest becomes the boss."

"The Peter Principle," I observed.

"That's it. The guy who keeps his nose clean, who went to the right schools, who has the attractive wife."

The attractive wife?

"Yes, It's much more important in business today than most people realize. The right wife can be a big help. There's a great deal of after-hours socializing in these executive groups, and the right wife gets friendly with the other right wives and helps her husband along. But he may not be the best man for the job at all, so the wife's work may be bad for the company although good for her husband.

"Another problem is that *so many numbers come off these computers that often the manager doesn't know how to handle them all:* he gets swamped."

I observed that these were all human problems, rather than problems of technology.

"You can usually correct business problems," Tisch said. *"The human problems are the ones that are harder to correct."*

Going back to the subject of his portfolio, I asked him what else he owned that might be interesting.

"Well," he said, "Studebaker Worthington is one, and Northwest Industries is another. Studebaker's an excellent company with excellent management. The whole group's underrated: the mixed industrial products area."

I noted that it didn't have a flashy image or concept, and so it was harder for a broker to sell. Speaking of which, did he have any favorite brokers?

"I don't get much from brokers. They call you after a stock has already gone up 50 percent, and then they don't tell you when to sell. We have a couple of guys around here who work on our portfolio and that's where the ideas come from. We make our own ideas."

What about the trust companies—did he know any bank that had done a good job in recent years?

He shook his head.

"Terrible," he said.

And the banks themselves, were any of *them* good investments?

Again he shook his head. "If you go into the balance sheets and analyze the less-developed countries loans, the real estate and all the rest of it, you'll find that the big money-center banks are very thinly capitalized.

"We don't do anything dramatic around here. We're pragmatic. Our philosophy could change from one day to the next. We just try to buy what's good value and sell it when it isn't good value anymore."

So you make money trading stocks?

"Yes, we make money at it. But it's not that we buy for a trade. If a guy called up and said that IBM would go up 10 percent we wouldn't buy it. We buy the stocks as *investors*. When they reach our target and we find something else we want to buy, then we sell them again. We just go along from day to day."

I visited Tisch again in the summer of 1979. He was concerned about the economic outlook, believing the U.S. to be closer to a recession than was generally thought. As a result he was ultracautious, and his portfolio very conservatively invested.

The forthcoming recession, he thought, could be more painful than most economists are prepared to discuss. "There are too many people talking a soft landing. I don't think we can have expanded the credit system the way we have in the last couple of years and get away with a soft landing."

Might any stocks hold up if the market in general went down? "I don't know. It doesn't pay to look for a needle in the haystack."

Many low-multiple stocks look attractively priced, but if a stock falls from 5 times earning to 4 times earnings, then you have lost 20 percent of your money. The key question, of course, is how seriously earnings might be hurt in a deep recession.

"If Aetna went from 4.3 times earnings to 5 times earnings because the earnings went down, there wouldn't be any problem. But what if it went to 10 times earnings? That's happened in the past." Tisch is not predicting that sort of a decline, but neither can he say it's impossible.

One of his major concerns is what inflation is doing to corporate earnings. One could make the argument that most corporate earnings are very much overstated.

Another serious problem in the forthcoming recession will be that government is not really intent on bringing the inflation rate down sharply. "The government is talking about reducing it gradually, over a seven-to-eight-year period. That means that the recession might not have the proper effect on inflationary psychology, which might persist even through the recession."

Asked if foreign investors might not reenter the market if they saw the dollar strengthening, Tisch replied, "Why should the dollar strengthen? With the new price of oil, our balance of payments should start deteriorating again; the next big question is, how big will the federal deficit be when the recession comes? Would we get back to a $60 billion to $70 billion deficit? The combination of a big deficit and a worsening balance of payments problem

could wreak havoc with the dollar. That's what we could be looking for in 1980."

I have included this description of a large-scale "gut" investor
at work not because he is a model to be commended to investors
in general but rather so that they can have an impression of
how he operates. Particularly I draw to their attention Tisch's
simple, experienced realism in comparing alternatives, and the
flexibility that follows from this attitude. Stocks have an indicated
total return higher than bonds: buy stocks. Bonds have more in
them than stocks, and are safer: buy bonds. Cyclical stocks have
been knocked down and should bounce: buy them for a bounce.

Tisch can make these judgments with masterful ease because
he knows the world of business and finance backward and forward; he's at home in the medium. Most investors who tack back
and forth à la Tisch, inspired by emotion rather than by experience and reason, will get it all wrong. Tisch makes money precisely because he acts in *opposition* to the mass of investors, who
lose a few percent to Tisch and his like every time they change
course. They can't beat the market; they *are* the market.

9

Robert Wilson

Pumping Up the Tulips

Some retail investors have the impression that their brokerage firms are in business to enrich *them*. Robert Wilson has no interest in disabusing them of that impression, but he knows better. For Wilson, the retail brokerage firms—the wire houses, as they're called—from dawn to dusk, every business day of the year, are hard at work for *him*—not that he's a customer of theirs.

Wilson's favorite acitivity is exploding such Wall Street balloons as the stocks of mediocre "concepts" companies that get wildly puffed up by hungry stockbrokers in need of something to sell to impressionable customers. There's always a new fad running around: above-ground swimming-pool companies, uranium stocks, dieting aids, cancer cures, antipollution schemes, computer software companies, double-knit clothing manufacturers—something, with no numbers attached, that's going to change the world, a tree that will grow all the way up to the sky. As the speculators rush in, the price rises from 5 to 10, let's say. The speculators, confirmed in their wisdom, buy more, putting the price still higher. New speculators rush in. Soon the whole self-confirming perpetual motion machine is grossly overinflated beyond any reasonable investment value. Robert Wilson, watching this fatally familiar process, sees the rubber beginning to stretch taut; more and more puffers don't seem able to blow up the concept any bigger. The stock hits 15. He borrows some shares in the company from a broker, promising to give them back later, and sells them in the market at 15, say, planning to repurchase them at 10, 5, or even 2.

Thanks to the brokers' enthusiasm the retail investors, with a final huge effort, run the stock up to 20. Wilson has lost a third of his investment. Does he panic? No. It's all routine. He sells short thousands of additional shares. The stock falters and eases back to 15. Now Wilson scents victory: the enemy is in retreat! He explains to his friends, to brokers, reporters, anybody who will listen, why the stock is absurdly overpriced, why the outlook is grim: the plant is antiquated, management insincere, competition intensifying, costs are rising, the market is drying up, a better product is arriving from Japan, the company owes a lot of money to the bankers, perhaps there are regulatory headaches.

While the original brokers rally their troops and seek to enlist new recruits under the banner of "It's a bargain at 15, down from 20," and "It'll earn $5 sure two years from now and go to 40," Wilson, his broker, and other short-side sharpshooters close in for the kill. That is, hundreds of thousands of shares sold short, brokers inventing explanations for the decline, sinister intimations circulating in the Wall Street lunch clubs, odd-lot sellers panicked, margin calls, the works. The stock goes into a free fall and Wilson meets his obligations by repurchasing all his borrowed stock between 7 and 10, ending up a quarter of a million dollars to the good.

So for Wilson, the energetic brokers who puff up "concept" stocks are like the beaters in a European hunt, driving the pigeons toward him as he waits at his post. Bang! A hundred thousand dollars. Bang, bang! A hundred thousand more.

That's what I mean when I say that as far as Wilson is concerned the beaters—I mean the brokers—are working for him, not for the pigeons.

Wilson is a thin man, with a trim brown beard and thinnish hair surrounding a slender face. He speaks in a bright and humorous way, in a slightly strangled midwestern voice. Simply and neatly dressed, he has the figure of a man in his thirties and the face of one about forty. He is, in fact, fifty-two. He believes in keeping fit, and indeed in his line of work he has to be fit, as would an airport tower controller.

Wilson sits with his sandaled feet on his desk in a large, clean Scandinavian-modern office in a commercial building on New York's West Fifty-seventh Street and buys and sells stocks. He spends about two-thirds of his working day on the telephone (a tiny headset and mike gadget which he answers himself: "Wilson") and about one-third of it reading business magazines and telephone messages taken by his secretary. He also goes out a lot at night with stock market friends.

The output of this information system is the investment ideas that have made Robert Wilson, after Warren Buffett and Larry Tisch, perhaps the richest of our subjects. In 1958 he received an initial stake of $15,000 from his father and has multiplied his assets into the tens of millions of dollars purely by buying and selling in the stock market—and in spite of a fearful setback in 1978.

To keep this moneymaking apparatus in good order, Wilson gives much attention to his health. Things start with a big breakfast, which used to include eggs and bacon; he quit the bacon and cut down on the eggs when he discovered his cholesterol was too high. He drinks a great deal of water—about half a gallon a day. He finds it good for his complexion, which is, indeed, that of someone twenty years younger. He started drinking all the water as a stool softener when he suffered from hemorrhoids, and kept up the habit after he recovered.

He takes vitamins E and C, has a low-key form of jogging that he likes, and practices yoga and other exercises. He goes around to the New York Athletic Club for calisthenics, but not to engage in sports, of which he dislikes the competitive side. He says he has always been weak and uncoordinated. His facial exercises, which he finds helpful in avoiding wrinkles and a baggy chin (he has neither), involve ominous grimaces, thrusting the corners of the mouth out sideways and down like an actor in a Japanese painting. When he started to go bald, he began grabbing his hair and pulling it about to stimulate the scalp, which has stabilized matters. He says that the blood flow of the body slows down with age, and one must keep it moving along.

According to Wilson his predilection for the short side derives from the circumstances of his youth in Detroit. His father, a fire and casualty insurance agent, was not wealthy but owned some bank stocks, which in those days carried unlimited liability. If the bank failed, the shareholders were individually liable to the depositors; if a shareholder went bankrupt as a result, his liability carried back to the shareholder he had bought his stock from. Because of this law, Wilson's father was wiped out in the Depression, even though the family went on living comfortably. That experience, says Wilson, made him conscious of the risk of disaster, and gave him a feeling that the market boom of the sixties could not last.

Although reasonable in large things, Wilson's father was niggling in small ones, and irritated young Robert about money matters to the point, he says, that he resolved to be able to "buy and sell him" some day.

After graduating from college and spending two years in law school Wilson became a trainee at First Boston Corporation, where, he claims, he learned nothing but how to dress properly. (He was not allowed to wear his usual sandals, and so padded around in stocking feet.) In 1951, during the Korean War, he was drafted, and spent two years as an Army clerk-typist. He came back to First Boston upon emerging from the service, but after a year and a half returned to Detroit, where he spent five years in the trust department of the National Bank of Detroit. He did not like the job, but found his fellow workers outstandingly able, and regards the experience as having been extraordinarily valuable. In 1958 he returned to Wall Street with General American Investors, a closed-end fund, and thereafter went on to join A. G. Becker & Co.

Wilson mentioned that in the mid-fifties he had tried to join de Vegh & Company. The head of the firm, Imrie de Vegh, was an encyclopedia, and gave him a frightful grilling. At the end he mentioned that if Wilson wanted to work there he would have to give up the idea of speculating on his own. Wilson said he would never do that, and so the possibility foundered. (I got around the de Vegh house rule by paying the full fee for the firm to look after my own funds, which gave me the right to be treated as a client as well as a manager.)

In 1968 he went out on his own, starting a small hedge fund for some friends and relations who put up $3 million. At the bottom of the bear market in 1970 the fund had declined 38 percent and only $300,000 was left, since most of the investors had pulled out. Wilson gets 20 percent of the amount by which the fund outperforms the Standard & Poor's 400-stock average on a cumulative basis. The fund has now recovered to $3 million again.

By far Wilson's most important activity, however, is managing his own money, which in recent years has been in the tens of millions of dollars. He points out that people who could do so most often fail to make fortunes because they think that "40 percent of a little bit of money is still a little bit of money." But making 40 percent a year of any amount of money becomes a huge amount soon enough, as Wilson's career demonstrates. Conversely, a very rich man who says, "I made $3 million last year" hasn't done well at all if he is working with $100 million.

The Best Revenge

Wilson is doing up a huge, light apartment on Central Park West, where he lives alone. He is an important patron of several New York institutions, including the Metropolitan Opera, the Brooklyn Botanic Garden, and the Whitney Museum, where his acumen is much appreciated. He loves music, particularly Mahler, Wagner, Richard Strauss, Puccini, Mozart, and Beethoven, but walks out of two-thirds of the movies he attends. He has a keen practical sense, and is interested in the problems of doing things right. His manner is simple, amused, sympathetic, and unostentatious.

What makes Wilson tick? He reiterates that more than anything else he wants to be rich, and yet he seems to like money as a token, not for what it can buy. He has simple tastes and no expensive hobbies. He doesn't want to have servants or a big, black car, which he feels would insulate him from life; ostentatious spending "reduces vitality." He does like being in a position to make generous donations to cultural institutions and serve on their boards, and enjoys dining out in style a couple of times a week.

He frequently measures himself against other investors. Speaking of Warren Buffett, for example, he says, with a slight smile, "I guess he's more successful than I am . . . he made his money when he was younger." I told him I doubted that cash was what Buffett was really interested in. Wilson was puzzled. He talks about how much money he had, or has, or will have: $10 million, $20 million, $40 million, hundreds of millions. He expects in the forthcoming bull market to run his stake up to a "significant part of a billion." He adds, "Everybody asks me *what* part of a billion, but I'm not ready to say." Rowe Price's talk about percentages— "up 20 percent in eighteen months"—he finds only mildly interesting. How much *money* does Price have? Not that much. And yet what does Wilson gain by making more money in material terms? Not too much either. He enjoys what he has, but has more than he needs. Perhaps he is indeed getting back at the old man, or settling scores with bullies in the schoolyard.

Life he describes as a process of enjoyment. "An up day in the market is as good as a performance of *Electra.*" He suffers when losing money, but not unbearably. A high tolerance for pain is necessary for success in his type of investment. "This business doesn't get to me too much—not fundamentally," he says.* He quotes Bernard Berenson: "In order to be comfortable, one

---

* Alexander Pope was constantly subjected to merciless lampoons. One day a friend called and found him perusing a handful. "These things are my diversion," said Pope airily—but the friend noticed that his face was working.

should have a little more money and a little less time than one needs." He says that his other motto in life is "Living well is the best revenge."

Wilson is highly intelligent and articulate, with a lively philosophical awareness about the many things that he is interested in. When we came to discuss the obvious disinclination of outstanding investors to live ostentatiously, he pointed out that those with lavish life-styles tend to be captains of industry and persons with high income but low net worth. Investors, we agreed, have a more philosophical bent, and thus less taste for outward display. Wilson went further: "One of the dumbest things you can do with money is spend it."

He suspects, incidentally, that investment people are in general not fond of mankind, and thus not interested in impressing it.

Quem vult perdere deus . . .

In addition to exercises, Wilson keeps refreshed by periods of inactivity, following J. P. Morgan's dictum "I can do a year's work in nine months, but not in twelve." One of his vacations probably did more harm than good. In May 1978 he set forth on a six-month trip to Europe, the Far East, and Australia, having moved his portfolio into what he thought was a satisfactory posture; the diversified list of stocks he held long were balanced by another list that he had sold short, and whether the market rose or fell (and he did not expect much activity) he felt he would be all right. Previously, he had usually been able to make more money by being simultaneously long and short than by simply being out of the market. He had enjoyed a "godlike" success in his short-side trading until then, he says.

Unfortunately, at that time one of his positions was a short commitment of over 200,000 shares of Resorts International, at an average price of $15. (It has since split 3 for 1, so the price Wilson went short was $5 on today's stock.) The stock had moved up to about $20 before he left. "I'm getting crucified, but I may short more," Wilson announced in a widely noted interview in a national magazine. He predicted that Resorts International, which had just opened the first gambling casino in Atlantic City, would not do as well as the public believed, since Atlantic City's weather is not as favorable as that of Las Vegas. Also, Wilson explained, casino owners need the Mafia to help them collect debts; so if Jersey succeeded in its attempt to drive out the mob, then the casinos couldn't extend credit and wouldn't be attractive to the high rollers. On this confident note, Wilson set off on his planned junket around the world. As he meandered through Europe, Resorts International reported prodigious initial results from its new casino. The public, fascinated, poured into the stock. Since Wilson had announced his huge short position publicly, brokers were well aware of it, and told their customers that when the stock got high enough Wilson would have to buy all his shorts back, since his resources were not infinite; this, they said, gave a measure of support to the stock.

Only one person, Harold Charnow, had disagreed with the idea of going short in Resorts. Charnow thought the stock was going to be a great winner, and indeed forecast everything that happened. Wilson's other advisors, such as Dick Gilder, urged him to hold on. Neither Wilson nor they realized what a long, slow fight the other casinos would have before they were admitted to Atlantic City, and they forgot the huge size of the market. The entire state of Nevada did $1.5 billion in gambling business in 1978; Resorts International all by itself did $350 million.

So as Wilson wandered between beautiful views, cathedrals, palaces, concerts, and fine repasts in famous restaurants, his destruction was slowly being engineered back home.

Resorts started to pick up momentum. From 20 when he left, it advanced to 30—double his cost. Then, as the hapless Wilson drifted from one attraction to the next, Resorts moved to 40, to 50, to 60—four times his cost. Now it had become one-third of his entire short position. He had lost millions. He remembers a grim evening in the Norwegian fjord country. He couldn't shake a persistent dull couple he'd been drinking too much with, insistent cables from Wall Street were accumulating in a sinister pile, and he began to have a sick feeling of things coming unstuck.

Writers in the financial press started speculating openly about his plight. Resorts continued to report brilliant earnings. The brokers urged their legions forward: Wilson's on the run!

He reached the Far East: Singapore, Hong Kong. Resorts crept up relentlessly: five points, ten points. Even a minor move now meant a loss of $100,000.

Wilson began to crack. The situation had been building up in his mind all summer. Deep down, he knew he was doomed; he was in an entirely new and different investment climate. The underlying merits of Resorts International had got him, and the times in general, not just his stock market judgment. Who could have conceived that from making "one phony million dollars a year" Resorts could jump to $50 million a year? It was one of the biggest success stories in business history. To this day Wilson can't think of another company that has ever gone from $1 million to $50 million in eighteen months.

Neuberger & Berman were telephoning regularly now. We gotta have more margin! What do you want to sell? They gave him a dollar limit beyond which he couldn't go. They couldn't risk what might be catastrophic financial damage to their own firm if Wilson collapsed. And they were right: Wilson admits that without that limit he would have been ruined.

"Cover some Resorts," Wilson ordered. Now he was in the position of squeezing himself. His own purchases helped force the stock up further, increasing the pressure.

Resorts reached 120. He had lost $10 million.

Wilson went on to Formosa. The catastrophe gathered speed. Taipei in September is a bright, steaming Oriental town, chaotic, gay, and vital, unlike beautiful, melancholy Hong Kong. Wilson settled into the Grand Hotel, a monument built by the Kuomintang. He had a single room with high ceilings, like a pagoda. Every day he would sally forth in his rugby shirt, Adidas sneakers, pastel-colored pants and sun hat to go through the noisy, colorful streets by taxi from one temple to another, from museum to museum. Chiang carried off the best of China's art when he left the mainland, so the art museum in Taipei is one of the greatest in the world.

And every day Resorts International surged forward. In a week and a half it rose from 120 to 180. Wilson was losing up to half a million dollars on a bad day: $100,000 each hour the Stock Exchange was open.

He couldn't stand it. On September 4, he went to pick up his room key in the Grand and the clerk handed him the usual grim telex from New York. Up again! Wilson at last knew he was cooked. Rather than telex his reply (which would have been instantaneous) he decided to save a few dollars and went down to the communications desk to send Neuberger & Berman a cable: "COVER ALL RESORTS." That was it.

But it wasn't. The next day Wilson had a substantial breakfast: a couple of eggs, porridge, and a banana (which he describes as a "cornucopia of nourishment").

He set forth, as usual, in a taxi—marveling, as always, at how little they cost in Taipei—for his scheduled rounds: temples, cathedrals, paintings, sculptures. At noon, he suspended operations to enjoy an excellent lunch, and then resumed.

Late in the day he returned to the hotel and went to his room to get ready for dinner downstairs.

At 7:00 P.M. the telephone rang. Wilson, still dressed in his rugby shirt, Adidas sneakers, and light blue pants, sat down on the bed to pick it up.

It was his broker at Neuberger & Berman.

"Resorts is 190," he said. "What do we do?"

Wilson knew that 190 had to be the top, or within a hair's breadth of the top. The stock couldn't go any higher. It had no reason to be *that* high. It was a typical speculative blowoff—just froth. It would collapse in no time. But did he dare, even he, to sell everything else, his perfectly good long positions? If he was wrong, in another week, if it was like the one just passed, he'd be finished. He *had* to close out Resorts, even if it was surely the wrong move. He was done, exhausted, beaten. All the invisible suckers out there were getting their own back.

"Didn't you get my cable?" Wilson asked.

"What cable?"

"I told you to close out Resorts."

"Is that what you want us to do?"

"Yes! Close it out!" After a few more words, he hung up.

Wilson's disaster came during the newspaper strike, but received lavish coverage in the financial press, including a major story in the *Wall Street Journal,* and considerable attention in *Esquire* and other publications. It is, indeed, likely to be remembered as the most catastrophic short play in modern times, particularly since it was so elaborately telegraphed.*

Wilson says that his mistake in Resorts was not an error of market judgment, but a misunderstanding of the fundamentals of the company. However, he also thinks that just at that moment America changed tack. In the 1960s nothing went right, politically or otherwise. In business, new ventures usually failed. But in 1978 a better era started. Who would have thought that New Yorkers would start picking up dog droppings? Perhaps Resorts and the dog droppings are both harbingers of profound change. Resorts International's Atlantic City venture, says Wilson, was the first thing in America that has gone right on a colossal scale in a long time. ("Right" depending, of course, on what you think of incorporated vice.)

Wilson chuckled on thinking of a *New Yorker* cartoon of some years back. A hippie couple with frizzy hair and shabby clothes are lounging in their pad. Junior, a well-brushed tyke nattily

* Wilson may thus take a position alongside the never to be forgotten Ahmed Abd el-Aziz, who farted in the Great Mosque during a silent moment in Friday prayer. Every head swung around to glare at the scarlet Ahmed, who rose and crept out. All Damascus was soon buzzing. Finally, Ahmed decamped to Aleppo. Years later, with a gray beard, he returned, finding the city much changed: new shops, houses gone, others built, new faces. In the market he asked directions of a stranger, who complied, and then, looking at him keenly, said, "You are not from Damascus, then, brother?" "No, I live in Aleppo," said Ahmed; adding modestly, "I used to live here, though." "How long have you been away, brother?" asked the stranger. "Twelve years," said Ahmed. "There have been many changes." "Twelve years . . ." mused the stranger; "that is a long time." He smiled faintly: "Yes, yes, twelve years ago . . . that was the year that Ahmed farted in the Great Mosque."

decked out in a three-piece suit and armed with an attaché case, is walking with stern purpose out the door. The freaked-out parents are moaning, "Where did we go wrong?"

Wilson's Rule

Any successful approach in investing is bound to fail in due course. Things change. "Shorthand techniques are okay, but they finally blow up in your face. Then you have to do something different."

Without a Rope

Robert Wilson's *modus operandi* would terrify most of the other eminent investors in this book, who, however, generally make less money than he does. It is, in fact, the same approach that costs the small investor so much money every year. The difference is that Robert Wilson does it better, and is financially fearless. He can't be shaken out of a good idea if things go wrong for a while. Mountain climbers are well advised to wear proper clothes, carry the necessary equipment, not go out late in the day during periods when avalanches may occur, and move carefully on the mountain face with competent companions, an experienced guide, and a strong rope. Nevertheless, if someone is out to break records he may violate these rules: he may do away with the companions and the guide and thus have no need for the rope, may run up and down so fast that he needs only light equipment, and may even risk the avalanches.

Anyway, that's Wilson's technique: He virtually never visits companies or assesses their managment firsthand. Almost all his ideas come to him from stockbrokers, and he essentially works with concepts rather than the reality. When he buys a stock, he assesses what's going to make it go up, what will focus interest on the company, rather than worrying about the details of the underlying business.

That analysis he leaves to others. He's like the president of an advertising agency savoring a new slogan. " 'The Uncola.' Interesting . . . interesting. But will they buy it in Pocatello? Why not?" And if asked about the actual product he might say, "The quality control people tell me . . ."

Wilson's facility for imaginative synthesis, uncluttered by analytical baggage, lets him see the market outlook for a stock far more easily than a conventional analyst.

He describes himself as a "long-term trader." If things are going his way he may stay with a stock for a year or more. If not— and many of his ideas don't work out—he moves on.

Sources

Wilson hates to read long write-ups on stocks, and rarely does more than glance at them. In fact, his entire information system consists of only three file drawers. If he owns a company, he files any information he receives about it; when he sells the stock, he throws the information away again. Instead, Wilson gets his ideas from talking to others.

Wilson's prime brokers, from whom he obtains his best ideas and with whom he keeps his securities, are Furman Selz Mager Dietz & Birney (handling custody for his long positions), Neuberger & Berman (handling custody for his short sales), and Bob Birch of Oppenheimer & Company, whose ideas he particularly respects. But he also deals with dozens of other sources, brokers tending to specialize in serving small institutions or sophisticated individual investors. They also tend to be young—in their forties or younger—probably because of the demographic gap in Wall Street. From about 1934 through the Depression and war years into the early fifties, very little new talent was recruited, and the older generation is disappearing from the scene. Also, successful salesmen in brokerage houses often become independent money managers, which rids them of the necessity of calling up customers. (A few salesmen do prefer to stay in brokerage, since it suits their temperament and is somewhat safer.)

Peter Reiss at Paine Webber, who recommended that Wilson

go short Resorts International, was contrite when Wilson came back many millions poorer. Wilson said, "That's okay, Peter; so many people recommended the short that one way or another I'd have gotten stuck. But I hope you'll forgive me for not giving you the commission on the way out."

Though Wilson never attends meetings with institutional securities analysts (who to him are "just bureaucrats"), he does go every year to the conference given by WEMA—formerly Western Electronics Manufacturers Association; now it includes manufacturers from many parts of the country. About 100 member firms take rooms in a West Coast hotel and receive some 250 analysts. Wilson sees about fifteen companies in two days, for an hour each. He likes this procedure because he can get an impression, "with a minimum of bullshit."

An example of Wilson's indifference to exact data arose when we were talking about Engelhard Minerals, which both of us find intriguing. He mentioned it several times in our discussions, at one point revealing that he thought the sales of the company were on the order of $1 billion; actually, they were about $8 billion! Later I ran through a list of the companies he was long or short and asked him the names of their presidents; he knew only about half of them. Doubtless Wilson would observe that with each new president a company changes, fundamentally, no more than Italy does with each new prime minister. The general nature and position of the business is what Wilson wants to grasp, the key changes in its circumstances that the public does not yet understand—such as that Datapoint may go from a $20 million company to a $200 million company every institution will have to own. When the public finally does understand the business, realizes how good it is, and as a result wants to buy the stock, Wilson will have it for sale—at a much higher price.

New Wave Stocks

Wilson's cardinal principle is: *Buy companies that are doing something new and different, or doing it in a different way.*

As an example, he cites the catalogue merchandisers, whose business has become huge in recent years. Among them, Best Products and Modern Merchandising have revolutionized the jewelry business, which generates one-third of their profits, at the expense of the "Mom and Pop" local jewelry stores. Wilson says that only the catalogue merchandisers are selling jewelry properly: their markup is modest, and they offer a much better deal than the conventional jeweler, thus creating a new market.

Other new wave companies include Federal Express, which revolutionized small package transport, Sensormatic Electrics, which makes devices to reduce pilferage, and again, Engelhard Minerals, which in essence is a block trader of commodities on a huge scale, with an unmatched worldwide commodities intelligence system. Engelhard deals primarily in ores, but its Philipp Brothers division is a huge trader in oil. The developing countries are happier to sell their oil to Engelhard than to Exxon, which has colonialist associations. Wilson believes that the opening of China will almost certainly represent a business opportunity for the company, as will Iran's disaffection with its traditional trading partners, Israel and South Africa, who will have to be supplied by new and anonymous routes, which Engelhard can provide.

Another principle Wilson follows is: *buy technology companies that could go up ten times in five to seven years,* companies like Datapoint, Intel, Data General, Wang Labs, M/A Com, Inc., Management Assistance, Systems Engineering Laboratories, and Tandy; also Cray Research and AM International.

A special hazard of playing stocks of the hour with which the public is enchanted is that not infrequently unscrupulous brokers in league with management are pushing weak businesses so that insiders can sell the stocks to the public for more than they are worth, as happened with all the hot issues of the sixties that simply vanished. The speculator trying to stay just ahead of the public has to be nimble or he will be carried to ruin with them, as were most of the "new breed" of hotshots and gunslingers who flourished in the late sixties and early seventies.

So Wilson the speculator may well buy the same sort of merchandise that Wilson the balloon-pricker will attack when the time is right.

Playing the Surprises

If you are betting on an election you don't necessarily bet on the best man, you bet on the man you think will win.* Wilson uses his flair and skill to bet on the stock image that he thinks will excite the public in a few months or a year, not necessarily three years from now. The market in a "T. Rowe Price" company, clocking in its 20 percent earnings growth, quarter after quarter, probably reflects its prospects. You get a better move, says Wilson, "playing the surprises."

The Tiger in the Tank Is Fear

The major difference between Wilson's approach and that of most of the investors in this book is that a Graham, for instance, always sought situations where there is little risk of loss. Wilson, on the other hand, says that he insists on stocks in which there is a major risk, because only such a stock is likely to go way up.

"Unless there is fear in a stock, it probably doesn't have a great capital gains potential," he says, adding, "I'd be scared shitless if my portfolio consisted of only ten out of my seventy stocks."

I find that to be the most useful single idea I have heard him express, and urge the reader to contemplate it carefully. What most enrages him, incidentally, is a broker asserting that "there's no downside risk in this stock."

The Short Side

Wilson likes to see the brokerage fraternity get behind a stock and push. He knows that they are only wheeling his next target

---

* John Maynard Keynes (who, incidentally, made most of his money speculating on commodities and currencies) compares speculation to a wager on the outcome of a beauty contest. You don't bet on the girl you find prettiest, but on the one you think others will prefer.

into position: the next balloon to be pricked, the next tulip-bulb mania. In a pleasantly mixed metaphor he refers to the brokers "pumping up the tulips." He likes to short into strength in a stock, not when it's already on the way down.

Colonial Commercial was one of his famous shorts. Wilson describes it as a weak Long Island conglomerate. He started selling at $5 a share, beginning in early 1978. By October the stock had risen to about $20. The Wall Street fraternity, reasoning that Wilson would be unable to hold on in Resorts International, decided to force up Colonial Commercial too, hoping that, in order to cut his losses, he would be compelled to buy in his short position at higher prices. He was a big fish in that pool, and his own buying would have forced the stock up further: he would have squeezed himself. But the stock settled back down to 12, and Wilson shorted even more.

Wilson also once shorted Mostek, which makes semiconductors, at $6, and was forced to run for cover at $22. Such setbacks, however, are more than offset by his usual ability to wait out the rise and then finally cover at fire-sale prices.

Wilson's principal short positions had formerly included Graphic Scanning, Astrex, Tom Brown, Tampax, and British Petroleum. Other stocks he has been short include the heavy chemicals, notably Dow, W. R. Grace, Rohm & Haas; also Air Products, National Presto, Applied Digital Data, Centronics, Advanced Micro Devices, and International Systems and Controls.

Another of his famous shorts was Technicare. He began shorting at below $10, continued while the stock went over $20, and rode it down again to about 11, where he covered.

He also shorted Bowmar Instruments, at 20. They had one great year, with booming earnings; then they borrowed to finance a major expansion just in time for the entry of Texas Instruments and National Semiconductor into the market. Wilson covered his stock at 2½. Meanwhile, unfortunately, the stock had gone from $20 to over $40 at a time when the general market was going down. ("That was a rough one!") When Technicare went against him, at least he was making money on the long side to offset his losses on the short side. Before shorting Bowmar, he talked to a lot of people, almost all of whom were wrong. Neither they nor he had any idea that the calculator market would get as big as it eventually did, or that Bowmar would do as well as it did. After all, says Wilson, a calculator is just a couple of semiconductors in a metal box with some buttons.

Another category that he recently considered overpriced was the international container leasing companies, such as Flexi-Van, Interway, and Sea Containers. Rates and utilization have advanced spectacularly at what he thinks is an unsustainable rate.

Wilson points out that only in the U.S. market can one take short positions that can be kept in place month after month. If he had been born in England, he would never have been able to get rich.

The Whites of Their Eyes

According to Wilson, the single rule that would have saved him the most money as an investor is this: *Don't try to anticipate how fast competition will undercut an established company.* There's no use theorizing how competition will unfold; it's best to wait and see what really happens. With Tampax, for instance, one could have started worrying about competition fifteen years ago. However, one could have made a fortune in the stock before the problem became acute, as it finally has. Similarly, Eastman Kodak's pounce on the instant camera industry alarmed followers of Polaroid, yet Polaroid did marvelously well *after* Kodak's appearance as a competitor. The availability of the product opened up the market. Still another example is hamburgers: who could have dreamed that after McDonald's, Burger King, and all the others, the market could support still another major competitor? "How many hamburgers can America stuff in its face?" asks Wilson rhetorically. And yet Wendy's has enjoyed a prodigious success.

Companies are often destroyed not by the competition but by themselves. They get soft. How did foreign imports rise to a full 20 percent of the U.S. car market? The foreign manufacturers were keen and efficient while the American manufacturers got sloppy. And Interstate Department Stores, who virtually discovered discount merchandising, should be bigger today than K mart—but they aren't. New arrivals more often fill a vacuum than displace a strong existing company.

Free Lunch

Wilson is uninhibited in describing the stocks that he is long and short. If he is long, he wants the stock to go up, and describing its excellence may help that happen. If he's short, he wants the stock to go down, and explaining what's wrong may help that happen too. There has been criticism of this habit from a number of quarters, including the SEC. It has been alleged that Wilson and other members of his circle regularly feed ideas to Alan Abelson, whose front-page column in *Barron's* is exceedingly influential. Abelson likes to attack overpriced companies and Wilson finds it a congenial chore to furnish him with cannon fodder.

A story in the July 1977 *Institutional Investor* quoted Wilson's reply when asked if he tried to "use Abelson to promote his positions": "I use everybody. I am always trying to get my longs up and my shorts down, so I am constantly using people. I feel perfectly free to tell Alan anything I have in my mind as long as it isn't inside information."

The *Wall Street Letter* also quoted Wilson on the subject: "I do discuss many ideas with [Abelson] and urge upon him the merits of these."

Abelson commented: "Most of the people who send me information have a strong interest in one way or the other. They are long or short the stock." *Barron's* editor Robert Bleiberg added, "We assume everyone who sends us something is an interested party. There is no such thing as a free lunch."

Wilson himself, having attracted the attention of the SEC, commented to *Esquire:* "I'm not as anti-SEC as others on Wall Street, but they're trying to inhibit free speech, and I'm not going to let them do it. If I have a thousand ideas for Alan, I'll call him up with all of them. I'll shoot my mouth off if I see fit, talk to anyone I want . . . to whores or anyone else. I've made that clear to the SEC."

Abelson, in turn, as quoted in the *Institutional Investor,* comments: "Is it unethical to short the stock and call the press? I think it is. Is it done? You bet. But if the SEC doesn't like it, let *them* do something about it. I'm a reporter, not a policeman."

What's Ahead

While he was off on his 1978 tour, Americans were becoming disgusted with their lot as an "emerging second-class nation," Wilson says. They began to see that incentives had to be restored to the economy. For instance, the capital gains tax was cut, an extraordinary turnabout. If it had been predicted before he went away in May, he would have said it was simply inconceivable— as inconceivable as the prospect of Resorts going up 1,000 percent.

This momentous transformation in the United States should soon bring about a huge bull market.

In the 1940s and 1950s, the last time price-earnings multiples were at these low levels (and when the Russians seemed to be gobbling up the world), the investing public expected that there would be another great postwar depression. Instead, after the beginning of 1953 it became apparent that there would not be one, and price-earnings multiples began rising. The reason that price-earnings multiples got so low this time is that investors felt that the country was drifting into socialism. That drift, however, may be reversing direction.

Wilson believes that the bankruptcy of New York City means the discrediting of big government, that as a result there will be less government, and that things in general will go much better. From 1980's depressed levels the market could rise to twenty times doubled earnings, or almost fivefold in five to seven years. Wilson believes that he'll be worth hundreds of millions of dollars before it's over.

10

The Masters Compared

Techniques

Fisher, Price and in a way Buffett all practice variations on the same basic approach: plant the tree and watch it grow and grow and grow. Buy a successful, growing business and share in the building of value as it develops. The method isn't too risky if the price is right. Stick to what you can know a lot about: if the business *has been* growing, and *is* growing, you have reason to believe it should *go on* growing for at least a while.

Graham, Tisch and Buffett look primarily for what's so cheap right now that you almost can't lose.

Buffett understands business and thinks like a businessman (which Graham did not). Thus he emphasizes the importance of a business franchise, and of excess assets in a company, which can be redeployed for the benefit of the owners. A modest, slowly growing well-run bank with more capital than it needs would suit him fine (that's the Graham influence), but might not interest Fisher, Price, or Templeton. Buffett won't pay a high multiple of earnings. Specifically, he feels the "earnings yield" should be as high as the prevailing bond yield, and he's glad to sell when a stock becomes high-priced.

Fisher lives in San Francisco, next door to "Silicon Valley," where so many semiconductor and other high-tech companies are found. He therefore understands growth through technology, with which Templeton and Buffett are uncomfortable, as was Graham (essentially a New York merchant), and which Price approached through the economic idea, the "fertile field," rather than a specific company. Fisher has always liked running around in his old car talking to managements, so his checklist requires a deep study of the men who run each business. He observes that great managements create their opportunities—even create new industries—so management has to be the key. While every enterprise has its dull spells, a great management will maneuver it back into position. Price felt that growth will *attract* good management.

Of all our subjects Price took the longest view: he was a futurologist, for whom high growth over the long term was of greatest importance. Since he foresaw growth so vividly, he would if necessary pay a premium for it—indeed, he expected to. (But not as high a premium as his followers did, making this principle a religion, not a discipline.) Price once told me that he found it more likely that a company squarely in the line of progress would be able to develop good management and become highly successful, and less likely that good management could push a dull company into a high-growth area. Once a company has successfully navigated into the middle of the river of rapid growth and has the management skill to stay there, Price wanted to ride it for years, rather than switch about like Templeton. But he emphasized *high* growth, while Buffett, Fisher, and Price emphasize *solid* growth. Both approaches are valid. You can make vast amounts of money with a machine like Procter & Gamble or MMM endlessly compounding at 12 percent or so, and you can make even more, but with less certainty and with a probable need to sell sooner or later, in a Xerox, a Polaroid, an Avon, or a McDonald's.

Templeton is always looking for bargains, as was Graham, but whereas Graham wanted a financial bargain, a furnished house selling for less than the furniture, Templeton wants a company that in a few years will be worth more than its present market price, even if it isn't today. So he's both a growth investor and a value investor. Templeton doesn't understand technology and isn't in a position to analyze managements, as Fisher does; is less interested in excess working capital and supposedly bulletproof business franchises than Buffett; and is more wary of endless growth than Price was. He thinks as a stock market operator, not —as Buffett and Fisher do—as a businessman. He, like Larry Tisch, wants a stock so cheap in earnings terms that it really has to go up, giving him a chance to sell at a profit. He doesn't dream of a chance to float all the way down the Mississippi River like Price and Buffett. Since he's out for maximum performance, he doesn't like to wait for the plan to work out if things get dull for several years. The same is true for Larry Tisch: no profound insights, no extraordinary visions; just a business selling for less than he, or a friend of his, would buy it for.

Of both Paul Cabot and Larry Tisch one can, I think, say that the method is that there is no method, except thoroughness and realism. Everything is specific. Let the *public* have the big ideas, the exciting theories—and sell them your stock. Let the public get panicked and disillusioned—and buy the stock back again.

Cabot and Tisch are looking for quality merchandise only, but not the best possible companies, as Buffett is. Cabot will look farther ahead and take bigger risks. Only Price could have shared Cabot's killing in Dome Petroleum. Certainly neither Cabot nor Tisch would touch the wormy situations that Graham was happy with, nor would they profess to understand the offshore exotica that have done so well for Templeton. In the quality spectrum Graham would be at the bottom and Buffett and Cabot at the top. Templeton and Tisch will take anything that seems pretty good at the right price.

Graham thought mathematically, like a banker, not a business-man. The beauty of his method is that it's safe—bankerly. Very few people have ever lost money by following it. If you use your analytical X-ray to discover that inside a box selling for $10 lies $20, you can't go wrong; you don't guess about the future.

At one time I was living in Italy, at the base of a mountain north of Florence called Montemorello. Up the side of the mountain, looking west over the plain, was an abandoned convent. Every so often someone would think of buying it, but, on a bad road with no neighbors, it was not easily accessible, and it lacked a good water supply. It would also have been difficult to adapt the structure for family living or, since the location was inconvenient, to turn it into a hotel; remodeling would have been fiendishly expensive either way.

Finally it was bought by an antique dealer, who had figured out that he could recover his costs from what was *inside* the building—some valuable old objects and many newer, less interesting ones—and that once he had done that, someone would eventually want to buy the structure for some reason.

And someone did. Monasteries and convents in Italy are often sold *a porte chiuse*—"with doors closed": in other words, as is, sight unseen, with no right of inspection. The religious order doesn't want the fuss of buyers traipsing around. That limits the market, which creates an opportunity for a specialized class of experienced buyers who can do well making low bids without giving thought to where the master bedroom will go or what potential a place may have for tourism—a technique that might not work when a single property is being considered, but does when a whole series is purchased.

Another time I was in Western Australia as the financial man for a well-sponsored syndicate interested in developing ranching, real estate, mining, or whatever. I flew and drove all over the state looking for likely projects. The rainfall in most of Western Australia is miserably low, and thus instead of being able to support four sheep to an acre, say, a rancher may need to have four acres per sheep. The ranches (called stations, pronounced *sty*-shuns) must therefore be large: a million acres isn't unusual. Under those conditions a rancher can't fence the sheep in—he'd need too much fence. Instead, he lets them roam about on their own and then rounds them up—if he can—for shearing or sending them to market. Buying such a sheep station really means getting a license to hunt sheep. The land (held under a ninety-nine-year grazing lease) has no other value, and the house, farms, and outbuildings are usually modest. So the clever buyer of a sheep station rents a light plane, flies carefully over the property, counting the animals, and makes a bid for less than the value of what he sees running around. If the owner accepts the bid, at least the buyer can't lose much. Of course he may not be able to sell it for very much either, when the time comes. Western Australia isn't Middleburg, Virginia. It lacks charm. Rich horse-fancying romantics don't come along and fall in love with such a place, giving no thought to its possible operating earnings or fire-sale liquidating value; they analyze it very carefully.*

These two approaches to buying—*a porte chiuse* and "counting the sheep"—are, of course, Grahamite techniques, far removed from how the public invests, or from what makes an appealing autobiographical book. How many have we not read: the war over, the new couple—he a decorated officer, she the daughter of a county family and with literary or artistic aspirations—resolves to make a new life far from dismal London, where even the fog is rationed. They strike off for the hills of Tuscany or the vales of New Zealand. They fall in love with the place at first sight, and for the next twelve years the Major bashes away at an unforgiving landscape while Sybil keeps house, hobnobs with the villagers, hatches little Desmond and Kate, and records it all, with charming photographs, in *Season in Arcadia* (Tasteful Books, Ltd: £60). The world is enriched by this classic and by their improvements to the landscape, but they lose money on the deal—probably quite a lot, counting inflation and opportunity cost. Finally her father dies, leaving some property that needs looking after; since it's time for the children to attend a proper school, back they go, hoping for a rich American buyer but all too probably having to settle for some glassy-eyed miser. So

---

* Incidentally, a sheep station in Australia is often purchased "walk in walk out." This means that the seller, who may be moving to another station a couple of thousand miles away, leaves everything in place except his most personal possessions. The buyer can resume operations instantly, and the seller, when he gets to his new station, can set up shop without a break. Since we're talking about well-used mail-order stuff which there'd be little point in moving vast distances, the system makes sense.

they've bought at retail and sold at wholesale. They have the life, but Graham gets the money.*

The essence of Graham, then, is that he always quantified the present, and refused to be distracted by a vision of the future. This object is worth more *now* than it's selling for; let's buy a share in it and wait. Either someone else will be attracted to the possibilities, or a liquidator will come along.

Across the table from him, or one step down the food chain (to use an idea from natural history)—the mullet to Graham's shark—is the romantic, who looks too far into the future, or not far enough.

Both Kroll and Wilson deal essentially in psychology, not in material things or businesses, but they approach the subject differently. Kroll, looking at his charts, guesses where the herd—like Ionesco's rhinoceroses—will stampede next, or best of all "catches one of the big grains roaring down the track like an express train," as he says, and makes half a million dollars by riding the trend. In either case he's judging the public's mood by what it's *doing*. He is, in other words, a technician. The underlying "facts" aren't very interesting to him.

Wilson is interested in the underlying facts of the companies he's long or short, but mostly focuses on the difference between what the public is thinking now, in its euphoria or despair, and what it will find out when it recovers from its present fit and has had a second look at the facts. He resembles an experimenter watching rats scurrying in a maze; he knows pretty well how they will progress.

Always, though, Wilson is dealing in *images*, not, like Kroll, squiggles on a graph. His human side lets him *feel* how the poor old public will respond to the latest vision of sugarplums: CB radios, pocket calculators, another highway hamburger chain, gambling casinos. His serpentine side lets him devour the prey without compunction: the tongue flickers, the jaws open, snap!

---

* Lest I sound depreciating, my human sympathies are with our gallant couple. *Graham* has the profit from his side of the deal, not us; but from the homesteaders' side we have *Out of Africa* or whatever.

Common Attributes

Each "master" in this book seems to have certain traits:

1. *He is realistic.*
2. *He is intelligent to the point of genius; or else*
3. *He is utterly dedicated to his craft.*
4. *He is disciplined and patient.*
5. *He is a loner.*

One could add flexibility, but that is implicit in realism. It's sufficient to be a master of one game, rather than trying to learn two or three, as long as you retire to the sidelines when the game you know is no longer being played; you don't need to understand both "growth" investing and "value" investing, for instance. And in any event, I am not sure that our "masters" are all that flexible: most only know a limited part of the entire range of investing, although they could doubtless have learned other techniques had they needed to.

The business of investment is reality, both present and future. If an investor has a tendency toward self-delusion, sooner or later he will come a cropper. There are too many ways to go wrong. I think realism is a quality you're born with. The mind is balanced; it works well, like a watch. Experience and learning regulate the watch, but only to the extent that it is a fine enough instrument to begin with.

As for intelligence, Templeton was a Rhodes scholar, while Buffett and Graham seem to merit the title of genius. Fisher, it will be recalled, entered college at fifteen.

What does it mean in practice to be dedicated to the craft? The great investor—or great anything—rejoices in his vocation. You know this by the hours he keeps and the way his eyes glitter when he talks about his work. Often he has an overwhelming competitive instinct, even if concealed, and usually he was poor as a boy and developed an intense desire for financial security. And, of course, he thinks endlessly about investing, and is prodigiously well informed. Fisher, Kroll and Wilson are practically monomaniacs when working. So was Price.

And within the craft one mustn't waste one's skill and time on unproductive inquiries or anything else that cuts the time available to do what works. That's one area where discipline enters; the other is in sticking to one's basic method. One should also abandon unattainable objectives, such as trying to make money in short-term trading, trying to discover the unknowable,* so-called technical analysis (than which nothing could in fact be less technical), or investing according to set formulas, particularily if they require a computer to apply. (If there's a true formula, it will fit on the back of an envelope.) Nor should one follow so many companies that one knows less, not more, than the person one is buying from or selling to. And one must bring to this competitive game the best one has. One will not succeed with less.

Patience, which comes from knowledge and discipline, seems to be the hallmark of the professional. If you *know* you're right, it's not hard to wait. If you don't know and aren't disciplined, you risk getting shaken out just at the wrong time, like the bird that bursts from cover at the approach of the hunter.

The last quality of the master investor, that he is a loner, I discuss at some length in *Preserving Capital and Making It Grow*, which is largely concerned with how to find and work with an investment manager. (Very rarely one finds "twin" masters: they are partners but work as one loner *contra mundum*, like a twin star.) The loner's truth is within himself, while his opposite, the externalizer, is constantly testing the reaction of others and positioning himself in relation to them—usually to enjoy their esteem, but sometimes to express hostility. All great leaders, artists, and thinkers have to be loners; it's often very hard to keep them on the team.

Since buying what the crowd spurns and selling what the crowd craves is the essence of the master investor's art, it follows that

* *Nec Babylonios temptaris numeros*, as Horace said of astrology and divination: "Don't fuss with Babylonian numerology."

he must be serenely able to do the opposite of the herd, even though the herd instinct is the strongest human emotion. This calls for at least a solitary thinker, probably a misanthrope, and perhaps even something of a monster: a de Gaulle, one might say. It takes a lot of emotional stability to be happy at it.

11

Conclusions

In summing up the lessons of our masters perhaps the first subject to consider is some of the investment techniques that they agree *don't* work.

Investment Dont's

1. *Avoid Popular Stocks.* First must come the general class of anything that's too popular at the time, stocks that are on everybody's list. If you buy Polaroid when everybody feels it's cheap, you can be fairly sure that the stock is overvalued. It's not that the business won't do well or even that the stock will never rise; it's just that you will first have to work off that overvaluation, which takes time. IBM, then selling for 300, was a "religion stock" in the late 1960s, a certified member of the so-called Vestal Virgins. The company fulfilled all its owners' dreams: earnings went up 700 percent over the next decade, and the dividend rose 1,000 percent. Still, for ten years the stock never rose above 300. I often save the lists of "consensus" stocks published in magazines and check the results a year or two later. One may safely expect that they'll do about 30 percent worse than the averages.

That's the sinister meaning of the term *glamour stock.* A glamour stock is a good company overpriced because it's everybody's darling at the time. It's hard to make money buying one.

The same principle works for bursts of short-range enthusiasm. If a stock has run up wildly over a period of days or weeks, it's better to let it rest for a while.

A highly favorable purchase is very likely to seem odd, uncomfortable, risky, dull, or obscure at the time you buy it. Propitious reactions are: "That dog?" or, "I can't see it doing anything for the next six months." Later, everybody gets the idea and feels comfortable or enthusiastic about it. Then it's too late.

2. *Avoid Fad Industries.* Fads and brokers' stories are variations on popular stocks. The number of them you can remember is limited only by how old you are: the atomic energy craze of the fifties, the computer mania of the sixties, the gambling stock intoxication of 1978–79. There's an easy way to spot the terminal phase of these bubbles: if mutual funds are formed to concentrate on the industry in question, or if companies' stocks jump in the market because they announce that they *propose* to enter the field, then the buying is speculative and disappointment will probably follow.

IBM and Xerox each made most of the money that was ever made in their respective industries. One would have been safer *selling* the stock of any other company that announced it was going into computers or copiers.

As I've mentioned, a good rule is that when a company changes its name to indicate that it's going into a new industry, it's time to have a skeptical look at that industry.

The easiest way to be sure you aren't buying into a fad or popular stock is to consult the index of the *Wall Street Transcript* or ask your broker to check his research file; if nothing's been written about a company for a few years, you're probably safe. If I'm interested in a company, I usually contact its shareholder relations officer and ask him what the best brokerage house writeup is on his company. If there isn't any that really gets the point, then the discovery (or rediscovery) period is ahead of you.

A few years ago, for instance, H & R Block, the tax preparation company, seemed like a gift. They had a prodigious growth rate and no significant competition. The industry is imperishable, and

the company was selling in the market for barely more more
than its cash in the bank. I asked Richard Bloch (that's how the
family name is spelt), who didn't enjoy this state of affairs and
was glad to be helpful, if there were any good current brokerage
house studies around. He said that there was only one he knew
of, by an obscure individual practitioner. I considered that very
bullish, and in fact the stock eventually did extremely well.

Perhaps the archetype of this principle was the first great American oil strike, the fabulous Spindletop Dome. It attracted so many
investors that at its height one was said to be able to walk across
the field stepping from one drilling platform to the next. Result:
more money went into the ground at Spindletop than ever came
out of the ground.

3. *Avoid New Ventures.* Venture capital is for pros, not passive
portfolio investors. By far the majority of new ventures—probably
nine out of ten—go bust.

Warren Buffett's argument is overwhelmingly convincing:
There's little point in buying a gamble, of uncertain prospects
and management, with the likelihood of financial asphyxiation
in the future, and with the promoters getting a big free cut. If
you wait a few years for the next bear market, you know you'll
be able to buy the greatest companies in the world with superb
managements already in place, for no more than their net quick
assets, and with the company itself free—the plants, the patents,
the goodwill.

4. *Avoid "Official" Growth Stocks.* Stocks that have the growth
label—and corresponding price tag—often are no longer growing
rapidly enough to justify their prices. You might call them the
"old champs." Many famous companies that have "Growth Stock"
printed on the back of their robe and still wear the championship
belt and buckle they won in 1958 are really over the hill.

5. *Avoid Heavy Blue Chips.* A similar disappointment is likely
to come from buying cyclical heavy-industry "blue chips" with
static earnings, which sell for too high a price because of their
"security." When you buy U.S. Steel and its famous peers you
buy a cross-section of the modern world—whose problems for

the investor exceed its opportunities. After realistic depreciation the profits of these companies are usually substantially lower than reported, and even if there is a profit in accounting terms, there may be a cash deficit, covered by increasing the debt.

When you buy either the old champs or the heavy blue chips, the key is price: Is the rate of return really there? Will the reasonable projected flow of dividends give you what you need without any particular "leap of faith" and without any speculative assumption about what the stock will sell for ten years down the road at the end of the rainbow?

6. *Avoid Gimmicks.* Gimmicky investment "products" with high transaction costs and no intrinsic growth of value, such as option programs and commodity flyers, aren't investments at all.* They're casinos. Forget about them.

The economic function of real investment is to provide the capital needed for industry, for a fair return. The economic function of the casino customer is to be fleeced.

7. *Bonds Don't Preserve Capital.* A final bad deal for the investor, generally, is bonds, unless he reinvests all the income. The notion that they're "conservative" is grotesquely unrealistic. Franz Pick, in his sardonic way, has called them "certificates of guaranteed expropriation." After tax, bonds generally yield less than the inflation rate. The present half-life of money is eight to ten years; so, if you spend the income only half your buying power will remain after eight to ten years in real terms, and only one-quarter after sixteen to twenty years. You'll have run through your capital without even realizing it.

Incidentally, the Dow stocks *plus their dividends* have vastly outperformed savings accounts, with dividends compounded, over every twenty-year period since 1928, and have more than kept up with inflation.

8. *Forget About Technical Analysis.* One "system" of stock market investing not represented in this book is so-called technical

---

* I can't help finding repulsive the term *products* which some Wall Street firms apply it to their services. It suggests—often with justice—that they think of themselves as being in the entertainment business rather than in a profession.

analysis. The reason is that I have been unable to find any successful practitioners. In *Preserving Capital* I have this to say on the
subject (pp. 88–89):

Technical analysis of stocks. The study of value is the basis
of stock investment. There are no shortcuts. The "technician," however, tries to predict stock movement through the
shapes on a stock's chart, without reference to value.

It is not knowable from what a stock did last month or
last year how it will do next month or next year. Brokers'
pronouncements on this subject are tea-leaf reading, fakery.
Imagine a bookstore in which the salesman didn't know what
was between the covers, and instead offered guesses on next
year's prices for the merchandise! What a broker can and
should do is establish facts and values, so the customer can
decide if he wants to buy what has been described. This
involves legwork, study, interviews with a company and its
competition, consultation with industry experts, and the like,
the whole then to be presented in a form which permits
an investment valuation, but also where errors will stand
out.

How much easier and what tripe to say that a stock at
50 "seems to be poised for a breakthrough to the 54–56 area,
although a stop-loss order should be placed at 47." One
reader-advisor can issue pronouncements on hundreds of
stocks on this basis, instead of clearly revealing his competence (or incompetence) on one.

I have a naughty bet that I offer any "technician" I meet
and that none has accepted. It goes like this. He is asking
his readers to accept his word for it that if they do what
he says they will make money; that is, if he says Polaroid is
"technicially" a buy, and they buy a hundred shares, then
they will come out ahead reasonably soon, after round-trip
commissions and taxes. That is no joke. If Polaroid costs 50,
they are supposed to put $5,000 at risk, equal to the down

payment on a small house, on the strength of the wizard's readings of the wiggly lines.

Why not let him take a chance too?

So my bet goes like this: Somebody digs out some charts done on a daily basis from a few years back. He removes any identification and cuts each chart in the middle. He gives the first half to the technician.

All that worthy has to do is tell me, on a $100 bet, whether a stock was higher or lower at any specified point in the second period than at the end of the first. Since he claims the ability to prophesy, and is willing to have the rest of us take a substantial risk on his say-so—paying brokerage and tax whether we win or lose—he should be confident enough of his powers to give modest odds. Three to two seems fair enough.

So far, as I say, no "technician" has ever accepted the offer.

Personally, I do not think the SEC should allow any registered investment advisor to put out advice on stocks based on technical analysis. I consider it unprofessional.

Brokerage firms that I know have spent millions of dollars (literally) on computer programs for technical stock analysis and then quietly scuttled them.

I might add that even now no "technician" has ever offered to take this bet.

The best-known apostle of the technical approach, since John Magee died, is probably James Dines. In October 1974 Mr. Dines, who rightly had been gloomy all year, took a huge ad, THE DINES LETTER HAS NEVER BEEN SO BEARISH. The stock market jumped from 600 to 1,000 in little over a year; many issues tripled. Later in the month, more huge ads proclaimed, THE DINES LETTER FEELS GOLDS ARE ON THE VERGE OF A HISTORIC UPMOVE. Gold was about $220 an ounce at the time. After a last surge, it plunged for a year, to about half its former price. (Later it started its great rise.)

Winning Strategies

What *does* work?

One must of course start by asking, work *for whom*? As I've tried to show, Robert Wilson's technique of trading images works for him—and almost nobody else—precisely because he's so much better at it than the mass of investors, the losers. (And Kroll's technique is virtually impossible to execute—even for Kroll.) The next time you buy into some exciting rumor or alleged "sure thing" that your source doesn't know much about, remember that someone's selling what you buy—probably someone who knows everything you do, and possibly someone who knows a lot more, and who is also smarter, richer, and more interested in this particular situation.

If the investing public sat in a hall and *saw* Larry Tisch or John Templeton at the opposite side of the room trading against them, they'd be a lot more cautious, both buying and selling. They'd approach the situation with respect, like a dozen members of a local chess club playing simultaneous games with a visiting grandmaster who can easily beat them all.

I am going to limit my recommendations to strategies that can be practiced by investors who are serious and have common sense, but are not exceptionally qualified or dedicated.

What, then, are the main principles followed by the master investors we have considered, those which other investors can also execute? A few are accepted by almost all:

1. *Only buy a stock as a share in a good business that you know a lot about.* A stock is not a thing in itself, like a bird, that you hope will fly from 50 to 100. It should always be thought of as a specific share of a specific business, like owning a quarter-interest in a house.

Suppose, indeed, you contemplated buying a house, and got a week's option without much preliminary study. The silly way to spend that time would be to call the broker every hour or two and worry about what he said. The sensible approach would be to get an appraiser to check the house, finding out how much the necessary repairs and improvements would cost, and perhaps go around to other similar properties in the neighborhood and elsewhere to compare values. You would want to talk to the neighbors, find out about zoning and contemplated changes, visit the school, the mayor, the clergyman, the police chief, and the bank. That would be a week well spent, and you would be infinitely more likely to make a sensible decision than someone who sat at home badgering the broker.

So stated, it seems absurd to suppose that an investor would buy a stock without forming an accurate impression of what the underlying company was worth as a business: whether the management was competent, the research effective, how up-to-date the machinery was, whether the company was prosperous or strapped for cash, and so on; and yet in fact very few investors do know such things about the companies they own. It *is* absurd. And after they've bought, they look at the quotation in the paper rather than read the annual report. They often don't even bother to find out if the broker who sells them the stock really knows much about the company as a business, other than as a concept. Usually he doesn't.

Every good investor has specific, detailed knowledge of the companies he is interested in, has an idea of what the entire concern is worth, and thus knows what he can reasonably pay for 1 percent of it or 1 percent of 1 percent.

2. *Buy when stocks have few friends—particularly the stock in question.* One way of avoiding competition when buying is to have knowledge and nerve enough to buy good value when it's being dumped. Another is to know some class of company so well you're almost never outtraded.

3. *Be patient: don't be rattled by fluctuations.* They're to be expected, like rainy days. Particularly, don't sell just because a stock goes down from the amount at which you bought it, or when it thereafter recovers to your purchase price. Your cost is

an accident. It's not as if the stock knows about it and wants to cross you up; nor does the quotation affect the company's outlook. Watch the business, not the price.

4. *Invest, don't guess.* Swinging for the fences with a series of plausible half-baked speculations is fearfully expensive, both in the turnaround costs (brokerage and the spread between bid and asked prices, plus buying high and selling low) and perhaps even more so in opportunity cost. Trying, for instance, to catch the bounce off the bottom in a run-of-the-mill heavy industrial company without much intrinsic growth is fine for Larry Tisch, who has bought and sold companies for years and who doesn't want to hold anything forever; and fine for financial institutions that systematically cover every industry and know the values. But for the individual investor, even thinking about such things, let alone tying up money in them, prevents him from making the one great buy of an outstanding company, which is the best move most of us can hope for. Buffett's right: only buy something that you'd be perfectly happy to hold if the market shut down for ten years.

It's like your house. If you make a good buy of a house at $100,000, and then spend $50,000 adding a garage and improving things generally, you don't insist on knowing that you will immediately be able to sell it again for $150,000. You can have a reasonable expectation that should you need to sell again in the future and if you aren't in too much of a hurry, the market price will in due course reflect your additional investment. That's really all you have to know.

5. *High yields are often a trap.* The perfect company to invest in has opportunities to put its cash to work at very high rates of return: 15 percent, 20 percent, or better. Leave your money in the company to grow at that rate, rather than taking it out in taxable dividends and then putting what's left to work in bonds or another investment at a much lower real rate of return.

And many high-yield companies are Ponzi schemes anyway. A utility or domestic oil or chemical company that is adding to long-term debt faster than it's paying out cash in taxable dividends is on a fatal treadmill which must stop sooner or later. When it does the stock will take a beating.

6. *Only buy what's cheap right now, or almost sure to grow so fast that it very soon will have been cheap at today's price.* Sometimes, of course, you can get both. If for instance you buy a good bank stock at, say, two-thirds of hard book value (almost all cash or equivalents) and can determine that through reinvested earnings the value is growing at, say, 15 percent a year and paying a reasonable dividend, you're in fine shape. Someday, quite surely, the market will appraise the stock at two-thirds or more of its then much higher book value (15 percent growth compounded means doubling in about five years). Sooner or later it's likely to go to one times book value, or even 1.5 times. And of course the dividend should also double every five years or thereabouts, so whatever the market does you'll be all right, unless the world comes to an end. It sounds simple, and indeed it's not that complicated or difficult, if you confine yourself to realistic objectives, dealing with things you understand.

7. *If stocks in general don't seem cheap, stand aside.* The next bear market is rarely more than two or three years away.

8. *Keep an eye on what the master investors are doing.* They watch each other with keen attention, you may be sure. You can get the prospectuses and quarterly reports of the best funds just by asking for them. Buy a few shares of several, if you like. *Forbes* puts out an annual issue that analyzes fund performances over the previous years, from which you can get the names of the best ones. Other publications do the same on a smaller scale. My own "Smart Funds" column in *Forbes* regularly looks at what the most interesting fund managers are buying and selling.

9. *Buy investment management, if you find company analysis too difficult.* If you have $100,000 or less to invest, there's no chance that you can run your own portfolio as cheaply as you can buy management from outside. A good fund (or a good manager) costs around 1 percent, or $1,000 a year (tax deductible), for your $100,000. A sensible and industrious investor should be able to identify three or four good no-load or closed-end funds,

and through them get superior management. If the investor is good enough to analyze companies, then his time to do the job right will be worth more than $1,000; if he isn't that good, he should delegate the job anyway.

At what point does it become worth running your own money? At $200,000? $500,000? $1 million? There's no clear answer. Mostly it's a question of temperament. In general, humanity in its great choices responds to emotional needs rather than acting as the *homo economicus*. In practice, few large investors buy funds, and many hire professional managers. Probably, more of them should buy funds, rather than have professional counsel, but they want the personal, human reassurance that a counselor provides, like a doctor or priest. Also, the substantial investor likes to discuss with someone he has learned to trust whether his overall situation and point of view seem reasonable, and whether there aren't different ideas he should be considering in trust and estate matters, insurance, and other areas. After a certain level investment counsel includes quite a lot of personal financial planning.

Investment counselors are often inhibited in recommending funds run by other investment counselors out of a fear of seeming to endorse a competitor and a reluctance to have two levels of fees. For instance, if I buy Templeton Growth Fund for a client as a way of getting Templeton's management of a portfolio, the client may reasonably ask if I couldn't invest straight in the underlying holdings, saving Templeton's fees and costs. In general, he's right.

But there's every reason for the client to buy some Templeton on his own, saving my fees, and hold it outside of his professionally managed account. Reading what the managements have to say and trying to think through the logic of their investment moves ("reverse engineering," as it's called) will give him additional perspective.

10. *Decide on an appropriate investment strategy, and concentrate on it.* As to the choice of a "cheap right now" or "growth for the future" philosophy—assuming you can't get both—you must match your approach to three things:

a) your experience and skill (including how much time you can spend on this subject);

b) your tolerance for low yield and volatility, the two penalties of growth investing; and

c) your tax bracket. For instance, it makes no sense for a tax-free institution to buy municipal bonds, which are priced higher than corporates because of their tax exemption, and similarly it rarely makes sense for a tax-paying individual to hold preferred stocks, which are priced to yield less than debentures of comparable risk because they are largely tax-free in the hands of a corporate investor.

By the same token, it makes less sense for a high-bracket investor to look for cheap stocks he hopes to sell profitably a few years later—which if he succeeds will involve regular payment of capital gains taxes—than to buy a selection of "Price" companies that he may be able to hold for many years. Also, once the substantial investor has a big stake in a particular company he can justify taking time to understand that company fully and following it closely until he becomes desensitized to quotational fluctuations. A small investor can't justify spending (or paying someone else to spend) hundreds of hours studying a situation—particularly when by no means all such studies result in a positive conclusion. However, from a number of sources (see Appendixes VI, VII and VIII) he can come by the information he needs to buy a diversified spread of "Graham" investments that he won't have to study in detail and is unlikely to lose money on. So the small investor and the tax-free or institutional investor seem like the natural candidates for the Graham approach, and the large tax-paying investor for the Buffett-Price approach.

11. *Be Flexible.* Templeton, Tisch, and Wilson are right. The old order, as its principles are overused, must always yield place to the new—not that the new is ever really new.

From Theory to Practice

So much for the theory. Now, and more difficult: can you in practice follow the strategy you choose? There are both intellectual and emotional sides to the question, and they are closely linked. The more you know your subject, the less tempted you are to make irrational moves.

1. *Value Investing.* It seems to me—having worked with serious investors for many years—that there's no doubt the "Graham" approach can be executed with adequate success by any reader of this book who has made it to this point and has understood what he has read, as long as he reinforces his understanding with a study of Graham's *The Intelligent Investor,* and, if he is up to it, *Security Analysis.* At a guess I'd say that he should do a good 20 percent better than the market over a long period—although not during the most dynamic period of a bull market—*if he is rigorous about applying the method.* He must let no trace of sentiment intrude: he must never buy a stock because the idea appeals to him or fail to buy one because he finds it repellent. (In 1977 I bought Hillenbrand, a coffin manufacturer, for my wife, who made me sell it again. In 1978 it went up 50 percent, while the market declined). And of course he must have enough diversification to let the method work.

The charm of the Graham method is its mechanical simplicity. Anybody can do it. If many ever do, however, it won't work as well, because fewer stocks will get down to the point at which they meet his buying criteria, and there'll be a shortage of opportunities. But that time is not yet. And there will probably always be opportunities at the bottom of the four-year cycle, or whatever future cycles bear markets come in. Graham only tells us how low is low, based on history. One might similarly define how poor is poor in America or how cold is cold in the winter. But poverty and weather have both changed, and the standard limits of market fluctuations can also change.

The Graham approach seems particularly appropriate to institutional portfolios, such as bank-managed pension funds. The method is obviously "prudent" and systematic—bankerly, in fact. It deals with the here and now. Banks are in an unusually good position to assess the financial situation of companies—it's their daily business. And the capital gains tax penalties of the method won't bother a tax-free portfolio. A bank can execute such a program in-house, keeping costs down and preserving confidentiality, and it won't have to rationalize specific stocks to a client company's investment committee—only the method in general. Obviously, any large move toward "Graham" investing by even one bank will bring more money into this approach than has ever been dedicated to it and thus bring that much closer the day when the criteria will have to be changed; so far, however, that's never happened.

Further, if the criterion of "net current assets" becomes too popular and the opportunities dry up, the bank can go back to traditional ratio analysis of the type set out in *Security Analysis*, which can readily be done by a computer. In this analysis the institution can make full use of its inherent advantages over the private investor: a much larger continuing research capability, and training and experience in dispassionate evaluation. A financial institution gives up its built-in strengths when it departs from this approach, like a giraffe foraging under bushes instead of among high branches.

And the great merit of the Graham variation of the "value" strategy is that you can't lose any significant amount of money. Sooner or later objects selling well below their intrinsic value recover to their normal levels.

That idea is so simple that an investor who follows it can probably stick to his plan, even if he experiences setbacks en route. And as he gets used to the system, more and more he'll recognize fire sales as buying opportunities rather than an occasions for panic.

2. *Growth Investing.* For the substantial tax-paying investor I think the Fisher-Price approach is best, if possible applying Buffett criteria, if he really can do it himself or can hire someone competent to do it for him, either directly or through a mutual fund.

It does, however, offer a chance to lose money toward the end of a major bull market. Almost nobody—certainly not most fund managers—has the tough independence of spirit to get off the bandwagon when it is in full career.

A hot investment manager working for a big cut of the realized profits can put a fortune in his pocket in one year toward the end of a bull market, without having to disgorge it when the collapse follows, so he's very tempted to overstay the party. Even experienced professional men may well leave an investment advisor who "only" made them 30 percent in one year during a bull market to join one who has made their brother-in-law 45 percent by loading him up with frothy junk of uncertain value.

So the substantial investor dealing with an outside investment advisor must, in my opinion, impose his own restraints on the operation, based on his own wisdom and common sense.

Equally, however, he can *make* exceptional profits by buying authentic growth stocks during market collapses; that, indeed, is in my opinion the most practical strategy for the substantial experienced investor. And once he has acquired a portfolio of such issues during a bear market washout, the investor can if he likes forget the vagaries of the market and stay aboard the growth escalator. He must, of course, make sure that the values are actually still building. He can determine that by watching the profit margins, the growth of unit sales, the return on equity, and so on—all of which he can easily find in *Value Line*.

While this is a perfectly realistic approach, he should also always keep enough liquid reserves to see him through any likely emergency, and to provide ammunition for targets of opportunity. And a comfortable reserve means that the investor doesn't panic in bad times. He can, indeed, look forward to the possibility of acquiring some fantastic bargains, the foundation of a real fortune, if he has reserves to spend during a first-class panic.

That brings us to the emotional demands made on the investor by the "growth" approach. It doesn't do much good to know all the rules if you do not know the specifics, and during a major decline become panicked into selling at the bottom.

So you must ask yourself when adopting the growth philosophy, do I know enough about this company so that I can put up with the lack of yield and the quotational volatility that are the price of growth investing? If you don't know what you have, you're much more tempted to buy when a stock is popular—meaning when it is too high-priced—and then dump it if it falls: the opposite of the profitable strategy. So look over Fisher's tests of good management, for instance, and Price and Buffett's main principles. If you or your advisor have asked most of those questions and are satisfied by the answers, then you should have the confidence to hold on through bad times.

APPENDIXES

APPENDIXES

APPENDIX I: BUFFETT ON BONDS

BUFFETT PARTNERSHIP, LTD.

810 KIEWIT PLAZA

OMAHA, NEBRASKA 68131

TELEPHONE 342-4110

WARREN E. BUFFETT, GENERAL PARTNER
WILLIAM SCOTT
JOHN M. HARDING

February 25th, 1970

To My Partners:

This letter will attempt to provide a very elementary education regarding tax-exempt bonds with emphasis on the types and maturities of bonds which we expect to help partners in purchasing next month. I have tried to boil this letter down as much as possible. Some of it will be a little weighty—some a little oversimplified. I apologize for the shortcomings in advance. I have a feeling I am trying to put all the meat of a 100-page book in 10 pages—and have it read like the funny papers.

The Mechanics of Tax-Free Bonds

For those who wish our help, we will arrange the purchase of bonds directly from municipal bond dealers throughout the country and have them confirm sale of the bonds directly to you. The confirmation should be saved as a basic document for tax purposes. You should not send a check to the bond dealer since he will deliver the bonds to your bank, along with a draft which the bank will pay by charging your account with them. In the case of bonds purchased in the secondary market (issues already outstanding), this settlement date will usually be about a week after confirmation date whereas, on new issues, the settlement date may be as much as a month later. The settlement date is shown plainly on the confirmation ticket (in the case of new issues this will be the second and final ticket rather than the preliminary "when issued" ticket), and you should have the funds at your bank ready to pay for the bonds on the settlement date. If you presently own Treasury Bills, they can be sold on a couple of days notice by your bank upon your instructions, so you should experience no problems in having the money available on time. Interest begins to accrue to you on the settlement date, even if the bond dealer is late in getting them delivered to your bank. Bonds will be delivered in negotiable form (so-called "bearer" form which makes them like currency) with coupons attached. Usually the bonds are in $5,000 denominations and frequently they can be exchanged for registered bonds (sometimes at considerable expense and sometimes free—it depends upon the terms). Bonds in registered form are nonnegotiable without assignment by you, since you are the registered owner on the Transfer Agent's books. Bonds trade almost exclusively on a bearer basis and it is virtually impossible to sell registered bonds without converting them back into bearer form. Thus, unless you are going to own great physical quantities of bonds, I recommend keeping bonds in bearer form. This means keeping them in a very safe place and clipping the coupons every six months. Such coupons, when clipped, can be deposited in your bank account just like checks. If you have $250,000 in bonds, this probably means about fifty separate pieces of paper ($5,000 denominations) and perhaps six or eight trips a year to the safe deposit section to cut and deposit coupons.

It is also possible to open a custody account with a bank where, for a fairly nominal cost, they will keep the bonds, collect the interest, and preserve your records for you. For example, a bank will probably perform the custodial service for you for about $200 a year on a $250,000 portfolio. If you are interested in a custodial account, you should talk to a trust officer at your commercial bank as to the nature of their services and cost. Otherwise, you should have a safe-deposit box.

Taxation

The interest received upon the deposit of coupons from tax-free bonds is, of course, free from federal income taxes. This means if you are at a 30% top federal income tax bracket, a 6% return from tax-free bonds is equivalent to about 8½% from taxable bonds. Thus, for most of our partners, excluding minors and some retired people, tax-free bonds will be more attractive than taxable bonds. For people with little or no income from wages or dividends, but with substantial capital, it is possible that a combination of taxable bonds (to bring taxable income up to about the 25% or 30% bracket) plus tax-free bonds will bring the highest total after-tax income. Where appropriate, we will work with you to achieve such a balance.

The situation in respect to state income taxes is more complicated. In Nebraska, where the state income tax is computed as a percentage of the federal income tax, the effect is that there is no state tax on interest from tax-free bonds. My understanding of both the New York and California law is that tax-free bonds of entities within the home state are not subject to state income tax, but tax-free bonds from other states are subject to the local state income tax. I also believe that the New York City income tax exempts tax-free bonds of entities based within the state of New York, but taxes those from other states. I am no expert on state income taxes and make no attempt to post myself on changes taking place within the various states or cities. Therefore, I defer to your local tax advisor, but simply mention these few general impressions so that you will be alert to the existence of a potential problem. In Nebraska there is no need to have any local considerations enter into the after-tax calculation. Where out-of-state issues are subject to local taxation, the effective cost of your state or municipal income tax is reduced by the benefit received from deducting it on your federal income tax return. This, of course, varies with the individual. Additionally, in some states there are various taxes on intangible property which may apply to all tax-free bonds or just those of out-of-state entities. There are none of these in Nebraska, but I cannot advise on the other states.

When bonds are bought at a discount from par and later are sold or mature (come due and get paid), the difference between the proceeds and cost is subject to capital gain or loss treatment. (There are minor exceptions to this statement as, unfortunately, there are to most general statements on investments and taxes but they will be pointed out to you should they affect any securities we recommend.) This reduces the net after-tax yield by a factor involving the general rate of future capital gains taxes and the specific future tax position of the individual. Later on, we will discuss the impact of such capital gains taxes in calculating the relative attractiveness of discount bonds versus "full coupon" bonds.

Finally, one most important point. Although the law is not completely clear, you should probably not contemplate owning tax-free bonds if you have, or expect to have, general purpose bank or other indebtedness. The law excludes the deductibility of interest on loans incurred or continued to purchase or carry tax-free bonds, and the interpretation of this statute will probably tend to be broadened as the years pass. For example, my impression is that you have no problem if you have a mortgage against real property (unless the debt was incurred in order to acquire municipal bonds) in deducting the mortgage interest on your federal tax return, even though you own tax-free bonds at the same time. However, I believe that if you have a general bank loan, even though the proceeds were directly used to purchase stocks, a handball court, etc. and the tax-free bonds are not used for security for the loan, you are asking for trouble if you deduct the interest and, at the same time, are the owner of tax-free bonds. Therefore, I would pay off bank loans before owning tax-free bonds, but I leave detailed examination of this question to you and your tax advisor. I merely mention it to make you aware of the potential problem.

Marketability

Tax-free bonds are materially different from common stocks or corporate bonds in that there are literally hundreds of thousands of issues, with the great majority having very few holders. This substantially inhibits the development of close, active markets. Whenever the city of New York or Philadelphia wants to raise money it sells perhaps twenty, thirty or forty nonidentical securities, since it will offer an issue with that many different maturities. A 6% bond of New York coming due in 1980 is a different animal from a 6% bond of New York coming due in 1981. One cannot be exchanged for the other, and a seller has to find a buyer for the specific item he holds. When you consider that New York may offer bonds several times a year, it is easy to see why just this one city may have somewhere in the neighborhood of 1,000 issues outstanding. Grand Island, Nebraska, may have 75 issues outstanding. The average amount of each issue might be $100,000 and the average number of holders may be six or eight per issue. Thus, it is absolutely impossible to have quoted markets at all times for all issues and spreads between bids and offers may be very wide. You can't set forth in the morning to buy a specific Grand Island issue of your choosing. It may not be offered at any price, anywhere, and if you do find one seller, there is no reason why he has to be realistic compared to other offerings of similar quality. On the other hand, there are single issues such as those of the Ohio Turnpike, Illinois Turnpike, etc. that amount to $200 million or more and have thousands of bondholders owning a single entirely homogeneous and interchangeable issue. Obviously, here you get a high degree of marketability.

Marketability is generally a function of the following three items, in descending order of importance: (1) the size of the particular issue; (2) the size of the issuer (a $100,000 issue of the state of Ohio will be more marketable than a $100,000 issue of Podunk, Ohio); and (3) the quality of the issuer. By far the most sales effort goes into the selling of new issues of bonds. An average of over $200 million per week of new issues comes up for sale, and the machinery of bond distribution is geared to get them sold, large or small. In my opinion, there is frequently insufficient differential in yield at time of issue for the marketability differences that will exist once the initial sales push is terminated. We have frequently run into markets in bonds where the spread between bid and asked prices may get to 15%. There is no need to buy bonds with the potential for such grotesque markets (although the profit spread to the dealer who originally offers them is frequently wider than on more marketable bonds) and we will not be buying them for you. The bonds we expect to buy will usually tend to have spreads (reflecting the difference between what you would pay net for such bonds on purchase and receive net on sale at the same point in time) of from 2% to 5%. Such a spread would be devastating if you attempted to trade in such bonds, but I don't believe it should be a deterrent for a long-term investor. The real necessity is to stay away from bonds of very limited marketability—which frequently are the type local bond dealers have the greatest monetary incentive to push.

Specific Areas of Purchase

We will probably concentrate our purchases in the following general areas:

(1) Large revenue-producing public entities such as toll roads, electric power districts, water districts, etc. Many of these issues possess high marketability, are subject to quantitative analysis, and sometimes have favorable sinking funds or other factors which tend not to receive full valuation in the marketplace.

(2) Industrial Development Authority bonds which arise when a public entity holds title to property leased to a private corporation. For example, Lorain, Ohio, holds title to an $80 million project for U.S. Steel Corp. The development authority board issued bonds to pay for the project and has executed a net and absolute lease with U.S. Steel to cover the bond payments. The credit of the city or state is not behind the bonds and they are only as good as the company that is on the lease. Many top-grade corporations stand behind an aggregate of several billion dollars of these obligations, although new ones are being issued only in small amounts ($5 million per project or less) because of changes in the tax laws. For a period of time there was a very substantial prejudice against such issues, causing them to sell at yields considerably higher than those commensurate with their inherent credit standing. This prejudice has tended to diminish, reducing the premium yields available, but I still consider it a most attractive field. Our insurance company owns a majority of its bonds in this category.

(3) Public Housing Authority issues for those of you who wish the very highest grade of tax-free bonds. In effect, these bonds bear

the guarantee of the U.S. Government, so they are all rated AAA. In states where local taxes put a premium on buying in-state issues, and I can't fill your needs from (1) and (2), my tendency would be to put you into Housing Authority issues rather than try to select from among credits that I don't understand. If you direct me to buy obligations of your home state, you should expect substantial quantities of Housing Authority issues. There is no need to diversify among such issues, as they all represent the top credit available.

(4) State obligations of a direct or indirect nature.

You will notice I am not buying issues of large cities. I don't have the faintest idea how to analyze a New York City, Chicago, Philadelphia, etc. (a friend mentioned the other day when Newark was trying to sell bonds at a very fancy rate that the Mafia was getting very upset because Newark was giving them a bad name). Your analysis of a New York City—and I admit it is hard to imagine them not paying their bills for any extended period of time—would be as good as mine. My approach to bonds is pretty much like my approach to stocks. If I can't understand something, I tend to forget it. Passing an opportunity which I don't understand—even if someone else is perceptive enough to analyze it and get paid well for doing it—doesn't bother me. We will probably tend to purchase somewhere between five and ten issues for most of you. We will try not to buy in smaller than $25,000 pieces and will prefer larger amounts where appropriate. Smaller lots of bonds are usually penalized upon resale, sometimes substantially. The bond salesman doesn't usually explain this to you when you buy the $10,000 of bonds from him, but it gets explained when you later try to sell the $10,000 to him. We may make exceptions where we are buying secondary market issues in smaller pieces—but only if we are getting an especially good price on the buy side because of the small size of the offering.

Callable Bonds

We will not buy bonds where the issuer of the bonds has a right to call (retire) the bonds on a basis which substantially loads the contract in his favor. It is amazing to me to see people buy bonds which are due in forty years, but where the issuer has the right to call the bonds at a tiny premium in five or ten years. Such a contract essentially means that you have made a forty-year deal if it is advantageous to the issuer (and disadvantageous to you) and a five-year deal if the initial contract turns out to be advantageous to you (and disadvantageous to the issuer).

Such contracts are really outrageous and exist because bond investors can't think through the implications of such a contract form and bond dealers don't insist on better terms for their customers. One extremely interesting fact is that bonds with very unattractive call features sell at virtually the same yield as otherwise identical bonds which are noncallable.

It should be pointed out that most Nebraska bonds carry highly unfair call provisions. Despite this severe contractual disadvantage, they do not offer higher yields than bonds with more equitable terms. One way to avoid this problem is to buy bonds which are totally noncallable. Another way is to buy discount bonds where the right of the issuer to call the bond is at a price so far above your cost as to render the possible call inconsequential. If you buy a bond at 60 which is callable at 103, the effective cost to you of granting the issuer the right to prematurely terminate the contract (which is a right you never have) is insignificant. But to buy a bond of the Los Angeles Department of Water and Power at 100 to come due at 100 in 1999 or to come due at 104 in 1974, depending on which is to the advantage of the issuer and to your disadvantage, is the height of foolishness when comparable yields are available on similar credits without such an unfair contract. Nevertheless, just such a bond was issued in October 1969 and similar bonds continue to be issued every day. I only write at such length about an obvious point since it is apparent from the continual sale of such bonds that many investors haven't the faintest notion how this loads the dice against them and many bonds salesmen aren't about to tell them.

Maturity and the Mathematics of Bonds

Many people, in buying bonds, select maturities based on how long they think they are going to want to hold bonds, how long they are going to live, etc. While this is not a silly approach, it is not necessarily the most logical. The primary determinants in selection of maturity should probably be (1) the shape of the yield curve; (2) your expectations regarding future levels of interest rates; and (3) the degree of quotational fluctuation you are willing to endure or hope to possibly profit from. Of course, (2) is the most important but by far the most difficult upon which to comment intelligently.

Let's tackle the yield curve first. When other aspects of quality are identical, there will be a difference in interest rates paid based upon the length of the bond being offered. For example, a top-grade bond being offered now might have a yield of 4.75% if it came due in six or nine months, 5.00% in two years, 5.25% in five years, 5.50% in ten years, and 6.25% in twenty years. When long rates are substantially higher than short rates, the curve is said to be strongly positive. In the U.S. Government bond market, rates recently have tended to produce a negative yield curve; that is, a long-term Government bond over the last year or so has consistently yielded less than a short-term one. Sometimes the yield curve has been very flat, and sometimes it is positive out to a given point, such as ten years, and then flattens out. What you should understand is that it varies, often very substantially, and that on an historical basis the present slope tends to be in the high positive range. This doesn't mean that long bonds are going to be worth more but it does mean that you are being paid more to extend maturity than in many periods. If yields remained constant for several years, you would do better with longer bonds than shorter bonds, regardless of how long you intended to hold them. The second factor in determining maturity selection is expectations regarding future rate levels. Anyone who has done much predicting in this field has tended to look very foolish very fast. I did not regard rates as unattractive one year ago, and I was proved very wrong almost immediately. I believe present rates are not unattractive and I may look foolish again. Nevertheless, a decision has to be made and you can make just as great a mistake if you buy short-term securities now and rates available on reinvestment in a few years are much lower.

The final factor involves your tolerance for quotational fluctuation. This involves the mathematics of bond investment and may be a little difficult for you to understand. Nevertheless, it is important that you get a general grasp of the principles. Let's assume for the moment a perfectly flat yield curve and a noncallable bond. Further assume present rates are 5% and that you buy two bonds, one due in two years and one due in twenty years. Now assume one year later that yields on new issues have gone to 3% and that you wish to sell your bonds. Forgetting about market spreads, commissions, etc. you will receive $1,019.60 for the original two-year $1,000 bond (now with one year to run) and $1,288.10 for the nineteen-year bond (originally twenty years). At these prices, a purchaser will get exactly 3% on his money after amortizing the premium he has paid and cashing the stream of 5% coupons attached to each bond. It is a matter of indifference to him whether to buy your nineteen-year 5% bond at $1,288.10 or a new 3% bond (which we have assumed is the rate current—one year later) at $1,000.00. On the other hand, let's assume rates went to 7%. Again we will ignore commissions, capital gains taxes on the discount, etc. Now the buyer will only pay $981 for the bond with one year remaining until maturity and $791.00 for the bond with nineteen years left. Since he can get 7% on new issues, he is only willing to buy your bond at a discount sufficient so that accrual of this discount will give him the same economic benefits from your 5% coupon that a 7% coupon at $1,000 would give him.

The principle is simple. The wider the swings in interest rates and the longer the bond, the more the value of a bond can go up or down on an interim basis before maturity. It should be pointed out in the first example where rates went to 3%, our long-term bond would only have appreciated to about $1,070 if it had been callable in five years at par, although it would have gone down just as much if 7% rates had occurred. This just illustrates the inherent unfairness of call provisions.

For over two decades, interest rates on tax-free bonds have almost continuously gone higher and buyers of long-term bonds have continuously suffered. This does not mean it is bad now to buy long-term bonds—it simply means that the illustration in the above paragraph has worked in only one direction for a long period of time and people are much more conscious of the downside risks from higher rates than the upside potential from lower ones. If it is a fifty-fifty chance as to the future general level of interest rates and the yield curve is substantially positive, then the odds are better in buying long-term noncallable bonds than shorter-term ones. This reflects my current conclusion and, therefore, I intend to buy bonds within the ten-to-twenty-five-year range. If you decide to buy a twenty-year bond and hold the bond straight through, you are going to get the concentrated rate of interest, but if you sell earlier, you are going to be subject to the mathematical forces I have described, for better or for worse.

Bond prices also change because of changes in quality over the years but, in the tax-free area, this has tended to be—and probably will continue to be—a relatively minor factor compared to the impact of changes in the general structure of interest rates.

Discount Versus Full Coupon Bonds

You will have noticed in the above discussion that if you now wanted to buy a 7% return on a nineteen-year bond, you'd have a choice between buying a new nineteen-year bond with a 7% coupon rate or buying a bond with a 5% coupon at $791.60, which would pay you $1,000 in nineteen years. Either purchase would have yielded exactly 7% compounded semiannually to you. Mathematically, they are the same. In the case of tax-free bonds the equation is complicated, however, by the fact that the $70 coupon is entirely tax-free to you, whereas the bond purchased at a discount gives you tax-free income of $50 per year but

a capital gain at the end of the nineteenth year of $208.40. Under the
present tax law, you would owe anything from a nominal tax, if the
gain from realization of the discount was your only taxable income in
the nineteenth year, up to a tax of over $70 if it came on top of very
large amounts of capital gain at that time (the new tax law provides
for capital gain rates of 35%, and even slightly higher on an indirect
basis in 1972 and thereafter for those realizing very large gains). In
addition to this, you might have some state taxes to pay on the capital
gain.

Obviously, under these circumstances you are not going to pay the
$791.60 for the 5% coupon and feel you are equally as well off as with
the 7% coupon at $1,000. Neither is anyone else. Therefore, identical
quality securities with identical maturities sell at considerably higher
gross yields when they have low coupons and are priced at discounts
than if they bear current high coupons.

Interestingly enough, for most taxpayers, such higher gross yields over-
compensate for the probable tax to be paid. This is due to several factors.
First, no one knows what the tax law will be when the bonds mature
and it is both natural and probably correct to assume the tax rate will
be stiffer at that time than now. Second, even though a 5% coupon on
a $1,000 bond purchased at $791.60 due in nineteen years is the equivalent of a 7% coupon on a $1,000 bond purchased at par with the same
maturity, people prefer to get the higher current return in their pocket.
The owner of the 5% coupon bond is only getting around 6.3% current
yield on his $791.60 with the balance necessary to get him up to 7%
coming from the extra $208.40 he picks up at the end. Finally, the most
important factor affecting prices currently on discount bonds (and which
will keep affecting them) is that banks have been taken out of the market
as buyers of discount tax-free bonds by changes brought about in bank
tax treatment through the 1969 Tax Reform Act. Banks have historically
been the largest purchasers and owners of tax-free bonds and anything
that precludes them from one segment of the market has dramatic effects
on the supply-demand situation in that segment. This may tend to give
some edge to individuals in the discount tax-free market, particularly
those who are not likely to be in a high tax bracket when the bonds
mature or are sold.

If I can get a significantly higher effective after-tax yield (allowing
for sensible estimates of your particular future tax-rate possibilities), I
intend to purchase discount bonds for you.

You should realize that because of the enormous diversity of issues
mentioned earlier, it is impossible to say just what will be bought. Sometimes the tax-free bond market has more similarities to real estate than

to stocks. There are hundreds of thousands of items of varying comparability, some with no sellers, and some with reluctant sellers and some with eager sellers. Which may be the best buy depends on the quality of what is being offered, how well it fits your needs, and the eagerness of the seller. The standard of comparison is always new issues where an average of several hundred million dollars worth have to be sold each week—however, specific secondary market opportunities (issues already outstanding) may be more attractive than new issues and we can only find out how attractive they are when we are ready to make bids.

APPENDIX II: EXTRACTS FROM THE 1978 ANNUAL RE-PORT OF BERKSHIRE HATHAWAY, INC.

Sources of Earnings

To give you a better picture of just where Berkshire's earnings are produced, we show [opposite] a table which requires a little explanation. Berkshire owns close to 58% of Blue Chip which, in addition to 100% ownership of several businesses, owns 80% of Wesco Financial Corporation. Thus, Berkshire's equity in Wesco's earnings is about 46%. In aggregate, businesses that we control have about 7,000 full-time employees and generate revenues of over $500 million.

The table shows the overall earnings of each major operating category on a pre-tax basis (several of the businesses have low tax rates because of significant amounts of tax-exempt interest and dividend income), as well as the share of those earnings belonging to Berkshire both on a pre-tax and after-tax basis. Significant capital gains or losses attributable to any of the businesses are not shown in the operating earnings figure, but are aggregated on the "Realized Securities Gain" line at the bottom of the table. Because of various accounting and tax intricacies, the figures in the table should not be treated as holy writ, but rather viewed as close approximations of the 1977 and 1978 earnings contributions of our constituent businesses.

Blue Chip and Wesco are public companies with reporting requirements of their own. [In] this report we are reproducing the narrative reports of the principal executives of both companies, describing their 1978 operations. Some of the figures they utilize will not match to the penny the ones we use in this report, again because of accounting and tax complexities. But their comments should be helpful to you in understanding the underlying economic characteristics of these important partly-owned businesses.

Textiles

Earnings of $1.3 million in 1978, while much improved from 1977, still represent a low return on the $17 million of capital employed in this business. Textile plant and equipment are on the books for a very small fraction of what it would cost to replace such equipment today. And, despite the age of the equipment, much of it is functionally similar to new equipment being installed by the industry. But despite this "bar-

(in thousands of dollars)	Earnings Before Income Taxes				Net Earnings After Tax	
	Total		Berkshire Share		Berkshire Share	
	1978	1977	1978	1977	1978	1977
Total—all entities	$66,180	$57,089	$54,350	$42,234	$39,242	$30,393
Earnings from operations:						
Insurance Group:						
Underwriting	$ 3,001	$ 5,802	$ 3,000	$ 5,802	$ 1,560	$ 3,017
Net investment income	19,705	12,804	19,691	12,804	16,400	11,360
Berkshire-Waumbec textiles	2,916	(620)	2,916	(620)	1,342	(322)
Associated Retail Stores, Inc.	2,757	2,775	2,757	2,775	1,176	1,429
See's Candies	12,416	12,840	6,976	6,598	3,033	2,974
Buffalo Evening News	(2,913)	751	(1,637)	389	(738)	158
Blue Chip Stamps—Parent	2,133	1,091	1,198	566	1,382	892
Illinois National Bank and Trust Company	4,822	3,800	4,710	3,706	4,262	3,288
Wesco Financial Corporation—Parent	1,771	2,006	777	813	665	419
Mutual Savings and Loan Association	10,556	6,779	4,638	2,747	3,042	1,946
Interest on Debt	(5,500)	(5,302)	(4,509)	(4,255)	(2,333)	(2,129)
Other	720	165	438	102	261	48
Total Earnings from Operations	$52,384	$42,891	$40,955	$31,427	$30,052	$23,080
Realized Securities Gain	13,796	14,198	13,395	10,807	9,190	7,313
Total Earnings	$66,180	$57,089	$54,350	$42,234	$39,242	$30,393

gain cost" of fixed assets, capital turnover is relatively low, reflecting required high investment levels in receivables and inventory compared to sales. Slow capital turnover, coupled with low profit margins on sales, inevitably produces inadequate returns on capital. Obvious approaches to improved profit margins involve differentiation of product, lowered manufacturing costs through more efficient equipment or better utilization of people, redirection toward fabrics enjoying stronger market trends, etc. Our management is diligent in pursuing such objectives. The problem, of course, is that our competitors are just as diligently doing the same thing.

The textile industry illustrates in textbook style how producers of relatively undifferentiated goods in capital intensive businesses must earn inadequate returns except under conditions of tight supply or real shortage. As long as excess productive capacity exists, prices tend to reflect direct operating costs rather than capital employed. Such a supply-excess condition appears likely to prevail most of the time in the textile industry, and our expectations are for profits of relatively modest amounts in relation to capital.

We hope we don't get into too many more businesses with such tough economic characteristics. But, as we have stated before: (1) our textile businesses are very important employers in their communities, (2) management has been straightforward in reporting on problems and energetic in attacking them, (3) labor has been cooperative and understanding in facing our common problems, and (4) the business should average modest cash returns relative to investment. As long as these conditions prevail—and we expect that they will—we intend to continue to support our textile business despite more attractive alternative uses for capital.

Insurance Underwriting

The number one contributor to Berkshire's overall excellent results in 1978 was the segment of National Indemnity Company's insurance operation run by Phil Liesche. On about $90 million of earned premiums, an underwriting profit of approximately $11 million was realized, a truly extraordinary achievement even against the background of excellent industry conditions. Under Phil's leadership, with outstanding assistance by Roland Miller in Underwriting and Bill Lyons in Claims, this segment of National Indemnity (including National Fire and Marine Insurance Company, which operates as a running mate) had one of its best years in a long history of performances which, in aggregate, far outshine those of the industry. Present successes reflect credit not only upon present

managers, but equally upon the business talents of Jack Ringwalt, founder
of National Indemnity, whose operating philosophy remains etched upon
the company.

George Young's reinsurance department continues to produce very
large sums for investment relative to premium volume, and thus gives
us reasonably satisfactory overall results. However, underwriting results
still are not what they should be and can be. It is very easy to fool
yourself regarding underwriting results in reinsurance (particularly in
casualty lines involving long delays in settlement), and we believe this
situation prevails with many of our competitors. Unfortunately, self-
delusion in company reserving almost always leads to inadequate industry rate levels. If major factors in the market don't know their true
costs, the competitive "fall-out" hits all—even those with adequate cost
knowledge. George is quite willing to reduce volume significantly, if
needed, to achieve satisfactory underwriting, and we have a great deal
of confidence in the long-term soundness of this business under his
direction.

Although some segments were disappointing, overall our insurance
operation had an excellent year. But of course we should expect a good
year when the industry is flying high, as in 1978. It is a virtual certainty
that in 1979 the combined ratio for the industry will move up at least
a few points, perhaps enough to throw the industry as a whole into an
underwriting loss position. For example, in the auto lines—by far the
most important area for the industry and for us—CPI figures indicate
rates overall were only 3% higher in January 1979 than a year ago.
But the items that make up loss costs—auto repair and medical care
costs—were up over 9%. How different than year-end 1976 when rates
had advanced over 22% in the preceeding twelve months, but costs
were up 8%.

Margins will remain steady only if rates rise as fast as costs. This as-
suredly will not be the case in 1979, and conditions probably will worsen
in 1980. Our present thinking is that our underwriting performance
relative to the industry will improve somewhat in 1979, but every other
insurance management probably views its relative prospects with similar
optimism—someone is going to be disappointed. Even if we do improve
relative to others, we may well have a higher combined ratio and lower
underwriting profits in 1979 than we achieved last year.

We continue to look for ways to expand our insurance operation. But
your reaction to this intent should not be unrestrained joy. Some of
our expansion efforts—largely initiated by your Chairman—have been
lackluster, others have been expensive failures. We entered the business

in 1967 through purchase of the segment which Phil Liesche now manages, and it still remains, by a large margin, the best portion of our insurance business. It is not easy to buy a good insurance business, but our experience has been that it is easier to buy one than create one. However, we will continue to try both approaches, since the rewards for success in this field can be exceptional.

Insurance Investments

We confess considerable optimism regarding our insurance equity investments. Of course, our enthusiasm for stocks is not unconditional. Under some circumstances, common stock investments by insurers make very little sense.

We get excited enough to commit a big percentage of insurance company net worth to equities only when we find (1) businesses we can understand, (2) with favorable long-term prospects, (3) operated by honest and competent people, (4) priced very attractively. We usually can identify a small number of potential investments meeting requirements (1), (2) and (3), but (4) often prevents action. For example, in 1971 our total common stock position at Berkshire's insurance subsidiaries amounted to only $10.7 million at cost, and $11.7 million at market. There were equities of identifiably excellent companies available—but very few at interesting prices. (An irresistible footnote: in 1971, pension fund managers invested a record 122% of net funds available in equities—at full prices they couldn't buy enough of them. In 1974, after the bottom had fallen out, they committed a then record low of 21% to stocks.)

The past few years have been a different story for us. At the end of 1975 our insurance subsidiaries held common equities with a market value exactly equal to cost of $39.3 million. At the end of 1978 this position had been increased to equities (including a convertible preferred) with a cost of $129.1 million and a market value of $216.5 million. During the intervening three years we also had realized pre-tax gains from common equities of approximately $24.7 million. Therefore, our overall unrealized and realized pre-tax gains in equities for the three-year period came to approximately $112 million. During this same interval the Dow Jones Industrial Average declined from 852 to 805. It was a marvelous period for the value-oriented equity buyer.

We continue to find for our insurance portfolios small portions of really outstanding businesses that are available, through the auction pricing mechanism of security markets, at prices dramatically cheaper than the valuations inferior businesses command on negotiated sales.

This program of acquisition of small fractions of businesses (common stocks) at bargain prices, for which little enthusiasm exists, contrasts sharply with general corporate acquisition activity, for which much enthusiasm exists. It seems quite clear to us that either corporations are making very significant mistakes in purchasing entire businesses at prices prevailing in negotiated transactions and takeover bids, or that we eventually are going to make considerable sums of money buying small portions of such businesses at the greatly discounted valuations prevailing in the stock market. (A second footnote: in 1978 pension managers, a group that logically should maintain the longest of investment perspectives, put only 9% of net available funds into equities—breaking the record low figure set in 1974 and tied in 1977.)

We are not concerned with whether the market quickly revalues upward securities that we believe are selling at bargain prices. In fact, we prefer just the opposite since, in most years, we expect to have funds available to be a net buyer of securities. And consistent attractive purchasing is likely to prove to be of more eventual benefit to us than any selling opportunities provided by a short-term run-up in stock prices to levels at which we are unwilling to continue buying.

Our policy is to concentrate holdings. We try to avoid buying a little of this or that when we are only lukewarm about the business or its price. When we are convinced as to attractiveness, we believe in buying worthwhile amounts.

Equity holdings of our insurance companies with a market value of over $8 million on December 31, 1978 were as follows:

No. of Shares	Company	Cost	Market
		(000's omitted)	
246,450	American Broadcasting Companies, Inc.	$ 6,082	$ 8,626
1,294,308	Government Employees Insurance Company Common Stock	4,116	9,060
1,986,953	Government Employees Insurance Company Convertible Preferred	19,417	28,314
592,650	Interpublic Group of Companies, Inc.	4,531	19,039
1,066,934	Kaiser Aluminum and Chemical Corporation	18,085	18,671
453,800	Knight-Ridder Newspapers, Inc.	7,534	10,267
953,750	SAFECO Corporation	23,867	26,467
934,300	The Washington Post Company	10,628	43,445
	Total	$ 94,260	$163,889
	All Other Holdings	39,506	57,040
	Total Equities	$133,766	$220,929

In some cases our indirect interest in earning power is becoming quite substantial. For example, note our holdings of 953,750 shares of SAFECO Corp. SAFECO probably is the best run large property and casualty insurance company in the United States. Their underwriting abilities are simply superb, their loss reserving is conservative, and their investment policies make great sense.

SAFECO is a much better insurance operation than our own (although we believe certain segments of ours are much better than average), is better than one we could develop and, similarly, is far better than any in which we might negotiate purchase of a controlling interest. Yet our purchase of SAFECO was made at substantially under book value. We paid less than 100¢ on the dollar for the best company in the business, when far more than 100¢ on the dollar is being paid for mediocre companies in corporate transactions. And there is no way to start a new operation—with necessarily uncertain prospects—at less than 100¢ on the dollar.

Of course, with a minor interest we do not have the right to direct or even influence management policies of SAFECO. But why should we wish to do this? The record would indicate that they do a better job of managing their operations than we could do ourselves. While there may be less excitement and prestige in sitting back and letting others do the work, we think that is all one loses by accepting a passive participation in excellent management. Because, quite clearly, if one controlled a company run as well as SAFECO, the proper policy also would be to sit back and let management do its job.

Earnings attributable to the shares of SAFECO owned by Berkshire at year-end amounted to $6.1 million during 1978, but only the dividends received (about 18% of earnings) are reflected in our operating earnings. We believe the balance, although not reportable, to be just as real in terms of eventual benefit to us as the amount distributed. In fact, SAFECO's retained earnings (or those of other well-run companies if they have opportunities to employ additional capital advantageously) may well eventually have a value to shareholders greater than 100¢ on the dollar.

We are not at all unhappy when our wholly-owned businesses retain all of their earnings if they can utilize internally those funds at attractive rates. Why should we feel differently about retention of earnings by companies in which we hold small equity interests, but where the record indicates even better prospects for profitable employment of capital? (This proposition cuts the other way, of course, in industries with low capital requirements, or if management has a record of plowing capital into projects of low profitability; then earnings should be paid out or used to repurchase shares—often by far the most attractive option for capital utilization.)

The aggregate level of such retained earnings attributable to our equity interests in fine companies is becoming quite substantial. It does not enter into our reported operating earnings, but we feel it well may have equal long-term significance to our shareholders. Our hope is that conditions continue to prevail in securities markets which allow our insurance companies to buy large amounts of underlying earning power for relatively modest outlays. At some point market conditions undoubtedly will again preclude such bargain buying but, in the meantime, we will try to make the most of opportunities.

Banking

Under Gene Abegg and Pete Jeffrey, the Illinois National Bank and Trust Company in Rockford continues to establish new records. Last year's earnings amounted to approximately 2.1% of average assets, about three times the level averaged by major banks. In our opinion, this extraordinary level of earnings is being achieved while maintaining significantly less asset risk than prevails at most of the larger banks.

We purchased the Illinois National Bank in March 1969. It was a first-class operation then, just as it had been ever since Gene Abegg opened the doors in 1931. Since 1968, consumer time deposits have quadrupled, net income has tripled, and trust department income has more than doubled, while costs have been closely controlled.

Our experience has been that the manager of an already high-cost operation frequently is uncommonly resourceful in finding new ways to add to overhead, while the manager of a tightly-run operation usually continues to find additional methods to curtail costs, even when his costs are already well below those of his competitors. No one has demonstrated this latter ability better than Gene Abegg.

We are required to divest our bank by December 31, 1980. The most likely approach is to spin it off to Berkshire shareholders some time in the second half of 1980.

It is a real pleasure to work with managers who enjoy coming to work each morning and, once there, instinctively and unerringly think like owners. We are associated with some of the very best.

WARREN E. BUFFETT, CHAIRMAN

March 26, 1978

APPENDIX III: SEQUOIA FUND COMMON
STOCK PORTFOLIO (JUNE 30, 1979) UNAUDITED

COMMON STOCKS	Cost	Value
Shares		
ADVERTISING (10.67%)		
168,600 The Interpublic Group of Companies, Inc.	$ 2,442,914	$ 6,406,800
69,000 Ogilvy & Mather International, Inc.	807,000	1,336,875
	3,249,914	7,743,675
BANKS (6.49%)		
120,000 DETROITBANK Corporation	3,205,238	3,045,000
20,000 National Detroit Corporation	457,873	617,500
24,500 Pittsburgh National Corporation	910,913	1,044,312
	4,574,024	4,706,812
CONSUMER PRODUCTS MANUFACTURING (6.64%)		
120,000 McDonough Co.	2,659,676	3,615,000
20,000 Polaroid Corporation	522,013	627,500
17,700 Sturm, Ruger & Company, Inc.	219,950	570,825
	3,401,639	4,813,325
INDUSTRIAL PRODUCTS MANUFACTURING (12.96%)		
15,600 Duplex Products, Inc.	275,364	345,150
140,000 P. H. Glatfelter Company	3,305,252	4,410,000
58,100 Hillenbrand Industries, Inc.	1,505,449	2,062,550
34,700 Pittway Corporation	1,014,867	1,140,763
30,000 Western Pacific Industries, Inc.	785,505	1,440,000
	6,886,437	9,398,463
INSURANCE (4.77%)		
100,000 Western Casualty & Surety Co.	3,220,437	3,462,500
METALS (10.46%)		
230,000 Reynolds Metals Company	8,233,819	7,590,000
NEWSPAPERS (8.24%)		
260,000 The Washington Post Company (Class B)	1,454,183	5,980,000
PUBLISHING (6.37%)		
15,000 Harcourt Brace Jovanovich, Inc.	387,386	566,250
115,400 Houghton Mifflin Company	2,589,719	3,779,350
10,000 Meredith Corporation	216,629	275,000
	3,193,734	4,620,600
RETAILING (5.77%)		
34,000 Masters, Inc.	407,541	233,750
30,000 The Miller-Wohl Company, Inc.	368,110	600,000
77,300 Supermarkets General Corporation	1,052,063	1,140,175
70,000 Tandy Corporation	1,164,170	1,496,250
31,500 Weis Markets, Inc.	614,773	714,656
	3,606,657	4,184,831

(continued)

COMMON STOCKS	Cost	Value
Shares		
SERVICES (12.20%)		
200,000 Capital Cities Communications, Inc.	5,554,563	8,000,000
20,000 LIN Broadcasting Corporation	290,000	852,500
	5,844,563	8,852,500
TRANSPORTATION (4.28%)		
130,000 Consolidated Freightways, Inc.	3,521,683	3,103,750
TOTAL COMMON STOCKS	47,187,090	64,456,456

APPENDIX III (a): PRINCIPAL EQUITY HOLDINGS OF THE SEQUOIA FUND (JUNE 30, 1986) UNAUDITED

COMMON STOCKS

Shares		Cost	Value
	ADVERTISING (.20%)		
36,800	The Interpublic Group of Companies, Inc. $	94,702	$ 1,067,200
9,000	The Ogilvy Group, Inc.	47,950	317,250
		142,652	1,384,450
	BROADCASTING (7.00%)		
191,100	Capital Cities/ABC, Inc.	38,145,272	49,017,150
	CONSUMER PRODUCTS (7.87%)		
920,600	Hasbro, Inc.	41,284,750	53,394,800
42,400	Sturm, Ruger & Company, Inc.	361,700	1,749,000
		41,646,450	55,143,800
	FOOD (12.99%)		
770,000	Dart & Kraft, Inc.	14,748,080	48,798,750
600,000	Sara Lee Corporation	14,915,388	42,150,000
		29,663,468	90,948,750
	INDUSTRIAL PRODUCTS (5.36%)		
540,200	Duplex Products, Inc.	4,738,098	11,479,250
90,000	Kimball International, Inc. Class B	2,443,125	2,677,500
61,000	MacAndrews & Forbes Group, Inc.	2,766,840	3,416,000
145,300	Western Pacific Industries, Inc.	6,465,864	19,942,425
		16,413,927	37,515,175
	PAPER MANUFACTURING (13.08%)		
745,500	Consolidated Papers, Inc.	22,645,750	43,145,812
1,949,400	P.H. Glatfelter Company	12,726,070	48,491,325
		35,371,820	91,637,137
	PUBLISHING (2.17%)		
200,000	Meredith Corporation	3,743,830	15,200,000
	RETAILING (2.82%)		
240,500	Melville Corporation	8,449,248	17,075,500
67,500	Weis Markets, Inc.	439,297	2,657,813
		8,888,545	19,733,313
	SERVICES (.47%)		
102,900	PHH Group, Inc.	3,178,387	3,292,800
WARRANTS (.22%)			
28,160	Capital Cities/ABC, Inc. $	941,600	$ 1,576,960

APPENDIX IV: MANHATTAN FUND COMMON STOCK PORTFOLIO
SECURITIES OWNED AS OF DEC. 31, 1969

Shares		Market Value
65,000	Dasa Corp.	$ 2,405,000
35,400	Downe Communications	532,593
54,000	Teleprompter Corp.	5,297,400
6,000	Teleprompter Corp.	654,000
50,000	Amrep Corp.	2,387,500
190,000	Deltona Corp.	11,495,000
280,000	Fedders Corp.	9,520,000
185,000	GAC Corp.	11,470,000
105,000	Horizon Corp.	5,617,500
150,000	Rouse Co.	5,100,000
76,000	Tishman Realty & Constr.	2,023,500
50,000	U.S. Financial	2,037,500
100,000	Franklin Stores	2,875,000
30,000	Levitz Furniture	1,488,750
130,000	Mattel, Inc.	8,385,000
120,000	Polaroid Corp.	15,000,000
30,000	Sony Corp. ADR	4,110,000
50,000	Unishops, Inc.	2,156,250
50,000	Int. Industries	2,087,500
50,000	Ky. Fried Chicken	2,150,000
244,000	Natl. Student Mark.	6,148,800
100,000	Ryder Systems	4,625,000
100,000	Calif. Computer Prod.	2,430,000

Shares		Market Value
100,000	Computer Technology	1,300,000
55,500	Telex Corp.	5,022,750
65,000	American Medicorp	2,340,000
100,000	Bausch & Lomb	7,775,000
50,000	Four Seasons Equity	1,065,750
7,690	Four Seasons Franch. Centers, warrants	7,690
190,000	Four Seasons Nursing Centers of Am.	12,252,746
60,000	Amer. Motor Inns	1,612,500
141,000	Hilton Hotels	8,512,875
77,000	Parvin/Dohrmann	4,530,000
125,000	Ramada Inns	3,687,500
25,000	Burroughs	3,934,375
20,000	Intl. Bus. Machines	7,290,000
41,500	Nat. Cash Register	6,660,750
100,000	Saxon Industries	10,900,000
100,000	Xerox Corp.	1,575,000
105,000	Career Academy	5,302,500
285,000	King Resources	8,051,250
45,000	Natl. Pat. Devel.	3,600,000
	Other com. stk.	9,994,500
	Total com. stk.	$215,411,479

APPENDIX V: STATE STREET INVESTMENT CORPORATION INVESTMENT PORTFOLIO
(MARCH 31, 1979)

No. of Shares		Market Value
AIRLINE — 1.1%		
123,061	Northwest Airlines, Inc.	$ 3,599,534
AUTOMOTIVE — 2.4%		
162,500	Ford Motor Co.	7,129,688
49,600	B. F. Goodrich Co.	961,000
BANK — 1.1%		
26,000	Continental Illinois Corp.	659,750
61,000	First National Boston Corp.	1,631,750
33,960	Texas Commerce Bancshares, Inc.	1,332,930
BUILDING — 4.4%		
122,000	General Portland Inc.	1,799,500
323,131	Jim Walter Corp.	9,855,496
32,100	Masonite Corp.	906,825
89,000	Owens-Corning Fiberglas Corp.	2,514,250
BUSINESS SERVICE — 1.3%		
158,625	Servicemaster Industries, Inc.	4,520,813
CHEMICAL — 1.1%		
12,000	Dow Chemical Co.	336,000
47,000	Monsanto Co.	2,426,375
25,000	Rohm & Haas Co.	950,000
CONTAINER — 1.0%		
123,000	Continental Group, Inc.	3,520,875
DIVERSIFIED — 3.4%		
163,909	Dart Industries, Inc.	6,556,360
130,000	International Tel. & Tel. Corp.	3,705,000
14,000	Minnesota Mining & Manufacturing Co.	810,250
27,090	Scovill Manufacturing Co.	528,255

No. of Shares		Market Value
DRUG — 7.7%		
9,000	American Home Products Corp.	$ 239,625
105,100	Bristol-Myers Co.	3,625,950
2,537	Merck & Co.	167,442
184,000	SmithKline Corp.	17,526,000
122,500	Upjohn Co.	5,022,500
ELECTRICAL EQUIPMENT — 0.9%		
61,000	General Electric Co.	2,928,000
ELECTRONIC — 2.2%		
43,000	Hewlett-Packard Co.	4,020,500
20,000	Intel Corp.	1,280,000
8,300	Motorola, Inc.	318,513
35,000	Tektronix, Inc.	1,898,750
FINANCE — 1.3%		
90,000	American Express Co.	2,846,250
100,000	First Charter Financial Corp.	1,750,000
FOOD & BEVERAGE — 2.2%		
100,000	General Mills, Inc.	2,500,000
330,870	Norton Simon Inc.	5,128,485
FOREST PRODUCT — 5.4%		
100,000	Champion International Corp.	2,475,000
55,100	Kimberly-Clark Corp.	2,541,488
260,900	Mead Corp.	7,435,650
194,000	St. Regis Paper Co.	6,183,750
HOSPITAL SUPPLY — 1.2%		
6,000	American Hospital Supply Corp.	149,250
116,200	Abbott Laboratories	3,820,075
INDUSTRIAL EQUIPMENT — 0.3%		
20,000	Cooper Industries, Inc.	947,500

No. of Shares		Market Value
INSURANCE — 4.0%		
144,000	American General Ins. Co.	$ 3,870,000
59,000	Criterion Ins. Co.	1,150,500
14,800	General Reinsurance Corp.	2,516,000
60,000	INA Corp.	2,707,500
90,800	Travelers Corp.	3,416,350
METAL & MINING — 7.3%		
179,600	Aluminum Co. of America	9,765,750
60,000	Eastern Gas & Fuel Assoc.	1,155,000
51,200	Inland Steel Co.	2,048,000
400,000	Kaiser Aluminum & Chemical Corp.	8,150,000
80,000	Kennecott Copper Corp.	1,950,000
75,000	St. Joe Minerals Corp.	2,081,250
OFFICE EQUIPMENT — 12.3%		
85,000	Burroughs Corp.	6,024,375
38,400	Digital Equipment Corp.	2,068,800
98,000	International Business Machines Corp.	30,919,000
50,000	NCR Corp.	3,487,500
OIL — 18.7%		
148,732	Commonwealth Oil Refining Co.	520,562
320,000	Dome Petroleum Ltd.	36,640,000
199,660	Gulf Oil Corp.	5,266,033
253,740	MAPCO Inc.	8,119,680
59,600	Mobil Corp.	4,432,750
200,000	Phillips Petroleum Co.	6,875,000
54,000	Standard Oil Co. (Ohio)	2,686,500
OIL SERVICE — 2.4%		
79,500	Schlumberger Ltd.	8,168,625
PHOTOGRAPHY — 0.6%		
31,400	Eastman Kodak Co.	2,009,600
RECREATION — 2.7%		
150,000	American Broadcasting Cos.	5,156,250
77,000	Metromedia, Inc.	4,081,000
RETAIL TRADE — 2.4%		
25,000	Dayton Hudson Corp.	950,000
89,500	K mart Corp.	2,215,125
100,000	Macy (R.H.) & Co.	3,525,000
50,000	Payless Cashways, Inc.	762,500
48,000	Super Valu Stores Inc.	804,000

No. of Shares		Market Value
UTILITY — 4.5%		
126,000	Florida Power & Light Co.	$ 3,528,000
350,000	Middle South Utilities, Inc.	5,293,750
76,800	Panhandle Eastern Pipe Line Co.	3,763,200
125,000	Texas Utilities Co.	2,406,250
25,000	Wisconsin Electric Power Co.	650,000
MISCELLANEOUS SECURITIES — 0.3%		1,246,919
	TOTAL STOCKS — 92.2%	
	(Cost $190,590,024)	316,960,148

Par Value		Market Value
CORPORATE BONDS — 0.5%		
$1,000,000	Cadence Industries Corp. 5% Cv. Sub. Notes 6/15/88	570,000*
325,000	Digital Equipment Corp. 4½% Cv. Sub. Debs. 12/15/02	365,625
970,587	Great Western Savings and Loan Assoc. 5% Cv. Cap. Notes 12/15/83	873,528*
	(Cost $2,295,587)	1,809,153
U.S. GOVERNMENT AND GOVERNMENT AGENCIES — 1.7%		
	9.5%-9.8% maturing on various dates to 8/30/79 (Cost $5,881,350)	5,835,100
COMMERCIAL PAPER — 5.7%		
	9.5%-9.9% maturing on various dates to 4/30/79 (Cost $19,450,000)	19,450,000
	TOTAL INVESTMENTS — 100.1% (Cost $218,216,961)	344,054,401
	CASH AND OTHER ASSETS, LESS LIABILITIES — (0.1%)	(352,371)
	TOTAL NET ASSETS — 100.0%	$343,702,030

* May be restricted in whole or in part as to public resale. Such restricted securities with aggregate fair value of $1,443,528, which is 0.4% of net assets, were valued in accordance with methods adopted by the Board of Directors.

APPENDIX V(a): STATE STREET INVESTMENT
CORPORATION

INVESTMENT PORTFOLIO   *(September 30, 1986)*

No. of Shares		Value
AUTOMOTIVE—1.0%		
300,000	Echlin Inc.	$ 5,212,500
BANK—1.0%		
3,282	Chase Manhattan Corp. Fl. Rate, Ser. F Pfd.	172,305
100,000	Citicorp	5,012,500
11,000	Irving Bank Corp. Cum. Adj. Rate Pfd.	572,000
10,000	Wells Fargo & Company Cum. Adj. Rate, Ser. A Pfd.	490,000
		6,246,805
BUSINESS SERVICE—4.1%		
740,728	ServiceMaster Industries Inc.	15,555,288
130,000	Waste Management Inc.	6,272,500
		21,827,788
CHEMICAL—5.2%		
6,200	Dow Chemical Co.	332,475
70,000	E.I. du Pont de Nemours & Co.	5,608,750
30,290	Freeport-McMoRan, Inc.	609,586
130,000	Monsanto Co.	8,840,000
402,000	Rohm & Haas Co.	12,512,250
		27,903,061
DIVERSIFIED—1.5%		
125,000	Loews Corp.	7,703,125
2,460	Minnesota Mining & Manufacturing Co.	247,538
		7,950,663
DRUG—13.4%		
65,200	American Home Products Corp.	$ 4,775,900
215,200	Bristol-Myers Co.	15,279,200
9,400	Merck & Co., Inc.	925,900
150,000	SmithKline Beckman Corp. ...	12,056,250
150,000	Squibb Corp.	15,187,500
160,000	Upjohn Co.	13,860,000
184,600	Warner-Lambert Co.	9,783,800
		71,868,550
ELECTRICAL EQUIPMENT—2.3%		
100,000	General Electric Co.	7,175,000
100,000	Westinghouse Electric Corp.	5,250,000
		12,425,000
ELECTRONIC—4.4%		
40,000	Augat Inc.	650,000
372,000	Hewlett-Packard Co.	14,322,000
99,000	Intergraph Corp.	2,178,000
140,000	Motorola, Inc.	5,180,000
		22,330,000

No. of Shares		Value
FINANCE—1.7%		
160,000	American Express Co.	9,000,000
FOOD—4.0%		
472,500	Archer Daniels Midland Co.	8,386,875
140,000	General Mills, Inc...............	11,077,500
31,360	Kellogg Co.........................	1,454,320
20,000	SYSCO Corp.	565,000
		21,483,695
FOREST PRODUCT—2.6%		
145,842	Champion International Corp...........................	$ 3,773,663
12,300	Fort Howard Paper Co.......	544,275
103,048	Great Northern Nekoosa Corp..............................	5,693,402
50,272	Temple-Inland Inc..............	2,651,848
11,070	Union Camp Corp.	564,570
8,100	Westvaco Corp.	435,375
10,400	Weyerhaeuser Co.	361,400
		14,024,533
HOSPITAL SUPPLY—3.6%		
464,800	Abbott Laboratories...........	19,463,500
INSURANCE—9.4%		
9,000	AEtna Life & Casualty Co. Cum. Fl. Rate, Cl. A Pfd.	475,875
281,821	American General Corp.	10,850,109
95,057	CIGNA Corp.	5,144,960
12,640	CIGNA Corp. $2.75 Cum. Cv., Ser. A Pfd.	410,800
12,300	Capital Holding Corp.	365,925
5,535	Chubb Corp.	365,310
50,000	Continental Corp.	2,181,250
191,200	General Re Corp.	10,946,200
3,075	Ohio Casualty Corp............	236,775
2,500	Torchmark Corp. Adj. Rate Pfd.	267,500
180,000	Travelers Corp.	7,762,500
300,000	USF&G Corp.	11,212,500
		50,219,704
METAL & MINING—2.5%		
9,102	Alcan Aluminum Ltd.	$ 285,575
309,840	Aluminum Co. of America ..	11,464,080
4,612	AMAX Inc. $3 Cv. Serv. B Pfd.	153,927
80,000	Hanna (M.A.) Co.	1,520,000
3,075	Newmont Mining Corp.	183,731
		13,607,313
OFFICE EQUIPMENT—12.4%		
142,800	Digital Equipment Corp.	12,834,150
328,051	International Business Machines Corp..............	44,122,860
200,000	NCR Corp.	9,425,000
		66,382,010

No. of Shares		Value
OIL—7.1%		
8,600	Amoco Corp.	557,925
150,000	British Petroleum p.l.c. ADRs	5,925,000
56,093	Chevron Corp.	2,468,092
4,800,000	Dome Petroleum Ltd.	3,600,000
100,000	Exxon Corp.	6,725,000
286,400	Mobil Corp.	10,740,000
13,451	Murphy Oil Corp.	344,682
14,959	Sabine Corp.	209,426
52,000	Standard Oil Co	7,277,000
		37,847,125
OIL SERVICE—1.7%		
275,312	Schlumberger Ltd.	$ 9,222,952
PRINTING & PUBLISHING 1.0%		
100,000	McGraw-Hill, Inc.	5,400,000
RAILROAD—0.4%		
83,900	Burlington Northern Inc.	1,885,688
7,380	Union Pacific Corp.	418,815
		2,304,503
RECREATION—3.9%		
5,120	Capital Cities/ABC, Inc. Wts.	250,240
68,000	CBS Inc.	8,364,000
80,000	Taft Broadcasting Co.	9,220,000
115,200	Tele-Communications, Inc. Cl. A	2,678,400
19,200	Tele-Communications, Inc. Cl. B	448,800
		20,961,440

No. of Shares		Value
RETAIL TRADE—6.6		
140,000	Dayton Hudson Corp.	6,020,000
5,000	Sears, Roebuck & Co. Adj. Rate Pfd.	517,500
192,000	Super Valu Stores Inc.	3,936,000
320,000	Tandy Corp.	10,240,000
510,000	Toys "R" Us, Inc.	14,662,500
		35,376,000
TELEPHONE—0.5%		
7,000	American Information Technologies Corp.	$ 917,875
16,000	BellSouth Corp.	920,000
15,000	Southern New England Telephone Co	811,875
		2,649,750
TEXTILE—0.1%		
7,040	Associated Dry Goods Corp.	401,280
TOBACCO—0.1%		
6,150	Philip Morris Cos. Inc.	407,433
UTILITY—2.5%		
300,000	FPL Group, Inc.	9,075,000
355,000	Middle South Utilities, Inc.	4,570,625
		13,645,625
MISCELLANEOUS SECURITIES—0.8%		4,463,403
TOTAL STOCKS—93.8% (Cost $210,121,936)		502,624,633

APPENDIX VI: "STOCKS SELLING FOR LESS THAN NET WORKING CAPITAL"

	Market Price	Net Wkg. Cap. Per Share	Market Price as % of Net Wkg. Cap. Per Share		Market Price	Net Wkg. Cap. Per Share	Market Price as % of Net Wkg. Cap. Per Share
Wayne-Gossard	6	$13.69	44	Weyenberg Shoe	18	21.66	83
Oxford Indus.	9	15.22	59	Carter-Wallace	7	8.26	85
Amer. Distilling	9	15.00	60	Warnaco Inc.	10	11.58	86
Salant Corp.	7	11.32	62	Pier I Imports	7	8.04	87
Vendo Co.	5	7.93	63	Craig Corp.	11	12.47	88
Cooper Tire	12	18.33	65	McNeill Corp.	12	13.71	88
Cunningham Drug	9	13.42	67	Monarch Mach. Tool	27	30.41	89
Kroehler Mfg.	10	14.96	67	Stevens (J.P.)	15	16.80	89
Cluett, Peabody	11	16.03	69	Mirro Aluminum	11	12.20	90
Sterchi Bros. Strs.	10	14.24	70	Zale Corp.	17	18.87	90
Wean United	6	8.51	71	Lowenstein (M.)	16	17.37	92
Munsingwear Inc.	15	20.37	74	Tappan Co.	9	9.73	92
Helene Curtis Ind.	8	10.42	77	Tobin Packing	7	7.57	92
Phillips-Van Heusen	13	16.97	77	Bell & Howell	18	19.20	94
Cont. Copper & St.	5	6.39	78	Rockower Bros.	11	11.70	94
Dynamics Corp. Am.	5	6.44	78	Faberge Inc.	10	10.52	95
Superscope Inc.	9	14.43	79	Mesta Machine	21	22.22	95
Manhattan Indus.	10	12.53	80	Nat'l Presto	18	18.64	97
Hart, Schaffner & M.	13	16.34	80	Springs Mills	18	18.59	97
Jantzen Inc.	17	20.48	83	N. Amer. Philips	28	28.39	99

(Standard & Poor's *Outlook*, October 1978)

APPENDIX VI (a): "SELECTED NYSE STOCKS AT DISCOUNTS FROM BOOK VALUE"

Company	Book Value Per Share	7/8/85 Price	Market Price as % of Book Value
Manville Corp.	$37.55	5 3/4	15
Puerto Rican Cement	16.17	6 3/8	39
McIntyre Mines	66.12	28	42
Zapata Corp.	23.08	10	43
Lukens Inc.	24.12	14 1/8	58
Reynolds Metals	59.69	35 5/8	59
Amfesco Indus.	11.45	7	61
Gulfstream Aerospace	30.09	18 5/8	61
Ampco-Pittsburgh	19.88	12 3/8	62
Murray Ohio Mfg.	29.49	18 1/2	62
Fieldcrest Mills	44.50	28 1/4	63
Moore McCormack	39.58	25 1/2	64
National-Standard	22.50	14 1/2	64
Southmark Corp.	10.41	6 3/4	64
Burlington Indus.	41.82	27 3/8	65
Texaco Inc.	55.66	36 1/2	65
Union Carbide	68.89	45 3/8	65
Southwest Forest Ind.	20.00	13 1/4	66
Springs Industries	50.10	33 1/4	66
Ameron, Inc.	52.18	35	67
Hayes-Albion	14.37	9 3/4	67
Overseas Shiphldg.	24.22	16 1/2	68
Jewelcor, Inc.	15.54	10 7/8	69
U.S. Steel	38.41	26 7/8	69
Goodrich (B.F.)	45.18	31 5/8	69
Transcon Inc.	11.65	8 1/4	70
Modular Computer Sys.	9.12	6 1/2	71
Borman's Inc.	10.75	7 3/4	72
Stevens (J.P.)	30.84	22 1/2	72
Timken Co.	66.43	48 1/2	73
International Paper	66.04	48 3/4	73
Armstrong Rubber	21.65	16	73
Wolverine World Wide	15.37	11 3/8	73
Cenergy Corp.	11.26	8 3/8	74
Firestone Tire & Rub.	28.49	21 1/4	74
Elgin National Ind.	19.07	14 1/4	74
Williams Cos.	37.43	28 5/8	76
Rowan Cos.	10.62	8 1/4	77
Sea-Land Corp.	29.83	23 1/4	77
General Homes	8.91	7	78
Gordon Jewelry Cl. A	21.34	16 7/8	78
Proler Int'l	50.02	39 1/2	78
Fruehauf Corp.	28.28	22 3/8	79
Twin Disc	$21.46	17	79
Lone Star Indus.	30.78	24 1/2	79
Cleveland-Cliffs	25.36	20 3/8	80
CCX Inc.	6.51	5 1/4	80
Huffy Corp.	12.29	10	81
Reece Corp.	12.17	10	82
Alcan Aluminium Ltd.	29.36	24 1/4	82
Ford Motor	52.86	43 3/4	82
Ceco Indus.	29.48	24 1/2	83
McNeil Corp.	32.22	26 7/8	83
Aluminum Co. of Amer.	40.23	33 7/8	84
Southeastern Pub. Sv.	8.16	6 7/8	84
Newmont Mining	40.70	41 1/8	84
Commercial Metals	19.70	16 3/4	85
Best Products	15.56	13 1/4	85
Anderson Clayton	47.19	40 1/4	85
Chevron Corp.	43.45	37 1/8	85
San Juan Rac. Assn.	12.66	10 7/8	85
CBI Indus.	26.18	22 5/8	86
SCM Corp.	54.29	47 1/8	86
ITT Corp.	36.09	31 3/8	86
Monarch Mach. Tool	18.12	15 3/4	86
Kerr-McGee	33.22	29 1/8	87
Trico Indus.	7.12	6 1/4	87
Dresser Indus.	24.73	21 3/4	87
American President	24.55	21 5/8	88
Quanex Corp.	8.77	7 3/4	88
Eagle-Picher Indus.	24.55	21 3/4	88
Commodore Int'l	10.56	9 3/8	88
Winners Corp.	6.76	6	88
Fabri-Centers Amer.	11.82	10 1/2	88
West Pt.-Pepperell	44.18	39 1/4	88
Deere & Co.	33.74	30 1/8	89
Zenith Electronics	20.00	17 7/8	89
Culbro Corp.	32.72	29 1/4	89
Todd Shipyards	33.27	29 3/4	89
Mobil Corp.	33.33	29 7/8	89
Dayco Corp.	20.08	18	89
Apache Corp.	11.14	10	89
Ingredient Technology	14.84	13 3/8	90
Amerada Hess	30.87	28	90
Ponderosa Inc.	14.10	12 7/8	91
Lowenstein (M.)	$50.21	45 7/8	91
Sterchi Bros. Stores	21.74	19 7/8	91
Purolator Courier	27.07	24 3/4	91
Lennar Corp.	15.30	14	91
Interlake, Inc.	$54.35	49 7/8	91
Roper Corp.	16.18	14 7/8	91
INTERCO, Inc.	70.43	64 7/8	92
Diversified Indus.	6.08	5 5/8	92
Allied Products	18.39	17	92
Clark Equipment	32.05	29 3/4	92
Rexnord, Inc.	15.02	14	93
Robertson (H.H.)	28.66	26 3/4	93
Cummins Engine	70.79	66 1/8	93
Belding Heminway	16.05	15	93
Cooper Tire & Rub.	16.31	15 1/4	93
Goodyear Tire & Rub.	30.07	28 1/8	93
Olin Corp.	34.23	32 1/8	93
Harnischfeger Corp.	11.04	10 3/8	93
Koppers Co.	18.57	17 1/2	94
Halliburton Co.	31.24	29 1/2	94
Jim Walter	37.45	35 3/8	94
Wynn's Int'l	17.82	16 7/8	94
Staley Continental	23.48	22 1/4	94
First City Indus.	10.94	10 3/8	94
Mohasco Corp.	32.81	31 1/8	94
Fox-Stanley Photo	10.64	10 1/8	95
Jorgensen (E.M.)	26.10	24 7/8	95
XTRA Corp.	26.76	25 1/2	95
Tandycrafts, Inc.	15.47	14 3/4	95
GATX Corp.	30.39	29	95
Brockway Inc.	26.45	25 1/4	95
Champion Spark Plug	9.25	8 7/8	95
Morse Shoe	23.95	23	96
Florida Steel	15.03	14 1/2	96
Varo Inc.	11.85	11 1/2	97
Grace (W.R.)	42.32	41 1/8	97
Joy Mfg.	24.06	23 1/2	97
Murphy Oil	28.13	27 1/2	97
Potlatch Corp.	36.65	36	98
McDermott Int'l	24.82	24 1/2	98
Oneida Ltd.	12.95	12 7/8	99
Cyclops Corp.	49.67	49 3/8	99
North Amer. Philips	34.96	34 3/4	99
Eastern Gas & Fuel A	22.62	22 1/2	99

APPENDIX VII: "STOCKS AT DISCOUNT FROM LIQUIDATING VALUE"

Stocks whose recent prices do not exceed the value of "net" working capital (i.e., current assets less all liabilities and preferred stock)

Page No.	Stock Name	Recent Price	"Net" Wkg Capital per sh.	Percent Price-to-"Net" Wkg Cap'l	Tangible Book Value per sh.	Percent Price-to-Book Value	Timeliness	Safety Rank	Beta	Pecent Est'd Yield	Current P/E Ratio	Industry
1064	SUPERSCOPE, INC.	5½	11.33	49%	26.78	21%	5	4	1.45	NIL	NMF	ELECTRONICS
884	KROEHLER MFG.	8½	16.69	51%	35.16	24%	5	4	0.95	NIL	NMF	BUILDING
146	FACET ENTERPRISES	4⅜	7.98	55%	15.31	29%	4	3	1:00	NIL	44.0	AUTO PARTS (REP)
1624	SALANT CORP.	6⅞	10.83	63%	15.71	44%	5	4	1.35	5.7%	4.1	APPAREL
1620	OXFORD IND.	9¾	15.21	64%	22.19	44%	—	4	0.85	6.8%	4.2	APPAREL
1566	STERCHI BROS. ST.	9½	13.57	70%	14.87	64%	4	3	0.70	7.1%	4.8	RETAIL (SPECIAL LINES)
1568	TANDYCRAFTS, INC.	4⅜	6.04	72%	12.30	36%	—	3	1.35	NIL	11.0	RETAIL (SPECIAL LINES)
370	VENDO CO.	5	6.82	73%	11.69	43%	5	5	1.10	NIL	NMF	INDUSTRIAL SERVICES
1609	HART SCHAFFNER & MARX	12	16.06	75%	23.10	52%	3	3	1.10	7.2%	5.3	APPAREL
628	HELENE CURTIS	7¾	10.18	76%	13.80	56%	5	4	1.20	NIL	6.5	TOILETRIES/COSMETICS
1628	WAYNE—GOSSARD CORP.	5¾	7.25	79%	14.98	38%	3	3	0.95	8.2%	7.2	APPAREL
1043	CRAIG CORP.	10	12.45	80%	13.03	77%	5	3	1.10	5.0%	9.0	ELECTRONICS
520	BAYUK CIGARS	9½	11.85	80%	15.29	62%	3	3	0.45	5.0%	7.2	TOBACCO
771	CUNNINGHAM DRUG ST.	11	12.98	85%	23.17	47%	3	3	0.75	2.8%	9.1	DRUG STORE
1682	PAMIDA INC.	4	4.63	86%	7.00	57%	5	4	1.20	3.0%	NMF	RETAIL STORE
626	FABERGE, INC.	8⅞	10.37	86%	18.05	49%	4	3	1.15	4.5%	7.0	TOILETRIES/COSMETICS
1610	JANTZEN, INC.	18	20.37	88%	26.73	67%	4	3	0.75	5.5%	5.7	APPAREL
1007	DYNAMICS CP. OF AMER.	5⅝	6.18	91%	8.57	66%	3	4	1.15	2.6%	6.8	ELECTRICAL EQUIPMENT
173	BELL & HOWELL	15	16.31	92%	33.52	45%	4	3	1.10	6.3%	7.5	PRECISION INSTRUMENT
1617	MCGREGOR—DONIGER INC.	1⅞	2.12	92%	4.55	43%	—	5	0.60	NIL	NMF	APPAREL
1618	MUNSINGWEAR	16	17.19	93%	29.53	54%	3	3	0.70	7.5%	6.6	APPAREL
1326	MCNEIL CORP.	14	14.85	94%	27.74	50%	2	2	0.75	5.6%	6.6	MACHINERY
350	AMER. DISTILLING	13	13.63	95%	18.86	69%	3	4	0.70	NIL	65.0	DISTILLING
1430	NATIONAL PRESTO IND.	17	17.84	95%	27.60	62%	5	3	0.70	8.7%	8.2	HOME APPLIANCES
624	CARTER—WALLACE	7⅞	8.25	96%	12.51	63%	3	3	1.00	5.0%	8.5	TOILETRIES/COSMETICS
807	GATEWAY IND.	8	8.33	96%	13.37	60%	3	4	1.00	7.5%	4.2	AUTO PARTS (OEM)
770	ADAMS DRUG	3¾	3.90	96%	5.79	65%	4	4	1.20	1.5%	4.5	DRUG STORE
1648	STEVENS J.P.	14	14.65	96%	37.50	37%	3	3	0.95	8.5%	4.3	TEXTILE
1569	ZALE CORP.	16	16.35	98%	24.74	65%	3	3	1.05	6.8%	5.5	RETAIL (SPECIAL LINES)
195	SARGENT—WELCH SCIENTIFIC	14	14.22	98%	18.04	78%	4	3	0.85	6.5%	6.0	PRECISION INSTRUMENT
1327	MESTA MACHINE	20	20.32	98%	52.[illegible]	38%	4	3	0.90	3.0%	12.5	MACHINERY
1647	SPRINGS MILLS	16	16.08	99%	35.15	46%	3	3	0.80	8.0%	4.5	TEXTILE
374	BACHE GROUP INC.	8⅞	8.96	99%	15.88	56%	3	4	1.80	4.5%	8.7	SECURITIES BROKERAGE

(*The Value Line Investment Survey*, "Summary of Advices and Index," April 6, 1979, p.29)

APPENDIX VII (a): "STOCKS AT DISCOUNT FROM LIQUIDATING VALUE"

Recent prices do not exceed the value of "net" working capital (i.e., current assets less all liabilities including long-term debt and preferred)

Page No.	Stock Name	Recent Price	"Net" Wkg. Capital per sh.	Percent Price-to-"Net" Wkg. Cap'l	Tangible Book Value Per sh.	Percent Price-to-Book Value	Time-liness	Safety Rank	Beta	Current P/E Ratio	Est'd Yield	Industry
140	Chic. Pacific	34	52.16	65%	88.33	38%	–	4	0.60	15.2	NIL	Home Appliances
1122	CPT Corp.	3	4.28	70%	7.50	40%	5	4	1.20	NMF	NIL	Office Equip & Supplies
1361	Egan Nat'l Ind.	15	16.13	93%	20.97	72%	3	3	0.55	NMF	NIL	Machinery(Const&Mining)
1682	Wolvenne World Wide	9	9.52	94%	15.98	56%	4	4	1.10	42.9	NIL	Shoe
823	Swank Inc.	12	12.57	95%	17.22	70%	4	3	1.00	27.9	NIL	Toiletries/Cosmetics

(*The Value Line Investment Survey*, "Summary of Advices and Index," January 2, 1987, p. 37)

EDITOR's NOTE: Note the shrinkage of stocks selling below two-thirds of net working capital from five in the 1979 Value Line compendium to one in 1987 and below one times working capital from 33 in 1979 to five in 1987. The five stocks listed in 1979 as selling below two-thirds of working capital had advanced an average of 188% by yearend 1986, incidentally (adjusting for splits).—J.T.

APPENDIX VIII: FORBES'S "LOADED LAGGARDS"

We regularly monitor results for the stock portfolios we create in this column. Sure, the theory behind a particular list tends to be interesting in its own right. But try buying dinner with a theory.

One of our favorite features, which we usually label "loaded laggards," seems to beat the market with surprising regularity. The list of 105 loaded laggards that appeared in our Oct. 26, 1981 issue has reaped a return of 145%—excluding dividends. Not bad, especially when you consider that the market is up only 46% over the same period.

We use several criteria to create our loaded laggard portfolios. Basically, we try to find companies that look cheap and seem otherwise healthy.

(*Forbes,* Sept. 24, 1984, pp. 242–243).

Book-value bargains

These 92 stocks all sell below book value, as the ratios in column seven below indicate. Each company is currently making money and, as shown in column three, also has a positive earnings growth rate over the past four years. In addition, many of these firms have a price/earnings multiple well below the market average.

New York Stock Exchange

Name/business	Recent price	52-week high low	4-year earnings growth	EPS	P/E	Book value	Price/ book	Debt/ equity	Yield	Sales ($mil)
Adams-Millis/textiles	15¼	18⅞–11⅞	144%	$ 0.95	16.1	$15.97	0.95	65.0%	1.8%	$ 82.8
Anderson Clayton/food processing	29¾	33½–24½	8	2.83	10.5	46.18	0.64	6.1	4.4	1,390.4
Applied Magnetics/computers	10¾	33⅝– 8	1	0.80	13.4	14.02	0.77	2.8	—	101.6
Armstrong Rubber/tires	19	19¼–15	33	2.54	7.5	20.57	0.92	34.7	2.5	594.7
Burlington Inds/textiles	25¼	43 –23	3	4.11	6.1	42.70	0.59	37.1	6.5	2,990.4
Burlington North/transportation	44¼	54¾–35	7	7.02	6.3	50.39	0.88	73.0	2.3	4,508.2
Control Data/comp svcs and equip	33⅛	57¾–24⅜	4	3.42	9.7	47.13	0.70	290.5	2.0	4,582.8
Easco /tools	14	22⅞–12⅞	2	1.32	10.6	17.37	0.81	54.4	6.3	492.6
Fabri-Centers of Am/spec retail	10½	13⅞– 9⅝	6	0.89	11.8	11.73	0.90	10.3	2.7	209.4
Firestone Tire & Rubber/tires	18⅛	23⅞–15¾	5	1.83	9.9	26.66	0.68	24.0	4.4	3,866.0
Fischbach/electric contractor	43¾	55½–40¾	22	5.32	8.2	48.35	0.90	18.5	6.1	1,339.0
Ford Motor/autos	45½	47⅜–33	15	15.97	2.8	46.01	0.99	31.6	3.5	44,454.6
Goodyear Tire & Rubber/tires	27⅜	33¼–23	11	3.97	6.9	28.61	0.96	20.7	5.1	9,735.8
Grolier/publishing	3⅜	5⅝– 3	218	0.77	4.4	3.60	0.94	247.7	—	286.2
Intl Multifoods/food processing	24⅜	34 –23	19	3.44	7.1	25.03	0.97	45.9	7.2	1,067.2

Book-value bargains

New York Stock Exchange

Name/business	Recent price	52-week high low	4-year earnings growth	EPS	P/E	Book value	Price/ book	Debt/ equity	Yield	Sales ($mil)
Jewelcor/specialty retail	6⅞	9 – 5⅞	2%	$0.48	14.3	$14.32	0.48	51.0%	—	$ 195.7
Mohasco/home furnishings	19¾	24¼–16¼	17	2.47	8.0	30.90	0.64	28.6	1.6%	643.8
Morrison-Knudsen/construction	29⅜	32¾–26¼	8	3.99	7.4	33.09	0.89	17.1	4.8	2,166.0
Morse Shoe/retail	22¼	35⅞–21⅜	6	3.28	6.8	23.19	0.96	41.3	3.6	523.0
GC Murphy/retail	33¼	41½–26	21	4.34	7.7	35.29	0.94	42.3	4.2	872.2
Murray Ohio Mfg/bikes, mowers	20⅞	29¾–20	1	2.33	9.0	28.90	0.72	23.1	5.7	386.5
Pueblo Intl/supermarkets	11	11¾– 7⅛	4	1.18	9.3	11.39	0.97	88.7	1.5	476.8
Puerto Rican Cement/cement	8½	12¼– 5½	9	2.38	3.6	14.80	0.57	134.4	—	57.2
Scot Lad Foods/food processing	6⅞	12⅞– 6	27	1.30	5.3	8.82	0.78	76.6	—	886.7
Springs Inds/home furnishings	34⅜	40¾–31¼	1	4.59	7.5	48.09	0.71	10.6	4.4	894.4
Suave Shoe/footwear	7⅜	9⅜– 6¾	9	0.37	19.9	11.14	0.66	22.8	4.1	111.5
Tandycrafts/leather products	13½	17½–11⅞	17	1.07	12.6	14.44	0.93	0.0	—	61.1
United Brands/food processing	16¼	21¾–13⅛	9	3.43	4.7	17.37	0.94	172.9	—	3,360.4
West Point-Pepperell/apparel	39	54⅞–34⅜	20	5.97	6.5	43.87	0.89	22.5	5.6	1,206.3
Wolverine World Wide/footwear	11¾	20¾– 9¾	4	0.69	17.0	15.36	0.76	33.8	4.1	353.1
Zapata/construction, oilfield svcs	20¼	24⅞–15¼	27	1.42	14.3	22.39	0.90	112.5	4.1	443.0

American Stock Exchange

Name/business	Recent price	52-week high low	4-year earnings growth	EPS	P/E	Book value	Price/ book	Debt/ equity	Yield	Sales ($mil)
Alba-Waldensian/apparel	8⅜	17⅜– 8⅛	69%	$1.45	5.8	$12.48	0.67	24.8%	2.4%	$ 46.7
Avondale Mills/textiles	18¼	25¾–17¼	87	3.10	5.9	26.65	0.68	27.7	4.4	302.1
Barco of California/apparel	3⅜	6 – 3⅜	4	0.25	13.5	5.80	0.58	0.5	3.6%	24.3
Blessings/health care products	22¼	26 –17⅝	35	2.52	8.8	22.60	0.98	44.9	3.6	43.6
CHB Foods/food processing	11½	15½–10¼	6	1.49	7.7	13.00	0.88	18.1	1.7	291.7
Diamond Bathurst/containers	9¼	12⅛– 8	8	1.21	7.6	9.87	0.94	54.8	2.2	62.4
EAC/military equipment	8¼	14⅜– 7	5	0.95	8.7	8.66	0.95	81.3	4.8	38.8
Esquire Radio & Elec/electronics	30⅛	31¼–24⅜	24	5.11	5.9	41.59	0.72	0.5	2.4	67.6
Galaxy Carpet Mills/carpets	13⅛	22½– 9⅝	58	2.20	6.0	13.68	0.96	77.9	—	200.1
Gaylords National/retail	9⅝	11 – 7	62	0.73	13.2	11.85	0.81	81.0	—	142.9
Intercole/plastic and rubber	6⅛	10⅛– 5⅝	6	0.79	7.8	7.81	0.78	21.4	—	29.9
Metex/apparel	11⅞	15⅝–11¼	4	0.81	14.7	16.26	0.73	31.6	—	14.9
Mid-America Industries/auto parts	8⅝	10⅛– 8⅛	18	0.87	9.9	11.60	0.74	36.6	4.6	83.9
MSI Data/computers	10¼	21⅛– 9½	10	1.38	7.4	11.58	0.89	3.9	3.9	61.2
Newbery Energy/elec contracting	5⅛	10½– 4⅝	56	1.29	4.0	5.64	0.91	118.2	—	68.2
Noel Inds/apparel	2¾	5⅞– 2¼	59	0.30	9.2	6.45	0.43	10.0	—	36.0
Olla Inds/handbags	19¾	22⅝–16⅞	43	1.47	13.4	24.97	0.79	0.0	2.0	5.9
Pantasote/plastics and rubber	6⅝	11¼– 5⅛	7	0.32	20.7	7.97	0.83	39.8	—	139.9
Penn Traffic/supermarkets	18⅝	26½–17⅞	3	2.80	6.7	25.46	0.73	70.1	6.4	518.9
Perini/construction	26⅝	33¾–23	15	2.85	9.3	29.41	0.91	19.7	3.0	852.4
Riblet Products/mftrd housing	11⅛	18¼– 9⅝	12	1.32	8.4	13.53	0.82	7.3	1.8	119.2
SE Nichols/retail	7½	11⅞– 5⅛	17	1.52	4.9	8.54	0.88	78.6	—	277.3
Shopwell/supermarkets	12¼	24⅜– 9½	13	0.89	13.8	19.63	0.62	111.6	1.3	511.9
TeleConcepts/telecommunications	3⅝	27 – 3⅜	NM	0.54	6.7	6.71	0.54	8.0	—	34.5
Trans-Lux/info display	10⅛	16⅝– 9⅞	7	1.37	7.4	13.63	0.74	25.7	1.0	28.0
Virco Mfg/furniture	13¾	14½–10⅛	134	1.69	8.1	14.16	0.97	73.1	0.3	137.0
Vulcan Corp/footwear	14½	17⅛–12⅜	4	1.88	7.7	15.27	0.95	6.8	3.4	29.8

NM: Not meaningful.

APPENDIX IX: GRAHAM-REA INVESTMENT ANALYSIS

February 28, 1979

Buys:

Company (TIC) Exch.	($ Millions)				($ Per Share)		
	Total Debt	Total Tangible Book Value	% Dividend Yield	P/E Ratio	(Bid) Market Value	(Max.) Buy Price	(+50%) Sell Price
1. Monarch Mch.	27.1	30.7	6.3	4.7	29	34	51
2. Coachman Ind.	33.2	42.6	7.6	3.4	7 7/8	12 1/4	18 3/8
3. Tri Chem	4.9	10.9	8.7	3.2	6	7 3/8	11
4. Shaer Shoe	0.9	6.04	7.6	6.4	5 1/4	5 1/2	8 1/4
5. Std. Coosa	25.4	39.5	7.6	5.5	21 1/8	26 1/4	39 3/8
6. Cone Mills	102	226	6.6	4.4	27 1/8	32 5/8	48 7/8
7. Pioneer Elec.	394	463	1.0	2.6	21 3/4	36 1/4	54 3/8
8. Rodale Elec.	3.6	5.66	7.7	4.9	7 3/4	9 3/4	14 3/4
9. Blufield Co.	43.6	36.6	6.6	5.4	18 1/8	18 1/2	27 3/4
10. Pat Fashion	4.9	14.0	0	3.3	5 3/8	7 3/4	11 5/8
11. Ti Caro Inc.	42.7	80.4	8.9	3.7	22 1/2	24 7/8	37 3/8
12. Salant Corp.	66.8	46.9	6.3	4.5	6 3/8	7 7/8	11 3/4
13. Curtiss-Wrt.	138	200	5.6	7.3	14 3/8	16	24 1/8
14. Hittman Corp.	3.7	4.06	3.8	4.8	4	4	6 1/8
15. Stevens, J.P.	487	486	7.9	4.9	13 7/8	17 7/8	26 3/4
16. King Kullen	13.4	19.7	4.2	5.1	12	12 1/4	18 1/2
17. Altamil Corp.	12.3	18.9	8.2	4.1	9 3/4	13	19 1/2
18. Rockower	15.2	28.0	9.0	4.5	11 1/8	13	19 1/2
19. Craig Corp.	28.1	40.5	4.7	6.5	10 3/4	10 7/8	16 3/8
20. Movie Star	11.4	14.4	5.2	4.2	10	13	19 1/2
21. Michaels, J.	4.9	7.94	6.1	5.1	5 1/4	7	10 1/2
22. Garan Inc.	32.8	37.5	8.0	4.3	7 1/2	9 3/8	14 1/4
23. Kenwin Shop	1.3	6.11	8.5	4.8	9 3/4	11 1/8	16 3/4
24. Southwstn Drug	22.4	20.7	6.9	6.1	10 1/2	11 3/4	17 5/8
25. Keller Inds.	50.0	50.9	3.8	4.5	7 7/8	9 5/8	14 3/8

(Based on Benjamin Graham's criteria for common stock investments)

Buys:

Company (TIC) Exch.	($ Millions)				($ Per Share)		
	Total Debt	Total Tangible Book Value	% Dividend Yield	P/E Ratio	(Bid) Market Value	(Max.) Buy Price	(+50%) Sell Price
26. La-Z-Boy	19.6	67.1	7.2	5.4	10	10 1/8	15 1/4
27. Sarg-Welch	7.9	39.6	6.3	6.9	14	14 3/8	21 5/8
28. Sterchi Str.	18.7	19.6	5.7	4.8	9 7/8	11 3/8	17
29. Jaclyn Inc.	3.8	11.2	7.8	5.6	5 1/8	5 3/8	8
30. Hart Schfner	164	183	7.7	5.5	11 1/2	14 1/2	21 3/4
31. Oxford Inds.	49.5	63	7.1	4.5	9 5/8	13 3/8	20 1/8
32. Spring Mill	152	292	6.9	4.7	15 1/4	17 3/4	26 5/8
33. Bassett Furn.	22.9	145	8.3	5.0	15 3/4	17 1/4	25 7/8
34. Ryland Grp.	9.8	25.2	5.1	4.6	9 3/4	9 3/4	14 5/8
35. Blue Bell	212	308	7.0	5.7	22 7/8	24	36
36. Smith, A.O.	173	182	8.1	3.2	17 3/8	24 5/8	37
37. West Pt. Pep.	262	288	8.5	5.1	33	35 1/4	52 7/8
38. Zale Corp.	219	316	6.4	5.1	15 5/8	16 7/8	25 1/4
39. Brow Group	178	246	7.3	5.4	24 5/8	29 1/4	43 7/8
40. Std. Register	39.5	66	7.0	5.3	23	23 3/4	35 5/8
41. Hse. of Fabrics	36	47.9	6.1	7.5	5 7/8	5 7/8	8 3/4
42. Strawb. & Clo.	67.8	98.6	5.1	5.0	27 1/2	28 5/8	43
43. Hse. of Ron.	10.3	13.4	6.4	4.1	6 1/4	8 1/8	12 1/4
44. Marlene Ind.	21.8	36.8	2.2	5.1	13	13	19 1/2
45. Rival Mfg.	11.6	51.0	11.6	7.7	6 7/8	8	12
46. Weyenberg	11.4	25.5	6.1	5.3	17 3/4	18 1/4	27 3/8
47. Realex Corp.	3.3	9.6	5.6	4.4	8 1/2	9 3/4	14 3/4
48. Cunnghm. Drug	15.1	27.3	3.4	7.5	9 3/8	10 1/4	15 3/8
49. CRS Group	8.2	17.5	3.1	5.2	9 3/4	10 1/4	15 3/8
50. Electographic	2.9	13.1	6.0	5.9	16 5/8	16 5/8	24 7/8

APPENDIX IX (a): GRAHAM-REA FUNDAMENTAL VALUES
DECEMBER 31, 1986

(Based on Benjamin Graham's criteria for common stock investments)

Columns under "$ PER SHARE" heading: MONTH END PRICE, MAX BUY PRICE, (+50%) SELL PRICE.

BUYS	COMPANY / SIC/TIC	EXCH	NOTE	TOT TANG BOOK & DEBT $MIL	DEBT TO BOOK	12 MO PRICE HIGH & LOW	MONTH VOL [100] & SHRS OUT [MIL]	BOOK P/S	NCA P/S	INV TO CUR AST	CSH TO CUR LIB	(Y) CUR YLD	P/E	RISK RATING	MONTH END PRICE	MAX BUY PRICE	(+50%) SELL PRICE
001	CONCORD FAB / 2200 CIS	ASE	W	24.1 / 25.4	1.1	13.0 / 7.5	238.0 / 0.573	13.53	10.25	0.5	0.0	0.0	PG 8.0	1.2	8.7	10.1	15.2
002	ESQUIRE RAD / 3661 EE	ASE		19.7 / 6.2	0.3	41.0 / 33.4	397.0 / 0.483	40.88	39.80	0.1	3.5	2.0	[100+]	1.2	35.3	39.6	59.5
003	GEMCO NATL / 5199 GNL	ASE	W	5.39 / 8.80	1.6	2.4 / 0.7	1247 / 2.71	1.99	1.75	0.5	0.8	0.0	PG 4.1 DE	1.2	1.5	1.6	2.5
004	LITTLEFIELD / 5199 LFA	ASE	W	5.21 / 8.90	1.7	4.2 / 3.0	165.0 / 1.07	4.85	3.50	0.6	0.0	0.0	[100+]	1.2	3.2	3.4	5.1
005	MICHAELS(J) / 5712 MICH	OTC		11.8 / 4.8	0.4	11.4 / 8.4	133.0 / 0.876	13.46	11.74	0.1	1.4	4.1	8.5 DE	1.1	8.6	11.5	17.4
006	SWANK INC / 3199 SNK	NYS		54.0 / 34.6	0.6	16.3 / 11.6	974.0 / 3.46	15.63	12.78	0.6	0.1	0.0	PG 27.3 DE	1.2	12.0	12.6	19.1
+++++++++++++++++[HOLDS FOR NET-CURRENT-ASSET COMPANIES]+++++++++++++++++																	
001	BARDEN CORP / 3560 BARD	OTC		47.3 / 12.5	0.3	31.2 / 23.4	207.0 / 1.60	29.56	17.14	0.5	0.7	4.0	PG 12.5 DE	1.3	25.0	17.1	25.6
002	BELL INDS / 5065 BI	NYS		99.1 / 46.2	0.5	27.3 / 22.0	2423 / 5.36	18.49	13.84	0.6	0.1	1.6	PG 37.3 DE	1.5	20.4	13.6	20.6
003	BINKS MFG / 3560 BIN	ASE		67.7 / 28.7	0.4	32.1 / 22.2	310.0 / 2.99	22.68	16.74	0.5	0.1	4.4	PG 10.4 DE	1.4	22.5	16.5	25.0
004	CHATHAM MFG / 2200 CHAT	OTC		54.4 / 16.1	0.3	31.0 / 22.0	874.0 / 1.68	32.34	22.90	0.5	0.7	3.0	11.4	1.3	26.4	22.7	34.2
005	DECISION / 3683 DIC	NYS		89.6 / 38.3	0.4	14.6 / 7.4	4945 / 9.40	9.54	6.89	0.4	0.6	0.0	35.0 DE	1.3	8.8	6.7	10.2
006	DOUGHTIE'S / 2010 DOBQ	OTC		7.61 / 5.5	0.7	6.4 / 5.0	24.0 / 0.86	8.85	4.32	0.3	0.2	2.6	PG 7.0	1.3	6.2	4.2	6.3
007	FISCHR & PR / 3823 FP	ASE		66.1 / 62.1	0.9	22.7 / 12.3	1469 / 4.13	16.00	11.67	0.5	0.1	0.0	22.9 DE	1.3	14.4	11.5	17.4
008	FRIEDMN IND / 3310 FRD	ASE		32.6 / 5.2	0.2	11.0 / 7.5	176.0 / 3.66	8.92	8.20	0.3	7.5	3.2	PG 15.1 DE	1.3	8.6	8.1	12.2
009	GILBERT ASC	OTC		101	0.7	37.4	1720	38.18	23.78	0.1	1.0	4.9	PG 3.9	1.4	35.0	23.6	35.5

#	Name / Ticker	Ex															
009)	GILBERT ASC / 8911 GILBA	OTC	101 / 70.8	0.7	37.4 / 31.2	1720 / 2.64	38.18	23.78	0.1	1.0	4.9	PG 3.9	1.4	35.0	23.6	35.5
010)	GORDON JEWL / 5944 GOR	NYS	242 / 235.7	1.0	22.4 / 16.3	2107 / 10.5	23.01	16.40	0.7	0.0	2.6	PG 16.1	1.3	20.0	16.3	24.4
011)	INFOTRON / 3663 INFN	OTC	61.6 / 23.5	0.4	18.4 / 7.0	6820 / 5.12	12.04	6.06	0.4	0.7	0.0	20.9 DE	1.1	7.6	6.0	9.0
012)	KREISLER / 3720 KRSL	OTC	6.98 / 0.8	0.1	9.6 / 7.6	44.0 / 0.797	8.76	7.22	0.4	3.9	0.0	PG 7.3	1.4	8.2	7.1	10.6
013)	MEGADATA CP / 3683 MOTA	OTC	7.05 / 1.2	0.2	2.1 / 19.7	579.0 / 2.12	3.33	2.59	0.4	2.7	0.0	95.8 DE	1.2	2.7	2.4	3.7
014)	MONARCH MCH / 3540 MNO	NYS	67.2 / 16.2	0.2	12.7 / 27.4	1856 / 3.67	18.28	12.61	0.4	1.0	5.3	PG 33.3 DE	1.3	15.0	12.5	18.7
015)	MUELLER CO / 3443 MUEL	OTC	31.7 / 16.0	0.5	20.0 / 14.5	1463 / 1.17	27.13	17.18	0.4	0.7	** 8.4	PG 100+ DE	1.2	20.2	17.1	25.6
016)	PENOBSCOT / 3140 PSO	ASE	8.74 / 1.30	0.1	10.5 / 5.4	229.0 / 0.663	13.19	11.33	0.3	3.3	3.4	PG 12.2	1.3	11.7	11.2	16.7
017)	PRIME MED / 8091 PMSI	OTC	49.5 / 11.1	0.2	3.4 / 23.3	7824 / 8.41	5.89	2.86	0.0	1.6	0.0	31.8 DE	1.1	3.4	2.6	4.2
018)	RAGAN[BRAD] / 5500 BRD	ASE	46.9 / 44.4	0.9	16.5 / 18.5	448.0 / 2.19	21.42	15.16	0.4	0.0	0.6	PG 50.6 DE	1.4	21.2	15.1	22.5
019)	SHAER SHOE / 3140 SHS	ASE	11.5 / 3.0	0.3	11.2 / 20.7	141.0 / 1.02	11.26	10.44	0.1	2.4	** 5.8	13.2 DE	1.4	12.1	10.3	15.5
020)	TANDYCRAFTS / 5999 TAC	NYS	38.3 / 5.3	0.1	14.7 / 4.3	922.0 / 2.36	16.26	13.48	0.5	2.2	0.0	PG 17.2 DE	1.4	16.4	13.3	20.1
021)	3 D DEPT / 5999 TDD.B	ASE	14.5 / 4.3	0.3	3.4 / 18.6	48.0 / 3.31	4.40	3.18	0.7	0.7	1.5	PG 16.0 DE	1.4	4.0	3.1	4.6
022)	WEISFIELDS / 5944 WEIS	OTC	19.6 / 18.9	1.0	13.4 / 10.5	230.0 / 0.996	19.72	11.79	0.5	0.0	2.9	PG 13.3 DE	1.4	17.2	11.6	17.5
023)	WELDOTRON / 3560 WLD	ASE	17.9 / 17.9	1.0	6.6 / 14.0	695.0 / 1.82	9.66	5.70	0.5	0.1	0.0 #	PG 28.2 DE	1.2	7.5	5.5	8.4
024)	WRIGHT [NM] / 2200 WRIT	OTC	27.1 / 8.1	0.3	11.1	124.0 / 2.09	12.97	10.55	0.5	1.3	2.8	100+	1.4	13.3	10.4	15.6

Note: Some companies qualify as both performance and NCA companies.

Buy price ≤ NCA & P/E < 250/AAA (not a loss company).

Research has shown that buying at or below NCA value is better than buying at or below 2/3 NCA value.

Ave. AAA industrial bond rate: 8.534

W = Companies which meet our investment criteria but have a higher ratio of debt-to-total tangible book than the average for their industry.

** = High dividend yield.

Courtesy, James Buchanan Rea, Inc., 10966 Chalon Road, Los Angeles, California 90077.

APPENDIX X: ASSET INVESTORS FUND PORTFOLIO
(Dec. 31, 1978)

ASSET INVESTORS FUND, INC.

STATEMENT OF INVESTMENTS
December 31, 1978

Number of Shares or Principal Amount	Security (Common Stock Unless Otherwise Noted)	Quoted Market(a)
	CONSUMER PRODUCTS (38.3%)	
400	*American Music Stores, Inc.—In Liquidation	$ 200
4,900	Bates Manufacturing Co., Inc.	297,675
14,220	*Beck Arnley Corp.	40,000
2,000	Carter-Wallace, Inc.	13,750
24,300	*Certified Corp.	69,863
25,500	*Circle F. Industries, Inc.	117,937
1,300	Del Monte Corp.	58,338
2,900	Diamond Crystal Salt Co.	63,800
103,500	*Ero Industries, Inc.	219,938
1,200	*Esquire Radio and Electronics, Inc.	18,300
2,000	Hudson Pulp and Paper Corporation	102,250
2,000	Kroehler Manufacturing Company	17,750
23,000	*Lazare, Kaplan International, Inc.	290,375
4,200	Lilli Ann Corporation	25,200
20,500	*National Silver Industries, Inc.	94,812
74,900	*Nestle-LeMur Company	149,800
12,262	Noland Company	95,031
11,300	*Pat Fashions Industries, Inc.	60,737
9,900	Penobscot Shoe Co.	35,888
1,000	Rust Craft Greeting Cards, Inc.	30,438
30,000	Rust Craft Greeting Cards, Inc., 5.25% Cv. Deb.	36,750
4,600	*Shatterproof Glass Corp.	33,350
2,896	Southwestern Drug Corp.	30,408
9,000	Springs Mills, Inc.	132,750
18,700	Star Lite Industries, Inc.	43,244
10,805	*Toscany Imports, Ltd.—In Liquidation	9,725
		2,088,309

* Non-income producing security.

Number of Shares or Principal Amount	Security (Common Stock Unless Otherwise Noted)	Quoted Market(a)
	FINANCIAL SERVICES (17.4%)	
11,650	Caribbean Finance Co.	$ 72,079
1,000	First Empire State Corporation	9,250
3,600	First Texas Financial Corporation	199,800
6,000	Franklin Life Insurance Company	167,622
2,000	Girard Company	45,000
1,000	Hartford National Corporation	14,625
15,397	Hawthorne Financial Corporation	234,804
1,500	Manufacturers National Corporation	38,625
4,312	Marine Corporation	112,651
300	*Meridian Investing and Development Corporation	900
2,000	Union Bancorp, Inc.	57,000
		952,356
	INDUSTRIAL PRODUCTS (28.8%)	
2,200	American Manufacturing Company, Inc.	74,800
18,750	Brennand-Paige Industries, Inc.	93,750
268	Carrier Corp.	7,102
11,640	A.M. Castle Co.	173,145
1,600	Dorr-Oliver, Inc.	25,800
11,400	Ehrenreich Photo-Optical Industries, Inc.	141,075
12,430	Grief Bros. Corp. Class A	205,095
5,735	Handschy Chemical Co.	32,976
9,250	*Holobeam, Inc.	20,812
9,500	*Jaco Electronics, Inc.	16,031
22,100	Kewaunee Scientific Equipment Corporation	164,369
12,495	*Marshall Industries	54,666
500	Revere Copper and Brass, Inc.	6,625
18,300	Schenuit Industries, Inc.	260,775
5,185	Syracuse Supply Co.	136,106
15,900	*Wood Industries, Inc.	159,000
		1,572,127

Appendix X (Continued)

ASSET INVESTORS FUND, INC.

STATEMENT OF INVESTMENTS (Continued)
December 31, 1978

Number of Shares or Principal Amount	Security (Common Stock Unless Otherwise Noted)		Quoted Market(a)
	NATIONAL RESOURCES (8.7%)		
6,400	Aguirre Co.		$ 91,200
1,000	Amax Incorporated		48,750
2,700	*EDG, Inc.—In Liquidation		5,400
2,850	*Kirby Industries Liquidating Trust CBI		5,700
8,675	*Pasco Liquidating Trust CBI		28,194
1,600	Penn Virginia Corporation		104,800
4,355	Shenadoah Oil Corp.		175,289
18,200	*Westates Petroleum Corp.—In Liquidation		13,650
			472,983
	MISCELLANEOUS (1.9%)		
12,235	*Empire Financial Corporation—In Liquidation		979
2,418	*Federated Media, Inc.—In Liquidation		725
5,400	San Jose Water Works		102,262
			103,966
	SHORT TERM INVESTMENTS (2.1%)		
1,040	Oppenheimer Monetary Bridge, Inc.		1,040
113,130	First Variable Rate Fund, Inc.		113,130
			114,170
	MUNICIPAL OBLIGATIONS (9.2%)		
500,000	N.Y.C. Project Notes, 3.93% due 1979		500,033
	Total Investments	106.4 %	5,803,943
	Liabilities Less Net Cash and Receivables	6.4 %	346,367
	TOTAL NET ASSETS	100.0 %	$5,457,576

APPENDIX XI: SELECTED HOLDINGS OF T. ROWE PRICE PERSONAL PORTFOLIOS AS OF 12/31/78

Security	(1) Date 1st Acquired	(2) Lowest Cost	(3) 12/31/78 Market	(4) % Change	(5) 1st Year Owned	(6) Dividend 1978	(7) % Change	(8) Yield on Cost 1st Year	(9) 1978
Black & Decker	7/31/37	3/8	16 5/8	1937 +4333.3%	$0.0242	$0.62	+2483.3%	6.5%	165.3%
Honeywell	7/25/38	3 3/4	69 1/2	1938 +1753.3%	$0.125	$2.05	+1540.0%	3.3%	54.7%
Minn. Mining & Mfg.	3/04/39	1/2	63 1/8	1939 +12525.0%	$0.025	$2.00	+7900.0%	5.0%	400.0%
Square D	12/31/39	3/4	20 1/8	+2583.3	0.063	1.40	+2122.2	8.4	186.7
				+7554.2%			+5011.1%	6.7%	293.4%
Dow Chemical	3/12/41	1 5/8	24 7/8	1941 +1430.8%	$0.0315	$1.25	+3868.3%	1.9%	76.9%
*Shell Oil	5/23/41	1 1/2	32 1/8	+2041.7	0.11	1.80	+1536.4	7.3	120.0
Merck	11/05/41	3/8	67 5/8	+17933.3	0.035	1.70	+4757.1	9.3	453.3
				+7135.3%			+3387.3%	6.3%	216.7%
*Tri Continental	6/03/42	3/8	17 5/8	1942 +4600.0%	Nil	$1.06	+100.0%	0.0%	282.7%
Pfizer	9/30/47	1 5/8	33	1947 +1930.8%	$0.10	$1.17	+1070.0%	6.2%	72.0%
Motorola	4/29/54	3 1/4	39 7/8	1954 +1126.9%	$0.125	$1.00	+700.0%	3.8%	30.8%
Avon Products	1/26/55	7/8	50 3/4	1955 +5700.0%	$0.04	$2.55	+6275.0%	4.6%	291.4%
Warner Lambert	6/15/55	2 5/8	23 3/4	+804.8	0.135	1.175	+770.4	5.1	44.8
				+3252.4%			+3522.7%	4.9%	168.1%
PepsiCo	10/23/58	4 1/8	25 5/8	1958 +521.2%	$0.20	$0.97 1/2	+387.5%	4.8%	23.6%

Appendix XI (Continued)

Security	(1) Date 1st Acquired	Market (2) Lowest Cost	Market (3) 12/31/78 Market	Market (4) % Change	(5) 1st Year Owned	Dividend (6) 1978	Dividend (7) % Change	Yield on Cost (8) 1st Year	Yield on Cost (9) 1978
Xerox	4/27/60	2 3/8	53 1/4	+2142.1%	$0.017	$1.90	+11076.5%	0.7%	80.0%
Exxon	12/21/60	19 7/8	49 1/8	+ 147.2	0.95	3.30	+ 247.4	4.8	16.6
				1960 +1144.7%			+5662.0%	2.8%	48.3%
R.P. New Horizons	2/02/62**	2 1/8	9 3/4	+ 358.8%	Nil	$0.0975	+ 100.0%	0.0%	4.6%
McCormick	4/10/62	2	14 1/2	+ 625.0	$0.051	0.40	+ 684.3	2.6	20.0
*Cummins Engine	6/26/62	22 1/8	33 1/4	+ 50.3	0.297	1.71	+ 475.8	1.3	7.7
*Trane	7/26/62	26 7/8	38 3/4	+ 44.2	0.475	1.43	+ 201.1	1.8	5.3
				1962 + 269.6%			+ 365.3%	1.4%	9.4%
Texas Instruments	4/15/63	12 1/2	80	+ 540.0%	$0.16	$1.68	+ 930.0%	1.3%	13.44%
Gulf Oil	8/08/63	13 5/8	23 3/8	+ 71.6	0.80	1.90	+ 137.5	5.9	13.9
IBM	9/11/63	90 7/8	298 1/2	+ 228.5	0.884	11.52	+1203.2	1.0	12.7
				1963 + 280.0%			+ 763.6%	2.7%	20.0%
*ARA Services	2/03/64	22 3/8	36	+ 60.9%	$0.20	$1.545	+ 672.5%	0.9%	6.9%
*EG&G	9/01/64	8 1/2	29	+ 241.2	Nil	0.42	+ 100.0	0.0	4.9
				1964 + 151.1%			+ 386.3%	0.5%	5.9%
Walt Disney Prod.	1/03/66	4	40 1/8	+ 903.1%	$0.0378	$0.3188	+ 743.4%	0.9%	8.0%
Emery Air Freight	1/12/66	8 1/2	18 1/2	+ 117.6	0.1435	0.8775	+ 511.5	1.7	10.3
*FlexiVan	2/01/66	10	14 5/8	+ 46.3	Nil	0.70	+ 100.0	0.0	7.0
*A. H. Robins	8/23/66	9 5/8	8 3/8	- 13.0	0.17	0.34	+ 100.0	1.8	3.5
Continental Oil	8/31/66	13	28 1/8	+ 116.3	0.62	1.425	+ 129.8	4.8	11.0
*Millipore	8/31/66	7	29	+ 866.7	0.01	0.18	+1700.0	0.1	2.6
Hewlett Packard	10/07/66	19 3/8	89 7/8	+ 363.9	0.10	0.50	+ 400.0	0.5	2.6
Georgia Pacific	10/19/66	6 1/4	24 1/4	1966 + 288.0	0.1698	1.025	+ 503.7	2.7	16.4

Security	(1) Date 1st Acquired	(2) Market Lowest Cost	(3) Market 12/31/78 Market	(4) % Change	(5) 1st Year Owned	(6) Dividend 1978	(7) % Change	(8) Yield on Cost 1st Year	(9) Yield on Cost 1978
Louisiana Pacific	10/19/66	4 1/8	18 3/4	+ 354.5	Nil	0.5265	+ 100.0	0.0	12.8
*Scope, Inc.	11/02/66	5 3/8	23 1/4	+ 332.6	Nil	0.50	+ 100.0	0.0	9.3
Avery International	12/23/66	8 5/8	15	+ 73.9	0.08	0.48	+ 500.0	0.9	5.6
				+ 313.6%			+ 444.4%	1.2%	8.1%
	1967								
*Hudson's Bay Oil & Gas	3/23/67	26 1/8	44 3/8	+ 69.9%	$0.40	$1.60	+ 300.0%	1.5%	6.1%
*Tenneco	4/17/67**	23 1/2	30 1/4	+ 28.7	1.22	2.05	+ 68.0	5.2	8.7
Revlon	5/23/67	22 5/8	51 3/8	+ 127.1	0.433	1.20	+ 177.1	1.9	5.3
*Anglo Amer. So. Africa	6/15/67	5 3/4	4 9/32	- 25.5	0.153	0.351	+ 129.4	2.7	6.1
Schlumberger	7/11/67	6 7/8	94 3/4	+1278.2	0.1184	1.175	+ 892.4	1.7	17.1
*Castle & Cooke	10/07/67	9 1/2	17 1/2	+ 84.2	0.26	0.73	+ 180.8	2.7	7.7
*Southwestern Life	11/17/67	13	18 3/8	+ 41.3	0.192	0.80	+ 316.7	1.5	6.2
*Dome Mines	12/05/67	16 3/4	78 1/4	+ 367.2	0.266	1.00	+ 275.9	1.6	6.2
				+ 246.4%			+ 292.5%	2.4%	7.9%
	1968								
Lowes Companies	4/01/68	5 3/4	18	+ 213.0%	$0.06	$0.40	+ 566.7%	1.0%	7.0%
Florida Gas	4/17/68	9	25	+ 177.8	0.40	1.44	+ 260.0	4.4	16.0
Newmont Mining	4/26/63	16 3/4	21 1/2	+ 28.4	0.96	0.80	- 16.7	5.7	4.8
AMAX	5/29/68	31 3/8	48 3/4	+ 55.4	1.266	1.8625	+ 47.1	4.0	5.9
Fleetwood Enterprises	5/29/68	4 1/8	11 1/8	+ 169.7	0.05	0.49	+ 830.0	1.2	11.9
Weyerhaeuser	6/20/68	12 1/2	24 5/8	+ 97.0	0.35	0.85	+ 142.9	2.8	6.8
General Electric	11/22/68**	31 5/8	47 1/8	+ 49.0	1.30	2.40	+ 84.6	4.1	7.6
				+ 112.9%			+ 280.7%	3.3%	8.6%
	1969								
R.P. New Era Fund	5/28/69	10 1/4	11 5/8	+ 13.4%	Nil	$0.3238	+ 100.0%	0.0%	3.2%
*Ranchers Exploration	7/11/69	9 7/8	14	+ 41.8	Nil	Nil	0.0	0.0	0.0
*Union Pacific	10/10/69	21 3/8	51 1/2	+ 140.9	$1.00	2.00	+ 100.0	4.7	9.4
*Hexcel	10/14/69	6	18 1/2	+ 208.3	0.24	0.4575	+ 90.6	4.0	7.6
*ASA Ltd.	12/18/69	7	23 7/8	+ 241.1	0.17 1/2	1.00	+ 471.4	2.5	14.3
				+ 129.1%			+ 152.4%	2.2%	6.9%

Appendix XI (Continued)

Security	(1) Date 1st Acquired	Market (2) Lowest Cost	Market (3) 12/31/78 Market	Market (4) % Change	(5) 1st Year Owned	Dividend (6) 1978	Dividend (7) % Change	Yield on Cost (8) 1st Year	Yield on Cost (9) 1978
				1970					
Mobil Corp.	2/20/70	42 1/4	69 3/8	+ 64.2%	$2.40	$4.30	+ 79.2%	5.7%	10.2%
*West Driefontein	4/01/70	18 5/8	30 1/2	+ 63.8	1.162	3.718	+ 220.0	6.2	20.0
Union Camp Corp.	4/01/70	17 3/4	47 3/4	+ 169.0	0.6666	2.10	+ 215.0	3.8	11.8
Ocean Drilling	5/01/70	10	35 1/2	+ 255.0	0.10	0.25	+ 150.0	1.0	2.5
*Perkin Elmer	5/11/70	11 1/4	27 1/2	+ 144.4	Nil	0.40	+ 100.0	0.0	3.6
Burroughs	5/21/70	39 5/8	73	+ 84.2	0.30	1.35	+ 350.0	0.8	3.4
*DeBeers	6/19/70	5	5 5/8	+ 12.5	0.145	0.513	+ 253.8	2.9	10.3
Louisiana Land	6/19/70	23 7/8	21 1/2	- 9.9	0.956	1.22	+ 27.6	4.0	5.1
*Cross & Trecker	8/13/70	2 3/4	17 1/8	+ 522.7	0.10	0.60	+ 500.0	3.6	21.8
Eastman Kodak	11/06/70	42 5/8 in 78	58 5/8	+ 37.5	1.28	2.23	+ 74.2	3.0	5.2
*Koger Properties	11/09/70	4 7/8	15	+ 207.7	Nil	0.70	+ 100.0	0.0	14.4
				+ 141.0%			+ 188.2%	2.8%	9.8%
				1971					
Combustion Engineering	2/01/71	38 7/8	32 5/8	- 16.1%	$0.90	$1.70	+ 88.9%	2.3%	4.4%
*Anglo Amerc. Gold Inv.	2/04/71	15 7/8	21 1/2	+ 35.4	0.547	1.776	+ 224.7	3.4	11.2
*U.N.C. Resources	6/10/71	16	18 1/8	+ 13.3	Nil	0.40	+ 100.0	0.0	2.5
*Callahan Mining	8/24/71	8 7/8	13 3/4	+ 54.9	Nil	0.3921	+ 100.0	0.0	4.4
*Alico	9/20/71	6 7/8	17 1/4	+ 150.9	Nil	0.25	+ 100.0	0.0	3.6
*Day Mines	10/07/71	6 3/4	9 3/4	+ 44.4	0.05	0.25	+ 400.0	0.7	3.7
*Gold Fields of S. Africa	11/09/71	11 1/4	16 5/8	+ 47.8	0.516	1.293	+ 150.6	4.6	11.5
*Pres. Steyn Gold Mng.	11/16/71	6 3/4	9	+ 33.3	0.157	0.758	+ 382.8	2.3	11.2
*Vaal Reefs Exp.	11/16/71	9 7/8	18 3/4	+ 86.1	0.636	1.533	+ 141.0	6.4	15.5
*Homestake Mining	12/08/71	10	30	+ 200.0	0.20	1.325	+ 562.5	2.0	13.3
*Thermo Electron	12/14/71	8 5/8	24 3/4	+ 187.0	Nil	Nil	0.0	2.0	0.0
				+ 76.1%			+ 167.0%	2.0%	7.4%
				1972					
*Newhall Land & Farming	1/03/72	8	25 1/8	+ 214.1%	$0.30	$0.585	+ 95.0%	3.8%	7.3%
*Campbell Red Lake Mines	2/09/72	14 3/4	29 1/4	+ 98.3	0.203	0.765	+ 276.8	1.4	5.2
Digital Equipment	5/18/72	27 5/8	53 5/8	+ 94.1	Nil	Nil	N.C.	0.0	0.0
*Scientific Atlanta	9/27/72	3 3/4	32 1/2	+ 766.6	Nil	0.17	+ 100.0	0.0	4.5

Security	(1) Date 1st Acquired	(2) Lowest Cost	(3) 12/31/78 Market	(4) % Change	(5) 1st Year Owned	(6) 1978	(7) % Change	(8) 1st Year	(9) 1978
			Market			Dividend		Yield on Cost	
*Stilfontein	5/08/72	1 1/2	4 1/8	+ 175.0	0.065	0.241	+ 270.8	4.3	16.1
*Federal Resources	10/17/72**	2 3/8	5 3/8	+ 126.3	Nil	Nil	N.C.	0.0	0.0
*Western Areas Gold Mng.	12/05/72	1 1/2	1 5/8	+ 8.3	0.093	0.124	+ 33.3	6.2	8.3
				+ 211.8%			+ 110.8%	2.2%	5.9%
1973									
*Pittson	1/19/73	11 1/8	17 3/8	+ 56.2%	$0.2698	$1.20	+ 344.8%	2.4%	10.8%
*Science Management	3/23/73**	2 5/8	3	+ 14.3	0.0884	0.10	+ 13.1	3.4	3.8
*Telesciences	4/16/73	4 3/8	15 1/8	+ 245.7	Nil	0.51	+ 100.0	0.0	11.7
C.R. Bard	4/30/73	11 1/4	11 5/8	+ 3.3	0.18	0.30	+ 66.7	1.6	2.7
Pinkerton's	4/30/73**	22 1/4	27 3/4	+ 24.7	0.757	1.75	+ 131.2	3.4	7.9
American Hosp. Supply	6/26/73	20	26 1/4	+ 31.3	0.28	0.65	+ 132.1	1.4	3.3
*Rosario Resources	7/25/73	19 3/8	16 1/4	- 19.4	0.2111	0.6372	+ 201.8	1.1	3.3
*Kloof Gold Mine	8/15/73	3 7/8	6 3/4	+ 74.2	0.518	0.367	- 29.1	13.4	9.5
Polaroid	12/04/73**	14 5/8	51 3/4	+ 253.8	0.32	0.90	+ 181.3	2.2	6.2
*Viacom	12/24/73	3 1/8	24 5/8	+ 688.0	Nil	0.225	+ 100.0	0.0	7.2
*Sanders Associates	8/29/73	2 1/2	17	+ 580.0	Nil	0.10	+ 100.0	0.0	4.0
*United Park City	10/03/73	1 3/4	1 1/2	- 14.3	Nil	Nil	N.C.	0.0	0.0
*TelePrompTer	11/13/73	3 7/8	12 7/8	- 232.3	Nil	Nil	N.C.	0.0	0.0
				+ 167.2%			+ 103.2%	2.2%	5.4%
1974									
*Tosco	5/10/74	2	6	+ 200.0%	Nil	Nil	N.C.	0.0%	0.0%
*Thomas & Betts	12/10/74	26 1/8	41 5/8	+ 59.3	$0.66	$1.18	+ 78.8%	2.5	4.5
Cox Cable	8/12/74	4 1/8	36.48***	+ 784.4	Nil	0.299 1.00	+ 100.0	0.0	7.2
*United Keno Hill Mine	3/20/74	9 1/4	8	- 13.5	1.00	0.70	- 30.0	10.8	7.6
*Duicker Explor.	12/05/74	3 1/8	2 3/8	- 24.0	Nil	0.329	+ 100.0	0.0	10.5
				+ 201.2%			+ 49.8%	2.7%	6.0%
1975									
*Houston Oil & Minerals	2/19/75	5 5/8	15 3/8	+ 173.3%	$0.133	$0.80	+ 501.5%	2.4%	14.2%
*Randfontein Estates	3/31/75	13 5/8	39	+ 186.2	Nil	3.864	+ 100.0	0.0	28.4
*Harmony Gold Mng.	12/22/75	4 1/4	4 1/8	- 2.9	0.169	0.631	+ 273.4	4.0	14.8
*Heath Tecna	4/09/75**	2 7/8	19 1/2	+ 578.3	Nil	Nil	N.C.	0.0	0.0
*AZL	9/19/75**	3 5/8	4 3/8	+ 20.7	0.10	Nil	- 100.0	2.8	0.0
				+ 191.1%			+ 155.0%	1.8%	11.5%

Appendix XI (Continued)

Security	(1) Date 1st Acquired	Market (2) Lowest Cost	Market (3) 12/31/78 Market	Market (4) % Change	(5) 1st Year Owned	Dividend (6) 1978	Dividend (7) % Change	Yield on Cost (8) 1st Year	Yield on Cost (9) 1978
				1976					
St. Joe Minerals	4/22/76	36 3/8	22 3/4	− 37.5%	$1.275	$1.30	+ 2.0%	3.5%	3.6%
*Dome Petroleum	12/08/76	33 5/8	80 1/2	+ 139.4	Nil	Nil	N.C.	0.0	0.0
				+ 51.0%			+ 1.0%	1.8%	1.8%
				1977					
*Magma Power	3/17/77	8 3/4	9 1/8	+ 4.3%	Nil	Nil	N.C.	0.0%	0.0%
Jack Eckerd	4/19/77	24	26 5/8	+ 10.9	$0.52	$0.68	+ 30.8%	2.2	2.8
K mart	4/20/77	25 1/2	22 1/2	− 11.8	0.50	0.68	+ 36.0	2.0	2.7
U.S. Fidelity & Guranty	4/20/77	32 1/4	30 1/2	+ 5.4	1.6545	1.9181	+ 15.9	5.1	5.9
*East Driefontein	6/10/77	6 1/4	9 1/8	+ 46.0	Nil	0.785	+ 100.0	0.0	12.6
Johnson & Johnson	8/09/77	70 1/2	73 3/4	+ 4.6	1.40	1.70	+ 21.4	2.0	2.4
*Payless Cashways	8/23/77	8 1/8	11 3/4	+ 44.6	0.075	0.10	+ 33.3	0.9	1.2
Kerr McGee	9/29/77	46 1/8	47 3/4	+ 3.5	1.25	1.25	N.C.	2.7	2.7
Harris Corp.	11/25/77	20 7/8	28 3/4	+ 37.7	0.45	0.55	+ 22.2	2.2	2.6
*Hecla Mining	12/13/77	5 1/8	5 1/8	N.C.	Nil	Nil	N.C.	0.0	0.0
				+ 13.4%			+ 26.0%	1.7%	3.3%
				1978					
*Rite Aid	2/07/78	17	19 3/4	+ 16.2%	$0.395	$0.395	N.C.	2.3%	2.3%
*Camflo Mines	9/12/78	11 5/8	13 1/4	+ 14.0	0.50	0.50	N.C.	4.3	4.3
*Ethan Allen	9/28/78	20 7/8	24 1/2	+ 17.4	0.625	0.625	N.C.	3.0	3.0
*Frigitronics	10/10/78	14	14 3/4	+ 5.4	0.22	0.22	N.C.	1.6	1.6
*McCulloch Oil	5/15/78	4 3/4	4 7/8	+ 2.6	Nil	Nil	N.C.	0.0	0.0
*Penn Central	11/22/78	17 1/2	14 7/8	− 15.0	Nil	Nil	N.C.	0.0	0.0
				+ 6.8%			N.C.	1.9%	1.9%

*Not on approved list of T. Rowe Price Associates, Inc.

**Original purchase has been sold. Cost shown is for later date.

***Merged into Cox Broadcasting 7/22/77. Basis 46/100 shs. Cox Broadcasting and $10.83 cash.

APPENDIX XII: PRICE MODEL NEW ERA PORTFOLIO (GROUP A)

T. Rowe Price model new era portfolio

(inception 8/31/77)
performance—growth of income and market value

shares	Group A company	price (2/28/79)	value	change since 8/31/77	dollar income 1977	dollar income 1978	change 1977-78
727	Castle & Cooke	15⅛	$ 10,995.88	+10.0%	$480.68	$581.60	+21.0%
196	Dome Mines*	85¾	16,807.00	+68.1	156.80	196.00	+25.0
265	Dome Petroleum	97¼	25,771.25	+157.7	—	—	—
402	Jack Eckerd	24⅛	9,698.25	-3.0	209.04	273.36	+30.8
563	EG&G	26	14,638.00	+46.4	202.68	236.46	+16.7
610	Flexi-Van	14⅝	8,921.25	-10.8	213.50	427.00	+100.0
740	Hexcel	17¼	12,765.00	+27.7	316.35	338.55	+7.0
261	Houston Oil & Mineral	16⅝	4,339.13	-56.6	174.09	208.80	+19.9
435	Lowes Cos*	18¼	7,938.75	-20.6	104.40	174.00	+66.7
1,176	Magma Power*	11¼	13,230.00	+32.3	—	—	—
552	McCormick	13½	7,452.00	-25.5	220.80	220.80	NC
1,212	Payless Cashways*	12¾	15,453.00	+54.5	90.90	121.20	+33.3
490	Perkin-Elmer	27¼	13,352.50	+33.5	156.80	196.00	+25.0
544	Scientific-Atlanta*	34¼	18,632.00	+86.3	70.72	92.48	+30.8
263	Thomas & Betts*	41⅝	10,947.38	+9.5	255.11	310.34	+21.6
576	Viacom*	26	14,950.00	+49.5	57.50	129.38	+125.0
976	Harris Corp.*[1]	26	25,376.00	+153.8	439.20	536.80	+22.2
397	Rite Aid[2]	19¼	7,642.25	-23.6	127.04	156.82	+23.4
728	Fleetwood[3]	10½	7,644.00	+86.3	313.04	356.72	+14.0
879	Teleprompter*[4]	12½	10,987.50				
578	Time 1.575 conv pfd B[5]	28½	16,473.00	+64.7	new issue	78.39	NA
	total Group A	—	$274,014.13	+37%	$3,588.65	$4,634.70	+29.1%
	NYSE comp index 52.93	53.93	—	+1.9	—	—	—
	Amex index 117.97	160.74	—	+36.3	—	—	—
	Dow Jones industrial 861.49	808.82	—	-6.1	$45.84	48.52	+5.8%
	Standard & Poor's 500 96.77	96.28	—	-0.5	4.66	5.09	+9.2
	NASDAQ OTC comp 100.10	122.56	—	+22.4	—	—	—

[1]Bought November 1977 at 20½ as replacement for Alcon Labs. [2]Bought April 1978 at 21⅝ as replacement for Sabine Corp. [3]Bought July 1978 at 13⅛ as partial replacement for ESL. [4]Bought July 1978 at 11⅛ as partial replacement for ESL. [5]Received October 1978 from merger of Amer. TV & Comm. into Time Inc. NC: no change. NA: not available.

(*Forbes* Magazine, April 2, 1979, p. 130)

APPENDIX XIII: PRICE MODEL NEW ERA PORTFOLIO (GROUPS B AND C)

shares	**Group B** company	price (2/28/79)	value	change since 8/31/77	dollar income 1977	dollar income 1978	change 1977-78
580	Black & Decker	19	$11,020.00	+10.2%	$278.40	$359.60	+29.2%
140	Burroughs	64¾	9,065.00	-9.4	114.80	189.00	+64.6
207	Digital Equipment	49½	10,246.50	+2.5	—	—	—
247	Walt Disney	37⅛	9,169.88	-8.3	36.26	78.74	+117.2
162	Eastman Kodak*	59⅝	9,659.25	-3.4	340.20	361.26	+6.2
510	Emery Air Freight	16⅞	8,606.25	-13.9	363.37	447.53	+23.2
187	General Electric	46	8,602.00	-14.0	374.00	448.80	+20.0
126	Hewlett-Packard*	85⅛	10,725.75	+7.3	50.40	63.00	+25.0
37	IBM*	300	11,100.00	+11.0	370.00	426.24	+15.2
138	Johnson & Johnson*	68¼	9,418.50	-5.8	193.20	234.60	+21.4
326	K mart	23¼	7,579.50	-24.2	163.00	221.68	+36.0
170	Merck*	65¼	11,092.50	+10.9	255.00	289.00	+13.3
192	3M*	56⅜	10,824.00	+8.2	326.40	384.00	+17.6
394	PepsiCo	23⅞	9,406.75	-5.9	325.05	384.15	+18.2
324	Polaroid	40¼	13,041.00	+30.4	210.60	291.60	+38.5
234	Revlon	47⅝	11,144.25	+11.4	222.30	280.80	+26.3
149	Schlumberger*	96¾	14,415.75	+44.2	130.37	175.07	+34.3
113	Texas Instruments*	78¾	8,898.75	-11.0	149.16	189.84	+27.3
324	Weyerhaeuser*	28¼	9,153.00	-8.5	259.20	275.40	+6.3
190	Xerox	52⅞	10,046.25	+0.5	266.00	361.00	+35.7
	total Group B	—	$203,214.88	+1.6%	$4,427.71	$5,461.31	+23.3%
	Dow Jones industrial	808.82	—	-6.1	$45.84	$48.52	+5.8%
	Standard & Poor's 500	96.28	—	-0.5	4.66	5.09	+9.2

shares	**Group C** company	price (2/28/79)	value	change since 8/31/77	dollar income 1977	dollar income 1978	change 1977-78
784	Alico*	18⅞	$14,798.00	+48.0%	$156.80	$196.00	+25.0%
225	AMAX*	48½	10,912.50	+9.1	393.75	419.06	+6.4
580	Anglo Amer Gold Inv*	25⅛	14,572.50	+45.7	944.82	1,030.08	+9.0
735	Callahan Mining*	16¼	11,943.75	+19.4	244.90	279.89	+14.3
362	Campbell Red Lakes Mine*	33⅛	11,991.25	+19.9	244.35	276.93	+13.3
1,212	Day Mines	11¾	14,241.00	+42.4	242.40	303.00	+25.0
1,454	East Driefontein Gold*	10⅜	15,085.25	+50.9	1,027.98	1,141.39	+11.0
255	Homestake Mining	34¼	8,733.75	-12.7	318.75	337.88	+6.0
169	Kerr-McGee*	50⅝	8,555.63	-14.4	211.25	211.25	NC
2,162	Kloof Gold Mining	9⅛	19,728.25	+97.3	583.74	793.45	+35.9
544	Newmont Mining*	24	13,056.00	+30.6	761.60	435.20	-42.8
410	Pittston	19⅜	7,943.75	-20.6	528.90	492.00	-7.0
1,403	Pres Steyn Gold Mining	10⅛	14,205.38	+42.1	242.72	1,063.47	+338.1
296	Randfontein Estates*	42⅜	12,543.00	+25.4	712.47	1,143.74	+60.5
615	Ranchers Exploration	17	10,455.00	+4.6	—	—	—
507	Rosario Resources	24	12,168.00	+21.7	298.20	323.06	+8.3
334	St Joe Minerals	25⅞	8,642.25	-13.6	434.20	434.20	NC
447	UNC Resources	20	8,940.00	-10.6	—	178.80	+100.0
714	Vaal Reefs*	23	16,422.00	+64.2	782.54	1,094.56	+39.9
487	West Driefontein Gold	31⅜	15,279.63	+52.8	1,314.41	1,810.67	+37.8
	total Group C	—	$250,216.88	+25.1%	$9,443.78	$11,964.63	+26.7%
	total portfolio	—	$727,445.88	+21.2	$17,460.14	$22,060.64	+26.3%
	Dow Jones industrial	808.82	—	-6.1	$45.84	$48.52	+5.8%
	Standard & Poor's 500	96.28	—	-0.5	4.66	5.09	+9.2

NC: no change.

(*Forbes* Magazine, April 2, 1979, p. 131)

APPENDIX XIV: TEMPLETON GROWTH FUND INVESTMENT PORTFOLIO (APRIL 30, 1979)

	Number of Shares	Cost	Market Value
COMMON STOCKS: 89.4%			
Oil & Gas: 14.0%			
Amerada Hess Corp.	99,250	$ 2,769,901	$ 3,386,906
*Dome Petroleum Ltd.	20,000	1,209,791	2,404,372
El Paso Company	59,000	788,308	1,076,750
Gulf Oil Corp.	90,000	2,080,281	2,418,750
Houston Natural Gas	77,000	1,971,341	2,175,250
Husky Oil Limited	25,000	584,779	1,278,689
Mitchell Energy & Development	146,999	1,962,158	3,546,351
Northern Natural Gas	28,000	1,025,496	1,211,000
Royal Dutch Petroleum	100,000	5,035,021	6,874,999
Shell Oil Company	50,000	1,658,097	2,131,250
Standard Oil of California	20,000	591,685	985,000
Texaco, Inc.	50,000	1,301,586	1,356,250
Union Oil of California	77,000	3,861,886	5,351,499
		24,840,330	34,197,066
Insurance: 11.4%			
Aetna Life & Casualty	100,000	3,896,653	4,387,500
*American Income Life Insurance	11,200	151,200	205,800
American National Financial Corp.	20,000	250,000	260,000
Dai Tokyo Fire & Marine	100,000	110,796	138,900
Guaranty National Corp.	50,000	577,288	806,250
Hanover Insurance	49,500	1,409,750	1,299,375
INA Corp.	100,000	3,020,774	4,400,000
Kemper Corp.	150,000	3,660,863	4,218,750
Reliable Investors	37,400	454,800	490,875
Reliance Group, Inc.	61,200	1,620,863	2,409,750
Simcoe & Erie Investors	90,300	105,608	339,489
Sumitomo Marine & Fire	400,000	329,232	442,000
Travelers Corp.	37,300	1,304,899	1,342,800
USLIFE Corp.	105,000	1,862,527	2,493,750
U.S. Fidelity & Guaranty	120,900	4,048,424	4,337,288
Washington National Corp.	7,300	177,352	226,300
		22,981,029	27,798,827
Banks and Finance: 8.0%			
Australian & New Zealand Bank	165,000	607,385	756,030
Bancohio Corp.	16,900	369,450	367,575
Bank of Nova Scotia	105,862	1,942,738	2,151,949
Canadian Imperial Bank of Commerce	397,000	9,348,112	9,458,578
First Pennsylvania Corp.	192,500	3,063,097	2,550,625
Royal Bank of Canada	97,800	3,417,097	3,473,770
Toronto Dominion Bank	35,000	678,315	722,951
		19,426,194	19,481,478
Real Estate: 7.4%			
Allarco Development	61,325	544,409	2,064,274
Daon Development	511,600	326,763	5,143,956
Hooker Corporation	1,073,344	797,616	924,150

	Number of Shares	Average Cost	Market Value
COMMON STOCKS (continued):			
Real Estate (continued):			
S. B. McLaughlin Limited	39,000	$ 401,216	$ 349,508
Nu-West Development	465,285	2,582,293	6,508,905
Oriole Homes	10,000	70,296	101,250
Shapell Industries	103,900	2,277,617	2,987,125
		7,000,210	18,079,168
Mining and Metals: 6.7%			
Alcan Aluminum Ltd.	230,000	6,103,977	8,244,809
Kaiser Aluminum & Chemical	76,000	1,272,295	1,558,000
Noranda Mines Ltd.	100,000	2,199,870	3,781,421
*Pancontinental Mining Ltd.	123,300	1,348,005	1,442,856
Reynolds Metals Co.	36,000	1,149,718	1,327,500
		12,073,865	16,354,586
Merchandising: 6.3%			
Brooks Fashion Stores	141,200	2,635,853	3,088,750
G. J. Coles	340,500	601,432	789,279
Heck's Inc.	10,400	108,700	117,000
Ito Yokado Co., Ltd. ADR	31,307	197,595	817,896
Modern Merchandising	44,800	643,800	677,600
Scotty's Inc.	20,100	235,075	281,400
Service Merchandise Co.	153,000	2,684,500	2,562,750
Supermarkets General	56,100	630,568	729,300
*Tandy Corp.	160,000	2,859,690	3,660,000
Volume Shoes	31,200	579,894	776,100
Ward's Co., Inc.	35,000	433,501	455,000
Winns Stores Inc.	47,300	849,203	1,407,175
		12,459,811	15,362,250
Automotive: 5.9%			
Australian Motor Industries	206,200	222,740	200,427
Cummins Engine	52,900	2,024,471	1,944,075
Eaton Corp.	20,000	782,777	767,500
Ford Motor Company	260,000	11,664,657	11,602,499
		14,694,645	14,514,501
Food and Beverage: 5.0%			
Central Soya Co.	50,000	677,643	650,000
Church's Fried Chicken	179,200	2,031,195	4,345,600
Denny's Inc.	54,000	1,721,012	1,154,250
Furr's Cafeterias	84,341	712,657	1,275,658
Marudai Food Co.	195,518	257,681	697,413
Pepcom Industries Inc.	26,000	200,327	516,750
Pepsico Inc.	80,000	1,355,162	1,950,000
Royal Crown Companies	77,400	1,344,858	1,102,950
*Sambo's Restaurants	40,000	631,499	310,000
Spartan Food Systems, Inc.	7,200	115,871	174,600
		9,047,905	12,177,221

	Number of Shares	Cost	Market Value
COMMON STOCKS (continued):			
Electric and Electronics: 4.5%			
Amalgamated Wireless Australasia	56,280	$ 113,822	$ 150,380
Farinon Corp.	26,500	348,675	354,438
Hitachi Ltd. ADR	87,000	3,308,018	3,947,625
Matsushita Electric Industries ADR	45,210	580,905	1,537,140
*Teledyne Inc.	40,040	2,779,247	4,894,890
		7,130,667	10,884,473
Transportation: 4.1%			
Ansett Transport Industries	1,963,600	2,079,187	2,644,970
Flexi-Van Corp.	97,400	1,416,197	1,716,675
Gelco Corp.	71,500	1,966,560	2,010,938
Orient Overseas Containers	121,000	71,927	79,981
RLC Corp.	22,000	315,145	352,000
Sea Containers Group Units	37,900	1,996,127	814,850
Xtra Corp.	110,000	1,139,524	2,310,000
		8,984,667	9,929,414
Manufacturing: 3.4%			
Carboline Company	30,500	525,902	579,500
Cessna Aircraft	64,800	962,711	1,069,200
Coachman Industries	50,000	622,268	362,500
Envirotech Corp.	40,000	1,087,463	805,000
Hyster Company	30,000	1,118,209	1,128,750
International Harvester Co.	25,000	893,850	953,125
Sullair Corp.	10,000	72,527	158,750
Toyo Seikan Kaisha	633,450	556,173	1,645,069
White Consolidated Industries	58,000	1,101,380	1,558,750
		6,940,483	8,260,644
Construction: 3.2%			
Atco Industries	50,000	555,614	961,749
Jim Walter Corp.	173,300	5,393,392	5,610,587
Trane Company	60,000	624,805	1,125,000
		6,573,811	7,697,336
Diversified Holding Companies: 2.6%			
Canadian Pacific Investments	50,300	896,979	1,264,372
Fuqua Industries	318,400	3,336,385	3,582,000
Versatile Cornat Corp.	118,400	581,728	1,526,907
		4,815,092	6,373,279
Pharmaceuticals and Cosmetics: 1.8%			
Fujisawa Pharmaceutical	242,550	196,623	1,159,389
Redken Laboratories	70,000	1,197,948	910,000
S. S. Pharmaceutical	949,003	564,367	2,447,479
		1,958,938	4,516,868
Chemicals: 1.8%			
Monsanto Company	80,000	4,247,938	3,950,000
Olin Corp.	20,000	314,723	417,500
		4,562,661	4,367,500

	Number of Shares	Cost	Market Value
COMMON STOCKS (continued):			
Communications: 0.8%			
News Ltd.	529,000	$ 1,502,861	$ 1,489,135
Nippon Television Network	16,830	370,960	504,648
		1,873,821	1,993,783
Consumer Specialty: 0.7%			
Hanimex Corporation	421,900	514,988	605,427
Olympus Optical	210,000	524,393	748,020
Pacific Film	784,999	512,671	381,510
		1,552,052	1,734,957
Other Industries: 1.8%			
American Medical International	77,000	824,992	2,011,625
General Medical Corp.	110,000	1,643,415	1,278,750
Grantree Corp.	119,300	1,670,406	924,575
*Leasco Corp.	10,200	—	109,650
Tokai Pulp Co.	200,000	175,716	166,000
		4,314,529	4,490,600
Total Common Stocks		171,230,710	218,213,951

	Principal Amount	Cost	Market Value
BONDS: 2.5%			
The Commercial Banking Company of Sydney Limited. 10%. Convertible Notes. 1988	$ 1,125,000 Aus.	1,351,926	1,325,000
Hitachi Ltd. 5.4%. Convertible Debenture, 1983	485,000,000 Yen	1,575,319	2,178,116
Hitachi Ltd. 7.8%. Convertible Debenture. 1981	45,100,000 Yen	146,936	457,551
Ito Yokado Ltd. 6%. Convertible Debenture, 1992	$ 300,000 U.S.	292,752	411,750
Matsushita Electric. 6¼%. Convertible Debenture. 1990	$ 200,000 U.S.	230,278	371,500
Riegel Textile. 5%. Convertible Debenture. 1993	$ 329,000 U.S.	252,988	233,590
South Africa Electricity Supply Commission. 12.15%, 1982	1,300,000 Rand	919,100	1,137,500
Total Bonds		4,769,299	6,115,007
SHORT-TERM OBLIGATIONS: 9.5%			
Certificate of Deposit: 0.4%			
Bank of Montreal. 10.313%. May 23, 1979	$ 1,000,000 U.S.	1,000,000	1,000,000
Repurchase Agreements: 1.1%			
Short-term securities under repurchase agreements with New England Merchants National Bank. 9.0%. collateralized by U.S. Treasury Notes	$ 2,700,000 U.S.	2,700,000	2,700,000
Goverment Securities: 8.0%			
U.S. Treasury Bills. with various due dates to July 26. 1979, 9.060% to 9.660%	$ 19,750,000 U.S.	19,471,308	19,471,308
Total Short-Term Obligations		23,171,308	23,171,308
TOTAL INVESTMENTS		$199,171,317	247,500,266
OTHER ASSETS, Less Liabilities (1.4%)			(3,511,934)
TOTAL NET ASSETS: 100%			$243,988,332

*Non-income producing.

The accompanying notes are an integral part of these financial statements.

APPENDIX XIV(a): TEMPLETON GROWTH FUND
INVESTMENT PORTFOLIO
(SEPTEMBER 30, 1986)

	Number of Shares	Market Value
COMMON STOCKS		
Energy Sources		
Amerada Hess Corp.	780,000	23,939,604.00
Royal Dutch Petroleum Ltd	619,000	75,992,896.80
Schlumberger Ltd	510,000	23,700,312.00
Total Francaise Petrol	338,000	31,837,096.30
Valero Energy Corp	230,000	2,353,038.00
		157,822,947.10
Utilities—Electrical & Gas		
General Public Utilities Corp.	357,900	11,356,954.38
Building Materials & Component		
USG Corporation	120,000	6,720,984.00
Walter (Jim) Corporation	187,500	11,639,475.00
		18,360,459.00
Chemicals		
Akzo ADR	83,130	7,207,371.00
Akzo NV	22,352	1,953,920.33
Akzo Warrants	1,117	34,680.30
Bayer A.G.	64,285	12,783,379.42
Hoechst A.G.	172,000	30,500,632.91
Imperial Chemicals Ind. ADR	473,500	40,559,820.60
Monsanto Company	650,200	61,333,105.92
		154,372,910.49
Forest Products & Paper		
Amcor Limited	693,344	2,049,005.54
B.C. Forest Products	250,171	3,158,408.87
Champion International Corp.	432,048	15,507,844.50
Domtar Limited	550,000	17,393,750.00
Georgia-Pacific Corporation	150,000	7,308,810.00
Great Lakes Forest Products	400,000	10,200,000.00
Pentair Inc.	104,627	3,592,179.72
Rolland Inc. (CLASS A)	116,600	1,719,850.00
Westvaco Corporation	37,500	2,796,075.00
		63,725,923.63
Mining & Metals		
Alcan Aluminium Limited	1,649,903	72,183,256.25
Aluminium Suisse	2,750	1,411,175.26
CRA of Australia	15,100	91,292.51
Minerals + Res Corp Ltd ADR	100,000	1,070,745.00
Pancontinental Mining Limited	1,248,411	2,990,811.24
Reynolds Metals Company	600,000	38,286,720.00
Sandvik AB B	1,173,333	34,841,168.00
		150,875,168.26
Data Processing & Reproduction		
Honeywell, Inc	20,000	1,945,548.00
Electrical & Electronics		
Email Limited	593,337	1,812,025.71
Hitachi Limited	407	3,932.25
		1,815,957.96
Electronic Components, Instruments		
Siemens A.G.	21,176	9,717,017.56
Industrial Components		
SKF (Class B)	404,000	27,073,071.91
Automobiles		
Ford Motor Company	600,000	44,112,960.00

	Number of Shares	Market Value
Food & Household Products		
General Mills Inc.	30,000	3,292,866.00
Textiles & Apparel		
Winsor Industrial Corp Ltd	1,700,000	2,373,052.69
Broadcast, Advertising, Publishing		
News Ltd.	3,670,000	91,119,147.55
News International Limited	702,500	24,608,763.27
		115,727,910.82
Business & Public Services		
American Medical International	100,000	1,959,420.00
Charter Medical Corp. CL A	785,000	22,867,992.00
Humana Inc.	350,000	11,288,340.00
Moore Corp.	473	13,894.37
		36,129,646.37
Merchandising		
American Stores Company	1,249,658	94,910,525.37
Cifra SA B	10,320,268	25,264,016.06
Dixons Group PLC (ORD IOP)	400,000	2,658,296.91
Hawley Group PLC	2,073,125	4,149,835.68
Peoples Jewellers CL A	100,000	1,200,000.00
Service Merchandise Company	833,000	11,410,933.80
Supermarkets General Corp	224,400	8,132,390.64
U.S. Shoe Corp	1,200,000	34,333,200.00
		182,059,198.46
Telecommunications		
Bell Canada Enterprises Inc.	186,800	7,028,350.00
Northern Telecom Ltd	250,000	9,531,250.00
Telefonos de Mexico ADR	203,124	26,416.28
Telefonos de Mexico ADR New	38,085	4,343.74
Telefonos de Mexico 86B	15,094,500	1,888,623.84
Telefonos de Mexico 87A	4,495,277	489,086.14
		21,462,374.98
Transportation		
Laidlaw Transportation CL A	54,000	816,750.00
Laidlaw Transportation CL B	737,650	10,511,512.50
Orient Overseas Contnr	825,892	292,257.15
Orient Overseas Wts	51,500	18,315.81
Sea Containers Limited	420,000	9,758,952.00
TNT Limited JN 07/91	858,000	1,043,226.91
TNT Ltd.	4,790,050	12,936,013.63
		35,377,027.99
Banking		
ANZ Banking Group Limited	12,858,191	56,007,811.22
Banco Popular Espanola	100,000	6,769,244.18
Bank of Montreal	454,490	14,827,736.25
Bank of Montreal Warrants	300,000	1,260,000.00
Bank of Nova Scotia	1,210,141	18,605,917.87
Barclays Bank PLC.	1,750,000	16,254,044.35
Fidelcor, Inc.	162,000	8,286,786.00
Mellon Bank Corp.	47,590	3,597,918.22
National Westminster Bank	2,163,050	22,168,787.00
Natl Australia Bank Limited	13,341,566	60,437,831.91
Republic New York Corporation	75,000	5,228,010.00
Royal Bank of Canada	422,788	13,582,064.50
Royal Bank of Scotland	500,000	3,282,836.54
Society Corp	53,500	4,360,143.00
Toronto Dominion Bank	728,276	16,386,210.00
Westpac Banking Corporation	15,352,192	60,585,307.86
		311,640,648.91
Financial Services		
Merrill Lynch Company Inc.	1,600,000	79,625,280.00

	Number of Shares	Market Value
Pargesa Holding Ord	1,100	1,827,587.63
		81,452,867.63
Insurance		
Hanover Insurance Co..	100,000	8,704,680.00
Jackson National Corp	258,000	17,536,982.40
Kemper Corporation..	648,000	24,045,724.80
		50,287,387.20

PORTFOLIO SUMMARY
  (Security Class)

Cash..		24,462,403.00
Short Term Notes...		559,365,643.78
Bonds		329,364,113.32
Preferred		10,613,849.82
Common Stock		1,591,309,500.97
TOTAL PORTFOLIO		2,515,115,510.89

INDEX